DREAM
SYMBOLS
——— *from* ———
A *to* Z

GEORG FINK

Sterling Publishing Co., Inc.
New York

Translated by Elisabeth Reinersmann

Library of Congress Cataloging-in-Publication Data Available

4   6   8   10   9   7   5   3

Published by Sterling Publishing Company, Inc.
387 Park Avenue South, New York, N.Y. 10016
Originally published in Germany under the title *Traumsymbol: Lexikon*
© 1997 by FALKEN Verlag, 65527 Niederhausen/Ts
English translation © 1999 by Sterling Publishing Company, Inc.
Distributed in Canada by Sterling Publishing
℅ Canadian Manda Group, One Atlantic Avenue, Suite 105
Toronto, Ontario, Canada M6K 3E7
Distributed in Great Britain and Europe by Cassell PLC
Wellington House, 125 Strand, London WC2R 0BB, England
Distributed in Australia by Capricorn Link (Australia) Pty Ltd.
P.O. Box 6651, Baulkham Hills, Business Centre, NSW 2153, Australia
Manufactured in the United States of America
All rights reserved
Sterling   ISBN 0-8069-4238-X

CONTENTS

THE VISUAL LANGUAGE OF THE SOUL

Dreams are the visual language of the soul. They arise from the unconscious, and if we fail to take note of them, they will be lost, depriving us of recollections and possibly even messages that could help us deal with the problems in our lives. Therefore, psychologists and psychiatrists alike encourage us to have paper and pencil on hand, so that immediately upon awakening we can jot down what we remember from a dream. An experienced dream interpreter would then be able to recognize what might be troubling us. Much scientific research has been carried out that measures physical processes during sleep and dreaming. The psychological aspects of dreaming had to be set aside during these experiments. But with the aid of an electroencephalogram (EEG), the person being observed could be questioned immediately about the content of a dream. During such experiments, electrodes connected to a computer are attached to the subject's head, making it possible to record the electric activity in the brain.

Having a record of our dreams is not only useful for psychotherapists; it is also important for us, because from the messages in a dream we can draw conclusions about our lives. But ordinary people do not need an electroencephalogram or a computer. Having a piece of paper and a pencil next to the bed before we go to sleep is all that is necessary. This allows us to write down a dream as soon as we wake up. After all, we all know from our own experience how fleeting and even bizarre dream images can be.

What Is a Dream?

What we see in our dreams has remained much the same throughout human history, perhaps with the exception that in the past people would not dream about airplanes and cars but about ox carts and wagons pulled by horses. The only difference lies in what we think dreams are.

In times past, dreams were considered to be messages from the gods, the result of an intestinal upset, or irrelevant nonsense. They were also understood to be a manifestation of the daily desires a person was hoping would find fulfillment. The strange visual language of the unconscious was interpreted differently by priests, physicians, and charlatans. It took a long time for the interpretation of dreams to be regarded seriously. People began to collect and compare dreams, and they tried to find out how the images, which could be interpreted as specific symbols, could be useful to a person's waking hours.

Thanks to Sigmund Freud, the famous Austrian psychiatrist and founder of psychoanalysis, dream research at the turn of the twentieth century began to take on a new direction. His analytical method led to completely new insights into our psychosexual life. His work established the concept of the unconscious, and made it part of all future psychological research. Freud made dreams part of psychiatry and psychotherapy, and established proof that dreams can identify the emotional state of a person when their symbols are interpreted properly.

Sigmund Freud's work led to intensive scientific research into the strange images that appear to many of us during sleep. The scientific community is still at odds regarding the interpretation of dreams and its relevance. However, the successes reported by psychoanalysts and other therapists who include dream interpretation in their treatment are proof that the practitioners are far ahead of the theorists. One example of the former is Carl Gustav Jung, the famous psychiatrist from Switzerland. Jung

and other practitioners have accumulated a wealth of empirical knowledge through their work with dreams. The successes that they have achieved are proof that the unconscious indeed provides dream images that can be interpreted as symbols that shed light on everyday life.

Scientific Dream Work—Available to the Layperson

This book seeks to make the results of scientific dream work available to the layperson. We felt that the easiest way to deal with the extensive material was to list dream symbols in alphabetical order. Certain other aspects, such as nightmares, we listed separately under Other Clues. We are sure that the attentive reader—after careful study of the book and personal observation—will even want to add to what we have listed.

Not everyone will go to a psychiatrist when he or she feels emotionally upset. Many people are ashamed to tell a stranger about their problems, or don't want to expose their innermost conflicts. This is precisely the problem faced by many psychotherapists who want to help their clients. Although the clients often answer questions willingly, they might falsify their dreams, simply because they may not want to stand in front of a stranger feeling totally naked. Such reticent people are the ones to whom we especially want to give a helping hand with this book. By starting to understand their dreams, they will get to know themselves better and thus be better able to identify their problems; then—if need be—they can see a psychotherapist, who can be helpful in finding the means to heal a particular condition.

But this book is written above all for the healthy among us, who want to use their dreams to uncover their emotions and thereby live more peacefully with themselves and the people around them. Problems that the unconscious points out to us in the form of dream symbols are not just indicators of illness.

How Dreams Can Be Interpreted

Before you begin to interpret your own dreams, take note of the following points:

1. It's important to write down your dream immediately upon awakening, describing everything exactly the way it occurred; this means no elaboration, no rose-colored glasses!
2. What we remember is a relatively small part of the whole dream. We see only fragments of what the unconscious or our soul wants to tell us.
3. Recurring dreams or dreams that seem to be a continuation of a previous dream should never be viewed separately but within the larger context.
4. It is seldom useful to analyze a single dream symbol, and might even lead to wrong conclusions. Always try to make use of several symbols when interpreting a dream.

5. The symbols described in this book are only meant as guidelines or possibilities. Take from them what seems to fit, and what you recognize from the events of the dream. A symbol that is a combination of several words can, and should, be examined by looking up the individual words in a dictionary.
6. If a certain symbol in a dream is not listed in the dictionary, look up words that describe something similar. You may also be able to find a connection by looking at other images or symbols in the dream.
7. Every dream image has several meanings. It is therefore possible that a specific meaning is accurate for one person but might be different in its nuances for another. In addition, various people might have the same dream, although its meaning could be completely different for each person.
8. When interpreting a dream for someone else, the interpreter must rely on the subjective report of the dreamer, who, in order to make the images in the dream clear, should share the issues and problems that he or she is facing in his or her life. The interpreter in turn must ferret out with well-targeted questions what is objective and what is emotional.
9. After listening to the person report the dream, the interpreter should try to gain access to the conscious state of the dreamer. In this phase, it is also important for the salient events and problems in the dreamer's life to be reviewed. If

nothing concrete develops from this, the interpreter ought to look to the dreamer's past to find the reasons for the dream. Then the dreamer should tell the dream again in more detail. The interpreter should use the specific dream symbols and the actual events that the dreamer has experienced to draw a final conclusion about the meaning of the dream.

10. Then it is up to the dreamer to decide if the interpretation makes sense and fits his or her particular situation. If the dreamer remembers any additional, relevant events from daily life or things that he or she left out when initially reporting the dream, they should be added now. Without this additional information, the picture of the dream might turn out to be completely different.

11. Those who are unfamiliar with dream interpretation, or have little or no training in psychology, should start by interpreting their own dreams first. When interpreting your own dreams, be as honest as possible; only then can you recognize and deal with the problems that the unconscious is trying to bring to your attention.

SYMBOLS FROM A TO Z

ABDOMINAL PAIN
Dreaming about abdominal pain only to feel no pain upon awakening indicates that you harbor a secret suspicion with which you should deal. Occasionally, a dream about abdominal pain points to a physical weakness that, when ignored, could develop into a full-blown illness. (See also "Stomach Pain.")

ABYSS To turn away from an abyss in a dream means to ignore reality. To go down into an abyss means that you ought to find the reason for a seemingly hopeless situation, in order to make solving it easier or to climb out of the abyss. To look into an abyss indicates that dangerous situations can be faced with courage, because the danger has been recognized early enough to make avoiding it possible. Falling into an abyss often is a signal that emotional heartache is imminent; sometimes a present, real-life situation is expressed in the dream (like falling out of bed while sleeping and then waking up). A bridge spanning an abyss suggests that real-life difficul-

ties can be "bridged." In ancient Egypt, this symbol meant that business losses are imminent. (See also "Bridge.")

ACCIDENT If the accident that you dreamt about is not a memory of an actual event, the scope of the dream will depend on other symbols. But often an accident in a dream only refers to careless actions in real life, which you needn't take too seriously.

ACORN The seed of the oak tree stands for life, or for a new beginning with few resources. Collecting acorns in the forest means that you will bend your back gladly in order to get ahead.

ACQUAINTANCE Meeting an acquaintance in a dream could point to someone in real life who not only thinks as you do, but could even be a mentor who will be providing support. (See also "Friend.")

ACTOR The actor in a dream is the person who puts on an act in real life. When an actor appears in a dream, it is a message to beware of people who only say what others tell them to say. Seeing yourself as the actor in a dream means that you want to be noticed; whether you are noticed or not depends on other symbols in the dream. (See also "Opera" and "Theater.")

ADHESIVE Dreaming about adhesives means that you are either holding fast to a decision or plans you have made, or not following through with them. This image may also imply that you cannot let go of something (perhaps an intimate relationship), even if the consequences are painful. (See also "Glue.")

ADULTERY Dreaming about being an adulterer is an indication that you want to change something in your marriage or relationship. If the adulterer in the dream is someone else, it is a message not to get involved in the affairs of others but to take care of your own.

ADVENTURE An adventure, even if it involves a stranger, points to your own ego and the tendency to be cavalier about your personal well-being, or a bit loose with your morals in matters of love or marriage.

ADVERTISEMENT Dreaming about reading and enjoying an advertisement is a hint to take advantage of an offer that is being made in real life. However, a general dream about advertisements has to do with advertising yourself or portraying yourself in a way that you want others to see. (See also "Poster.")

AIRPLANE Dreaming about airplanes racing back and forth, above and below, points to confusion in real life. Red airplanes often have something to do with sexual urges or a sexual disorder. In general, airplanes, no matter what their color, are a message from the soul to adjust to a more moderate lifestyle. Traveling by plane indicates that you want to leave your burdens behind. Although air travel, next to space travel, is the fastest means of transportation in the world, don't expect your troubles or difficulties to be over soon, because the soul considers traveling in the air to be more dangerous than it actually is. On the positive side, traveling by air might indicate that you entertain far-reaching ideas, which seem to fly right at you. (See also "Flying" and "Traveling.")

AIR-RAID WARNING If a dream about an air-raid warning is not connected to actual war experiences in the dreamer's past, the dream usually mirrors anxieties, whose causes should be explored.

AIRSHIP (SEE "ZEPPELIN")

ALARM (SEE "AIR-RAID WARNING")

ALARM CLOCK The shrill sound of an alarm clock in a dream usually has nothing to do with having to wake up. Often it is interpreted as described under "Clock/Watch."

ALCOHOL Even in our dreams, alcohol removes inhibitions and allows us to behave in a way that might be considered amoral. Intoxication in a dream may be an indication that you deal with your problems from a strictly logical point of view, and that becoming more relaxed could be a better approach. Being totally drunk in a dream could mean that you can count on the realities of life being ignored. Or, this could be a message to look at life more soberly. Being drunk may also indicate one way to reach a goal, even in the face of reality. If you are raising your glass in salute to many people, this may be a sign of ambivalent emotions or may point to compensating for something. (See also "Drunkenness.")

AMPUTATION In psychoanalysis, a dream about the amputation of limbs is usually understood in a sexual or erotic context. Such a dream alludes to a fear of castration or an impending separation from a loved one. According to modern dream interpretation, it's important to pay attention to which limb is being amputated. The amputation of the feet or the legs indicates that some obstacle is making life difficult for you. Losing your fingers, and thereby a means of tactile sensing, shows that you lack emotional expression. A missing hand suggests that you don't have enough freedom to deal with daily living. If you are decapitated in a dream, this could be a sign that you are about to "lose your head" in real life or that your love relationship is in trouble.

ANCHOR Throwing an anchor in a dream has to do with hoping that a problem in real life can be solved quickly with the help of others. When an anchor is hauled in, all hopes for help are dashed; this image also points to a change in your life most likely not being in your favor. A ship heading out to sea with a huge anchor on board shows that you can safely steer your life in a different direction; whether that direction will ultimately be in your favor or not depends on other symbols in the dream.

ANESTHESIA Dreaming about an anesthetic can be seen as the unconscious giving you a tranquilizer for real-life situations. In other words, the dream image is a message to be calmer in the future. (See also "Injury" and "Wound.")

ANGEL An angel in a dream may represent a proper emotional response, which would be helpful in handling a particular situation. An angel could be a message that you need help, because you won't make it alone. This image could also imply that you are being asked to let go of something that you love. Or, it could point to being taken to another, strange level of reality. If you are dreaming about being an angel yourself, examine your attitudes and behavior to see how closely they come to those of an angel.

ANGER Dreaming about being angry is a message to be aware of nasty situations in real life. Making others angry means that you have a streak of spitefulness. Sometimes dreaming about anger could point to the little things over which we become irritated during the course of a day.

ANIMAL JAWS The image of the wide-open jaws of an animal threatening to swallow you whole is a symbol for your anxieties. According to an interpretation from the Middle Ages, dreaming of an animal snapping at one indicates an existing heart or bronchial problem.

ANIMALS Animals in our dreams usually tell us about our motives, physical urges, desires, or inhibitions. They symbolize our basic instincts, the untamed but also the tamed within us. In a dream, we can instinctively find our way back in the order of creation. Animals in a herd or a pack, by the way, are a sign that we might fall prey to our physical urges. (See also individual types of animals.)

ANT HILL If you are dreaming of destroying an ant hill, this implies that you are worried that your own diligence and qualifications are not being recognized sufficiently. (See also "Ants.")

ANTLERS Dreaming about putting antlers on someone means that in real life you don't want to have anything to do with that person anymore. Dreaming about animals with antlers or horns points to the possibility of separating from a person or an object that you love.

ANTS In psychotherapy, the image of ants in a dream is often considered a sign that there is something wrong with the dreamer's autonomic nervous system. Such a dream, however, might simply be the result of the dreamer's limbs having "gone to sleep." In any case, consider a dream about ants as some kind of warning. If you literally feel industrious ants crawling over your body in a dream, it is a message from the unconscious to become more diligent. But this could also mean that something in your life is making you restless, such as big plans that call for some kind of action. (See also "Insects.")

ANVIL When someone is using an anvil in a dream, this means that a person in your life wants to bring you into submission or to lure you in a direction that does not bode well for you. When you are working on the anvil yourself, you want to rid your soul of something burdensome. Often the unconscious tries to encourage more perseverance during waking hours: Be the hammer and not the anvil! (See also "Hammer.")

ANXIETY (SEE "FEAR")

APARTMENT Dreaming about moving into an apartment is a sign that you can count on a positive change taking place in your living arrangements. However, dreaming about moving into a dilapidated apartment indicates that you may be suffering from an illness or may have reached "the bottom" in an interpersonal relationship. (See also "House," "Moving," and "Room.")

APE The ape is a dream symbol for the shadow or the caricature of ourselves. The ape often points to our

A more primitive urges. Dreaming about an ape can also be a sign that others think badly of you or are making fun of you. Being bitten by an ape suggests that someone is flattering you to gain an advantage. Unlike in India, where animals are considered sacred, in the West when we dream about apes, they often refer to physical urges and passions. How the ape appears in the dream will give you more information about the meaning of the dream. (See also "Gorilla.")

APPLAUSE Receiving applause in a dream points to getting positive recognition for a plan that you have yet to act upon in real life. In some dreams, hypocrites lure the dreamer into taking the wrong direction or following the wrong advice with their applause.

APPLE According to Carl Gustav Jung, apples are a symbol for life. A bright-red apple in a dream signifies love; an apple that is both red and green represents vitality. Eating an apple points to an intimate relationship between a man and a woman. If the apple has worms inside, this means that you have doubts about the honesty of your partner. A rotten apple implies that a love relationship is in question. The apple is an ancient symbol for fertility, which today has more of a nonmaterial connotation. The apple also stands for "the forbidden fruit," indicating what is good and what is evil. A distinction is made between biting into a sweet apple (a promise of love's pleasures) or a sour apple (meaning "swallowing a bitter pill" or "biting the bullet").

APPLE TREE The apple tree in the Christian West is the "tree of knowledge." The apple tree is used by the unconscious in our dreams, encouraging us not only to be responsive to the problems of others but also to move toward more self-knowledge.

APPRENTICE An apprentice in a dream may represent weaknesses in your past that you are now just beginning to realize. If you are a supervisor at your job, a dream in which you are an apprentice might well be a message from the unconscious to try to understand young people better. Often the apprentice in a dream actually has the role of the boss, telling the dreamer how to better deal with the affairs of life. (See also "School" and "Student.")

APRON Dreaming about wearing an apron indicates hard work in real life, which has to be done nevertheless.

ARENA An arena in a dream is the place where your ego is at the center of attention and your every step is observed. This is where you stand to fight for your emotional well-being, or where you meet a worthy opponent, a person against whom you must defend your innermost center. In an arena, you might not meet a person but an animal, which you will need to examine for its symbolic meaning and which might point out weaknesses that need to be addressed. (See also "Circus.")

ARIES Aries is a constellation between Pisces and Taurus, and is pictured as a ram. It symbolizes creative power, and doesn't appear in dreams very often. If you are dreaming about being attacked by a ram, you could be suffering in real life because someone is trying to gain your affection by forceful means and to make you totally dependent on him or her. Grabbing the horn of a ram, however, means that you are solving a problem by using your head.

ARM As an extension of the hand, the arm usually represents the basis from which we act. If you have an injured arm in a dream, your ability to act is impaired. A broken arm is a warning of an impending loss or conflict. Strong arms suggest that you are productive in both your work and your private life, which will lead to success. Arms appearing to be too short imply that you feel discouraged because nothing is working out. Arms that are too long connote that small but important details are missed. Weak or very thin arms may indicate helplessness. According to old folk wisdom, arms covered with a lot of hair indicate financial gain. Last but not least, arms encircling you in a dream could represent a helper giving you substantial support.

ARMCHAIR Sitting comfortably in an armchair in a dream is a message to provide for yourself more conditions of peace and quiet. Seeing others in armchairs shows that you can't expect a lot of help from them, but have to rely on your own skills and effort. (See also "Easy Chair.")

ARRESTED Being arrested, or seeing someone else being arrested, in a dream is a message to stop making nasty remarks about others because they just might backfire. Such a dream could also indicate that you feel too attached to the people around you and want to break free. (See also "Forest" and "Wandering About.")

ARRIVING Upon arriving somewhere in a dream, you are leaving one phase in life behind and hoping to have peace and equanimity. This image also points to a new beginning or a change for the better. (See also "Train" and "Traveling.")

ARROW An arrow coming toward you in a dream could represent a little trick that someone is trying to use to put something over on you; it could also represent the energy that you waste. Dreaming about shooting an arrow yourself can be a message to be cautious about making careless remarks.

ARTIST'S BRUSH An artist's brush is often seen as a sexual symbol. Therefore, when a man dreams of painting a picture with an artist's brush, this could express his desire for an intimate relationship. Try to remember what colors were used in the picture, because they will shed further light on the meaning of the dream. (See also "Painting," "Painter," and specific colors.)

ASHES Ashes in dreams point to the conclusion of an event or a situation: You have burned something, and rise, so to speak, from the ashes like a phoenix. You may have acted improperly, and want to "heap ashes on yourself." Or, perhaps you are sad, and walk around, in a biblical image, in a "sack cloth and ashes."

ASSASSINATION Witnessing an assassination in a dream indicates that something sensational is about to happen in real life; additional symbols in the dream will show you whether it will be a pleasant or a horrible occurrence. Dreaming about planning or carrying out an assassination suggests that you are trying to engage in something in real life that is hopeless.

ATOMIC POWER (SEE "NUCLEAR POWER")

ATTACK Dreaming about an attack indicates that something is taking its toll on your nerves in real life, or that you are not dealing very well with everyday stress and are about to "lose it."

AUTOMAT An Automat is a type of cafeteria in which food is obtained from vending machines. Freud would probably have given a sexual interpretation to a dream involving an Automat, because using one involves putting something in and taking something out. But it's more likely that the dreamer is being told to be less frivolous in matters of money or more cautious in handling the events that occur over the course of a day.

AUTOMOBILE The automobile often stands for our ego, which needs to be kept under control. If you keep a car under control in a dream, you will most likely keep things under control in real life too, and therefore make good progress. Having car trouble in a dream usually indicates that obstacles lie ahead. When traffic-warning signs are ignored, you may be suffering from angst and trying to cover it up. If you are the driver, you may appear as the person who you are in real life, or as what you would like to represent to others. If you are driving an expensive car that doesn't belong to you in real life, this means that you want to appear better than you actually are. If you are not driving the car properly, certain things in life are also handled badly. In many nightmares, we hit someone or our brakes don't work; both are usually a sign that there is some kind of problem with our ego, but could just as well be a message that a change in life is in order to avoid losses. (See also "Nightmares" under Other Clues, "Traveling," and various auto parts.)

AVALANCHE Dreaming about an avalanche roaring down a mountain represents a real-life danger that you see coming but can't escape or avoid. The dream is also a warning from the unconscious to be alert to an impending hazard that needs to be faced with courage.

AWAKENING A dream about awakening is a message to "wake up," to become more alive, or to go through life with more resolve. Dreaming about awakening is usually followed by actually waking up. (See also "Sleeping.")

AWL The awl is a tool used to mend leather (particularly shoes); symbolically, it can be seen as having the ability to temporarily restore us from an emotional crisis, so that we can continue with our lives. Being injured by an awl in a dream points to coming upon an emotional impasse, which needs to be avoided in the future. (See also "Shoemaker.")

AX Using an ax in a dream indicates that you are forcing your way to a goal. This image could also be a warning that you are wasting too much energy, and that at some critical point your energy will be depleted.

AXLE A fast-moving axle indicates a fast lifestyle (additional symbols in the dream will point to whether or not this is a critical message from the unconscious). A broken axle shows that a business deal is falling through; however, if the axle is intact, success is almost guaranteed. Sometimes an axle appears as a mobile in a dream, suggesting that in real life everything revolves around the dreamer.

BABY A baby in a dream symbolizes the unconscious desire for security. Being pregnant in a dream indicates having to carry something in real life for quite a while and with much effort until you reach your goal. Nursing a baby represents taking care of responsibilities, even if doing so is difficult. Looking at a beautiful baby means that you are likely to find good friends. Homely babies, on the other hand, point to small quirks in your character. A dead baby indicates that you suffer from painful memories. (See also "Child.")

BABY CHICK In the Middle Ages, people believed that dreaming about the hatching of baby chicks meant that a marriage would be blessed with many children. Baby chicks are generally associated with good luck in many forms. Should they be sitting in a box, chirping away happily, this indicates that a problem will be solved quickly.

BACK In dream interpretation, the back represents the shadow of our conscience. It is a place of vulnerability, or where unknown dangers are lurking. The back also points to having difficulty repairing emotional injuries. (See also "Spine.")

BACK DOOR Dreaming about leaving by the back door means that you are trying to avoid taking responsibility or trying to reach your goal by means of a detour. A back door also stands for secret thoughts or actions, which could refer to sexual matters. When interpreting a dream where there is a back door, it's important to determine if you were trying to get away or simply walking up to the back door. (See also "Door" and "Back Stairs.")

BACKDROP (SEE "THEATER SCENERY")

BACKPACK Dreaming about a backpack refers to the burden you

17

have to carry in real life, or it implies an intrigue taking place behind your back that could cause you emotional pain. A backpack taken off the back indicates that you are letting go of an emotional burden, or that you have recognized who the false friend is who misled and instigated against you. (See also "Knapsack.")

BACKSIDE
(SEE "POSTERIOR")

BACK STAIRS Back stairs that are hidden sometimes appear in erotic dreams, and might refer to a questionable relationship. (See also "Back Door.")

BACKYARD (SEE
"YARD/COURTYARD")

BAG Dreaming about an empty bag indicates that your relationships are empty. A full bag can be a hint that you are too occupied with yourself, and not concerned enough about the people around you. (See also "Sack" and "Pocket.")

BAILIFF A bailiff seizes property and objects that the courts have declared must be used to pay a person's debts. Dreaming about a bailiff is positive, because it points to emotional burdens being removed from the dreamer. (See also "Pledge" and "Security.")

BAKER A baker is a symbol for creativity, and points to your overall healthy development, or at the very least an improvement in your present circumstances. If the baker in the dream is tending a fire, this indicates that you are nourished intellectually.

BAKING Baking symbolizes the activity that gives us our daily bread. If you are the one in the dream doing the baking, this means that in real life you are taking your fate in your own hands. Baking small rolls indicates that you will have only small successes in life. Letting others bake the bread shows that you have little confidence in yourself.

BALCONY A balcony is a symbol for a house, and represents maternal love and female breasts, as well as a gift that does not need to be paid for later. (See also "House.")

BALDNESS Hair is a symbol for secondary sexual characteristics. This notion has been upheld for centuries, and led Artemidorus, who wrote an ancient book about dreams, to believe that when a man sees a bald head in a dream he will lose his virility. Today, we tend to think that such a dream has more to do with a disappointment in interpersonal relationships or with the fear that we could lose something dear to us.

BALL As with a globe, the ball that we play with is a symbol for completeness and wholeness. Its shape can be compared to that of the earth or the sun, and it can represent psychic energy in motion. Dreaming about playing with a ball indicates that you could be gambling with something in your life, be at the mercy of your emotions, or be getting hung up on a situation that is not worth it. Often we think that the game is easy, but then life presents us with an obstacle.

BALL OF WOOL OR YARN

A ball of wool or yarn in a dream represents a convoluted real-life situation that is almost impossible to untangle. Dreaming about rolling up wool or yarn or another twine indicates that it will take a long time for you to accomplish something. Hopelessly tangled-up yarn or wool points to jumbled thinking or ideas that can't be realized. (See also "Knot" and "Labyrinth.")

BALLOON This dream image represents that which is fleeting in our lives. It also has something to do with pursuing luck when we don't know if the winds will blow in our favor. A balloon that has burst, like burst soap bubbles, indicates that your hopes have not been fulfilled. (See also "Soap Bubbles.")

BALL/PARTY Going to a dance party in a dream means that you can expect joy and good cheer in real life. Or, this can be a message from the unconscious to make more of your life or to pay more attention to your surroundings. Dreaming about partying or going to a feast shows that you want to forget your everyday burdens for a while and simply relax.

BALM A dream about a balm, a healing substance applied to a wound, means that your psyche will be well again because you can trust in your surroundings. (See also "Salve" and "Medicine.")

BANANA In psychoanalysis, a banana is a symbol for the male sex organ. A banana often appears in sexual dreams of women, expressing desires that are rarely satisfied or a general lack of fulfillment in life.

BAND (SEE "ORCHESTRA")

BANDAGE Dreaming about applying a bandage to an injury indicates that you are indeed wounded in real life; the cause of the injury might be an insult, but it is just as likely related to your own poor behavior toward others. (See also "Physician," "Hospital," "Scar," "Pain," and "Wound.")

BAND AID (SEE "BANDAGE")

BANG Dreaming about hearing a bang coming out of nowhere without an apparent explosion means that in real life you are involved in a futile effort, perhaps to influence a certain person.

BANK A bank is often seen as the center of energy, where we can go and withdraw the energies needed to master life, including our love life. A bank account that is closed indicates that energies are also blocked. Breaking into a bank means that you are desperately trying to keep your ego from deteriorating, or that you want to appear to be more than you actually are. If you are depositing lots of money, this could mean that you are neglecting things in real life on which you should be spending more money. (See also "Piggybank.")

BANKNOTES

Dreaming about banknotes is a message to spend money wisely, and to never spend more than you have. (See also "Money.")

BANNER (SEE "FLAG")

BAPTISM Baptism stands for the "water of life," spiritual renewal, and emotional rebirth. Dreaming about a baptism, or being baptized yourself, means that you are planning on refocusing your efforts, or indicates a change that could be beneficial. A baptism with clear, consecrated spring water means that you will bring clarity to spiritual matters or judge the mistakes of others more compassionately. (See also "Spring" and "Water.")

BAR Dreaming about sitting alone in a bar implies that in real life you would like a change in scenery. Sitting in a bar with others is a sign that you are looking for easy company; however, it's important to determine with whom you were sitting for the dream to be interpreted correctly.

BARBER (SEE "HAIRDRESSER/BARBER")

BAREFOOT Dreaming about walking barefoot or having bare feet implies that you are returning to the solid ground of reality. Or, both can be a sign of modesty, poverty, or the humility with which one endures the highs and the lows of life. Bare feet also often indicate being connected to the earth, something that we may

not be aware of during our waking hours.

BARKING DOG Dreaming about a barking dog is a warning of impending danger. (See also "Dog.")

BARN A barn is a building where we store equipment and supplies, and in a dream it is considered a symbol for physical as well as intellectual energy. An empty barn in a dream indicates that you don't have much to look forward to in real life. A full barn, on the other hand, means that your wallet is full, or that you can live. (See also "House.")

BARRACKS The lives of people living in barracks are dictated by compulsory rules. Like a house, barracks also stand for the human body. Dreaming about barracks indicates that you are overtaxing your body in real life and are physically out of shape, which is making you tired in your personal life as well as on the job. (See also "House.")

BARREL Dreaming about the bottom of a barrel falling out points to something amiss in your mental attitude. A full barrel implies that you are well off financially; an empty barrel means that things are tight.

BARRIERS Barriers seem to appear in our dreams when we are unable to overcome our inhibitions. Only if you are jumping over the barriers, or are able to cleverly circumvent them, will you be able to deal with your inhibitions or limitations successfully in real life. (See also "Obstacle.")

BARS/RODS Dreaming about bars indicates a separation. You could be moving somewhere in real life. Or, you could be taking a trip, from which your return is somehow blocked. For the proper interpretation, additional symbols will need to be examined. (See also "Prison.")

BASEMENT The basement is a symbol for the unconscious. Dreaming about walking down into a basement means that you want to bring something out from the darkness to the light. Groping around a basement in the dark and being afraid is an indication that someone in real life wants to hurt you. Searching a basement for a burglar implies that you are afraid of a person who is intruding in your life without permission. Because a house is a symbol for the human body in the language of the unconscious, a basement usually represents the lower extremities. Thus, a collapsing basement means that your legs and feet are in danger, implying that in real life you are finding yourself in a hopeless situation. (See also "House.")

BASKET In psychoanalysis, a basket is a female sexual symbol. However, a basket in a dream often represents an obstacle.

BATS Bats appear suddenly from the darkness, spreading unrest and terror. Dreaming about bats means that your emotions are out of balance or that you feel persecuted; either way, you should take your anxieties seriously. (See also "Vampire.")

BATHING Here, the cleansing process of the soul is being addressed. The dream means that something bothersome is being removed. The water mirrors emotional energy. Many people have dreamt about a bath before they knew that a new phase in their lives was about to begin. When the bathwater is clear, you can expect to have clarity during waking hours. Taking a bath in muddy water means that you have gotten into a messy situation of your own doing. A bath taken outside is a positive sign, indicating a conscious attempt to be unencumbered and free of hang-ups. (See also "Water.")

BATHROOM This is the place for cleaning up or cleansing, and indicates emotional purification. It is here that people want to rid themselves of everyday dirt and slip into "another skin." The bathroom also suggests a place where you can scrub yourself clean before starting something new. Cleaning the bathroom of dirt and grime before taking a bath means that you are trying to forget things from the past. A geometrical shape of the bathroom (or bathtub) shows that you have substance.

BEAM A beam is not just something for the high jumper to jump over; it is also a reminder to the dreamer to jump over his or her own shadow and shed inhibitions.

BEANS Dreaming about beans could be a sign of too much materialistic thinking. As with every seed, the bean is also thought to be a symbol of the female sexual organs. Planting beans means that you are laying the groundwork for success. Seeing a seed germinate is a signal that luck will smile on you. Cooking beans implies that you are destroying that which would normally germinate, or that you cannot count on your luck to last. (See "Legumes.")

BEAR A bear represents earth-connected and protective maternal qualities. According to Carl Jung, a negative aspect of this symbol is that the bear, due to its strength, could make the dreamer feel superior. Dreaming about a bear sometimes connotes a danger or a threat.

BEARD In the past, a beard was considered a symbol for male superiority. Later, it was also seen as a mask behind which we could hide our real self; today, this interpretation is the more prevalent one. Losing a beard in a dream is a signal to let go of old attitudes or prejudices. Dreaming about brushing one's beard is a sign of vanity in real life. Making a gift of one's beard to a woman means that the dreamer is losing his virility. (See also "Hair.")

BEATING (SEE "THRASHING")

BED Dreaming about a bed, a place of safety, often involves feelings of deep apprehension; it's important not to dismiss such a dream, because it could indicate a hidden illness. Dreaming about being in bed with someone implies that you are dissatisfied with your sexual performance in real life, and that you want to perform better but do not trust yourself

to do so. A bed with fresh sheets, according to a dream book from the Middle Ages, shows that the dreamer will be lucky in love. Dirty sheets, unlucky in love. In contrast, today we believe that a bed with clean sheets is a reminder for us to practice better hygiene in our intimate life; dirty sheets, on the other hand, are a signal to clean up our relationship. Dreaming about an empty bed points to loneliness in real life. (See also "Mattress" and "Sleeping.")

BEDROOM This is the room where our intimate life plays itself out, where our real self can merge with another. This image often announces a heartache, particularly if the dreamer shares the room with a person whom he or she doesn't really like. If the bedroom in your dream is decorated in red, you may have unfulfilled sexual desires. Walking into the bedroom of another person in a dream means that in real life you want to have an intimate relationship with someone who has kept a distance so far, or that you want to have an affair. A stranger entering your bedroom in a dream indicates that someone will offend or embarrass you. (See also "Red" and "Bed.")

BEE The bee is a symbol for industriousness. Bees humming in a dream mean that you should rejoice in having strong nerves, which serve you well when you are in danger. The ancient Greeks believed that when a young girl dreams about being stung by a bee, the arrow of Cupid will find her. Now the general consensus is that a bee sting indicates that a decisive change will occur in the dreamer's life. (See also "Swarm of Bees," "Insects," "Honeycomb," and "Wasp.")

BEER Stale beer in a glass is an indication that a friendship is coming to an end. Freshly poured beer consumed in leisure is a promise of good a health, unless the beer is spilt. A glass of beer with a large foam head indicates that there could be a charlatan or a showoff in your circle of friends. (See also "Alcohol.")

BEGGAR Dreaming about a beggar is a hint not to feel superior to the people around you. The image of a beggar also points to an unpleasant memory that you want to erase from your mind. Or, it could be a message from the unconscious to live more simply. According to folklore, dreaming about giving a gift to a beggar means that the dreamer can expect good luck and plenty of money.

BELL Listening to the ringing of bells in a dream is a promise of good news; even the ancient Egyptians believed this to be true. Bells often also announce a family event, and sometimes are the voices of the heart. Bells that move but do not chime indicate that in real life you don't quite know what's up, or that a present situation is leaving you at a loss and you might do well to turn to something else. Dreaming about ringing a bell indicates that you are asking for attention from someone in real life.

BELLHOP Dreaming about a bellhop shows that we can expect help

in carrying the "baggage" that we haul around with us in life. In a woman's dream, a bellhop is the attentive young man who is standing in for her partner, who doesn't perform as well and is not as dashing as she would like him to be. (See also "Doorman.")

BELL TOWER Seeing a bell tower in the distance in a dream is much like seeing a signpost pointing the proper way out of a difficult situation. (See also "Tower.")

BELLY The image of a belly connotes a place where we digest the events of the day. If you dream about a full belly, consider eating in moderation. A belly in a dream may also refer to sexual matters.

BELT A belt is a symbol for female virtues (chastity belt) and male energy and virility. Dreaming about wearing a belt points to an intimate relationship where love is flourishing, or a strong bond between marriage partners. If you have to tighten your belt in a dream, a friendship in real life is not going as well as it had. A belt that brakes in two means that you have to let go of something dear to you.

BENCH Sitting on a bench in a dream means that in real life you are waiting for an adventure or for someone who will understand you. People often dream about a bench when they are disappointed in their relationship with their partner. (See also "Chair.")

BERRIES Picking berries in a dream indicates that you are facing tedious work in real life. Eating berries means that you get upset over small things but "swallow" your anger.

BICYCLE Young people often dream about a bicycle when they need to accomplish something on their own, or under their own power. This might have to do with getting a better grade in school or graduating with honors. Sometimes the dream includes riding with a partner, which could be interpreted to mean traveling happily and without a care together into the future. But if the dreamer or the partner gets a flat tire, this means that something is not quite right with the friendship or the sexual relationship.

BICYCLING The forward movement on a bike in a dream stands for getting ahead by your own volition in real life. Dreaming about pedaling forcefully means that you can count on accomplishing much in life; however, pedaling forcefully but not getting anywhere shows that you are having trouble finishing a job that you have started. (See also "Automobile" and other modes of transportation.)

BILL A bill in a dream needs to be interpreted according to the symbolic meaning of its amount (see individual numbers). If the bill is correct and paid, your life is in good shape, and you can expect a prosperous future and new projects. An incorrect or unpaid bill points to conflicts that can't be solved without your help, or indicates that you are afraid to start something new. (See also "Receipt.")

BIRCH TREE Dreaming of a birch tree with new, bright-green leaves in the spring has to do with the announcement of a joyful event in your life. Dreaming of climbing the trunk of a birch tree means that you will also reach greater heights in real life. In the Middle Ages, the birch tree was considered to be magic protection against witches and ghosts, and such ideas were carried over into the Catholic faith. Farms, stables, and houses are still decorated with the green branches of birch trees at the Feast of Corpus Christie. For religious people, this tradition mirrors a deep fear residing in their unconscious that they will be left helplessly at the mercy of evil powers. (See also "Tree.")

BIRD CAGE A bird cage, the prison of birds, stands for our own lack of emotional freedom or for an inferiority complex. Opening the cage in a dream and letting the bird fly free means that you can take a deep breath, for your soul is free and your emotions are unburdened.

BIRD'S NEST (SEE "NEST")

BIRDS Being creatures of the air, birds are interpreted to have spiritual and emotional meaning. Birds are a symbol for the soul. The owl represents innermost wisdom, and the raven stands for darkness and bad luck. Birds fluttering about helplessly in a room or a cage indicate that you are trying to escape from your emotional state. Birds flying free and unrestricted mean that you enjoy freedom of thought and have an unburdened soul. Specific birds cannot always be identified in a dream; the easiest, however, are the eagle, owl, chicken, peacock, raven, and dove. Check these symbols if you think they apply.

BIRTH Dreams about birth predict the beginning of a new, positive phase in the dreamer's life. In the case of women, a secret wish will be granted; the wish may be to have a child or for new possibilities to open up. When a man dreams of birth, it means that a new idea is coming to fruition. More specific information can be gleaned from the circumstances of the birth and from other symbols in the dream. (See also "Midwife," "Delivery," and "Child.")

BIRTHDAY Dreaming about your own birthday means that you have an excellent constitution and can look forward to living a long life. Celebrating a birthday with others indicates generosity toward other people. Dreaming about demanding birthday gifts from people is a sign to keep your selfishness in check.

BLACK Black is the color of grief. Dreaming about black usually has negative connotations, and sometimes is a message to change one's lifestyle.

BLACKBERRY The blackberry is seen as a sexual symbol having to do with bittersweet seduction. Dreaming about blackberries conveys the warning not to lose sight of the thorns.

BLACKBIRD Seeing a blackbird or hearing its song in a dream is a sign

that you will receive good news. (See also "Birds" and "Thrush.")

BLACKBOARD Dreaming about writing on a blackboard while others look over your shoulder is a sign that you are about to repeat an old mistake. Watching others laboring on a blackboard is a message to curb your fondness for mockery. Wiping away what is on the blackboard indicates that you want to ban a memory, or are trying not to repeat a mistake. (See also "Teacher" and "School.")

BLACKSMITH A blacksmith refers to a great misfortune that will, however, change your life in a positive way. The force of the blacksmith's forge can be seen as shaping your character or personality.

BLAZE A blaze in a dream may have to do with unconscious urges that are seeking expression in real life. According to Egyptian belief, seeing a blazing fire indicates that the dreamer will receive high honors. However, often a blaze stands for an intense fire (see also "Fire"), such as a fire of destruction or of passion, that brings pain. Dreaming about discovering the cause of a fire is a sign that you are about to experience a change in your life—that is, if the image is not a memory of an actual fire. Or, it could point to the onset of a physical or an emotional illness that needs to be explored and healed by taking better care of yourself. Try to determine where in the house (see also "House") the fire started. If it was the roof, you may be lacking intellectual growth. If a barn was ablaze, you may lack

B motivation. Dreaming about a blaze, in contrast to a fire, is a sign that you or your loved ones are in danger. In any event, you should explore your emotions and your conscience to detect the cause of the blaze, and then rebuild any inner qualities that may have gotten destroyed. (See also "Flame.")

BLIND Dreaming about being blind indicates that you are closing your eyes to a real-life problem that is usually emotional in nature. This could also mean that you lack farsightedness or knowledge of human nature, are easily taken advantage of, or are in need of help in order to find a way out of a dilemma. Leading a blind person implies that you are helpful and supportive of the people around you.

BLOOD Blood symbolizes vitality, consummate passion, and never-ending love. Dreaming about bleeding implies that you are suffering from emotional wounds, which you want to hide out of fear of being humiliated. Dreaming about seeing another person bleeding indicates that you are causing someone else pain. Losing blood could mean that you are losing out in love. A transfusion suggests that deep emotions are being revived. (See also "Scar" and "Wound.")

BLOOD VESSELS Seeing protruding veins in a dream is a signal to pay attention to your health, and, specifically, to that of your circulatory system.

BLOT Dreaming about a blot on a piece of paper could represent a dark

incident in your life that people who are envious of you may want to use against you. Ink blots, on the other hand, have a positive interpretation. (See also "Stain" and "Ink.")

BLUE Blue is the color of truth, emotional lightness, and intellectual superiority. A dream about the color blue is considered to be positive. (See also "Colors.")

BOAR (SEE "BUCK," "WILD BOAR," AND "PIG")

BOARDER Dreaming about a boarder means that limits have been set for your ego. This image could also signal limits to your standard of living.

BOAT A boat in a dream is a sign that you will safely reach the shore, where a life of happiness is awaiting you. A boat moving peacefully across the water suggests that you can expect quiet progress in your life. A boat struggling in rough waters indicates a hectic journey and instability in real life. A boat drifting in the dark implies that at the moment you are clueless as to how to proceed. (See also "Ship," "Traveling," and "Water.")

BODY In dreams, the human body and its functions usually refer to emotional issues. Dreaming about a physical defect points to an emotional or intellectual failing. If you dream that you are satisfied with your body, this means that you can rely on your intellectual strength in real life. Dreaming about a body dissolving into nothing means that your emotional state is in disarray. (See also individual body parts.)

BOLT Whatever is being locked up with a bolt in a dream is being denied to you in real life. A door bolted shut could describe the pain you are experiencing over a lost love, or the companionship for which you are longing. Unlocking a bolt, on the other hand, means that you are opening the door to the future or that lasting success is almost guaranteed.

BOMB The image of a bomb usually appears in dreams that have to do with the past, and generally mirrors a shocking event. However, a bomb may also represent an inability to change present, unfavorable circumstances. Dreaming about bombs connotes a threat to our existence, so they can be interpreted as a message to stay calm or to change our lifestyle in some way. Seeing an individual bomb in a dream can be a sign that a particular piece of news will hit us "like a bomb." (See also "Explosion" and "War.")

BONE Dreaming about bones could be a reference to your backbone. Seeing only the bones when dreaming about arms and legs means that you have weak extremities. Chewing on a bone indicates that lean times are ahead, or that you are too thrifty.

BOOK A book in a dream stands for "the book of life." The title and the contents of the book can tell you something about your own spiritual state. The color of the book cover can also be used in interpreting the dream. Sometimes the contents of the book have similarities to the dreamer's own life. Dreaming about a book may also express a desire to gain more knowledge in real life. According to Artemidoros, a book appearing in a dream often describes our own past, which we can make use of in the present.

BOOTS In general, boots are interpreted the same way as shoes are. A particularly klutzy pair of boots may represent a rather crude person who doesn't hesitate to kick people around in order to get his or her way. (See "Shoes.")

BORDER Crossing a border means that you are entering a new phase in life; other symbols will show if the change is positive. Crossing a border secretly is a sign that you want to change direction because of a precarious situation in real life. (See also "Path" and "Customs.")

BORDER GATE Dreaming about a gate at a border indicates that you are having a difficult time getting ahead in life. Sometimes this image points to having sexual inhibitions or being stuck in a relationship. If the barrier is raised and you are given permission to go through, there is some hope that certain things in your life may take a turn for the better. (See also "Barriers" and "Train-Crossing Barrier.")

BOSS When this image appears in a dream, the boss is usually part of the dreamer's own ego, and is very invested in the dreamer's fulfilling his or her responsibilities.

BOTTLE Dreaming about breaking a bottle foretells the end of luck or happiness; in Germany, there's this saying: "Luck and happiness—how easy it is for both to break." Dreaming about drinking from an unmarred bottle means that you will enjoy good luck; of course, the contents of the bottle also need to be taken into consideration. Sometimes a bottle in a dream can have male or female sexual connotations.

BOUQUET Arranging a bouquet of colorful flowers, or giving a colorful bouquet as a gift, expresses the dreamer's state of being. Both can also symbolize profound love.

BOWEL MOVEMENT This image in a dream has to do with freeing yourself of guilt, or at least uncomfortable feelings. You may also be trying to rid yourself of useless thoughts or bad memories, perhaps memories of a love affair gone bad. Or, it could represent being afraid of being asked to be more generous. (See also "Feces" and "Toilet.")

BOWL A bowl is a symbol for the womb but also for the collection plate, so it could indicate that the dreamer is making an offering in memory of someone else. A bowl also implies that the dreamer is offering him- or herself completely to a partner; this is especially the case when the dreamer is a woman. A broken bowl is a sign of a broken heart. (See also "Container.")

BRAID Dreaming of wearing a braid shows that you are hanging onto to old customs. You are against progress, but don't have the power to stop it. (See also "Hair.")

BRANCH A dream about a tree branch (symbolically, part of the "tree of life") is a reference to your emotional state. A green branch or one covered with blossoms is a sign of being balanced emotionally, whereas a dry or dead branch indicates that you might not be in very good shape. Stumbling over a broken-off branch shows that a specific subject is temporarily being put aside. Sitting on a branch of questionable stability implies that you are unsure of yourself. Sawing off the branch on which you are sitting is a warning to be careful about losing a grip on things. A thin branch that is green and also bears blossoms stands for desires that are being fulfilled. A branch that is brittle and has no leaves shows that you are hoping in vain for a positive change in your circumstances. (See also "Tree" and "Leaves.")

BRANDY (SEE "ALCOHOL")

BREAD Bread is the staff of life, nourishing both the body and the soul. Dreaming about bread indicates that your life is making sense again, because you are once more part of your social circle. Dreaming about a loaf of bread points to a loved one whom you want to call your own. (See also "Baking" and "Baker.")

BREAKDOWN Dreaming about a trip on which your car breaks down is a message that in real life you need to work much harder in order to reach your goal. Dreams about breakdowns always refer in some way to the dreamer's own failure or resignation. (See also "Automobile" and other transportation symbols.)

BREAKING (SOMETHING)

Breaking a glass in a dream is a warning to be more careful when dealing with a certain person or matter in real life. Breaking porcelain has a less severe meaning. (See also "Porcelain, Broken," "Glass," and "Container.")

BREAKING THROUGH

Dreaming about falling through the floor means that you are in danger of losing ground. Breaking through ice could be a sign that you will soon experience a loss on an emotional level.

BREAST Freud saw the breast as a symbol of early childhood, during which sexual feelings toward the mother were instilled. He believed that these early childhood experiences play a role in the dreamer's overly strong attachment to the mother, particularly in the case of men. Of course, dreaming about a breast also has maternal, life-sustaining connotations, and can represent spiritual and emotional nourishment for the soul. Dreaming of an injured breast means that you are searching for emotional understanding, or have troubles at home. Dreaming about a beautiful female breast could be a sign that a joyful love affair is in the making. Dreaming about the breast of an

old woman shows that you are fearful that your virility is diminishing.

BREATHING Dreaming about breathing well is a sign that you are in good shape emotionally, mentally, and physically.

BRICKLAYER A bricklayer, someone who patiently puts one brick on top of the other until a house is finished, describes a friend (or a physician) who makes sure that you are in good health, physically as well as emotionally. Dreaming about being a bricklayer, without actually being one in real life, means that you want to build something that is in your and your family's best interest. (See also "House" and "Wall.")

BRICKS/ROOF TILES Bricks are used to build houses, tiles to cover roofs. Together, they represent the building blocks of the human body. Using bricks in a dream means that you are taking care of your personal well-being. The dream could also mean that you are building a life for yourself or making a new beginning. (See also "House," "Roof Tile/ Shingle," and "Roof.")

BRIDAL SHOES According to folklore, dreaming about dancing a hole in bridal shoes means that the dreamer will have an affair. The shoes should be brought to a shoemaker for repair if the dreamer wants to put an end to his or her philandering. (See also "Shoemaker.")

BRIDE Dreaming about a bride wearing a white dress, the color of frugality as well as innocence, means that you have distanced yourself emotionally from someone in your life. A dream about escorting a bride to the altar, or being the bride at the altar yourself, is a sign that a wish might come true. Dreaming about carrying the train of a bridal gown means that you want somebody to take care of you, or that you don't want to take responsibility for yourself. If you are a man dreaming of sleeping with your bride, this is a message about being on an adventure, during which you are breaking a taboo. Sleeping with a strange woman who is wearing a bridal gown means that you could run into difficulty in real life as the result of your forceful behavior. If you are a woman dreaming of being a bride, this could point to a joyful love relationship, of which, however, you are afraid, because something in your life seems to caution against it. (See also "Wedding" and "White.")

BRIDGE A bridge in a dream is a positive sign, indicating a difficult problem being bridged or differing opinions being reconciled. Walking over a bridge means that you can expect a new, satisfying job, or that a joyful love relationship is beginning. A bridge is a symbol for an intimate connection with a loved one, and can also be a signal that a good friendship is being rekindled. The way the bridge is constructed indicates possible obstacles that you may face on life's journey. A bridge without a railing or one that is still under construction could be a message about lurking danger. Dreaming about a

bridge that has been destroyed means that you need to pay attention to your emotional health, or find a detour to happiness. (See also "Abyss" and "Building.")

BROOK A small, fresh brook in the spring is a symbol for vitality. Dreaming about a lively brook is a sign that your work and your personal life will flourish. A cloudy, foul brook shows that you are in a bad mood. The presence of many fish in the brook indicates that you will soon be blessed with lots of money. A dry brook is a warning of meager times ahead. (See also "Water.")

BROOM Dreaming about using a broom indicates that you want to straighten out or clean up your life. A stranger holding a broom calls forth an image of a witch riding around on a broom, which could represent someone who wants to start a fight with you, create havoc in your life, or "take you for a ride." A dream like this is a warning that should be taken seriously. Using a brand-new broom could be a good omen, or indicate that you are using a new idea to deal with something from the past. (See also "Witch.")

BROTHEL Dreaming about a brothel may be a message to try to solve an emotional dilemma without having moral compunctions. Similarly, this image may point to seeking the company of people who, regardless of their morals, try to establish emotional order in their lives. Here, sleeping with a prostitute is related to gaining life experience. However, going to a brothel can also indicate unfulfilled sexual needs and repressed sexual pleasure. (See also "Prostitute.")

BROTHER In a man's dream, the brother is usually the dreamer himself. Here, the dreamer is made aware of emotional imbalances or character flaws in himself, and urged to take inventory of himself. In a woman's dream, the image is also seldom the woman's own brother, but more likely a close person who, with brotherly concern, is trying to be helpful in a difficult situation; thus, the brother is a symbol for brotherly love. (See also "Siblings" and "Sister.")

BROTHER/SISTER-IN-LAW Even if you are dreaming about an actual brother- or sister-in-law, the dream probably has little to do with a relative. It has more to do with your unconscious feeling of competition with the one who has taken away your sibling. But this is on a symbolic level; although the dream points to conflicts within the family, these conflicts are actually about those within yourself. Sometimes a dream about a brother- or sister-in-law is a message that you can expect unwelcome visitors.

BROWN Brown is the color of the earth, and conveys comfort and maternal qualities. Putting on brown clothes in a dream may mean that you should moderate your rather flamboyant lifestyle.

BRUSHING Dreaming about brushing something off or out shows that in real life you don't want to have a speck of dust on your clothes—in other words, you want to appear flawless.

BUCK A buck, the animal that gores people with its horns, signifies emotional damage that you yourself have caused. During a sexual dream, a buck is an expression of fundamental male power that insists on having its conquest.

BUCKET The bucket was the vessel that was used to hoist water from a deep well. Dreaming about a bucket is a message from the unconscious that there is a way of bringing what caused a particular pain to the surface and dealing with it.

BUCKLE Dreaming about closing a buckle on a shoe or a garment indicates that you want to bring order into your life. Or, this shows that you want to deal with things that make you angry; even if these are only small things, you feel your anger toward them detracts from your personality. Unbuckling a buckle points to changes with negative consequences taking place in your home.

BUFFALO As is the case when dreaming about a steer, a dream about a buffalo has to do with your physical urges, and with realizing and living out your own desires. (See also "Buck" and "Steer.")

BUG Dreaming about bugs crawling everywhere shows that you are plagued by doubts and are about to have a breakdown. The cause could be a difficult love relationship or simply everyday stress. These little critters could also represent friends that are beginning to get on your nerves. (See also "Insects.")

BUILDING Dreaming about building something means that you want to get ahead in life. Complications while building indicate that you might have a difficult time overcoming certain problems. Accordingly, problems are easily taken care of when the building project is small and things go well. The bigger and taller the project, the bigger the problems. Building a bridge is a sign that you will soon have your problems solved. (See also "Bridge.")

BUMBLEBEES Dreaming about being surrounded by buzzing bumblebees means that your thoughts and ideas are in disarray, and that you need to reevaluate them. (See also "Bee" and "Wasp.")

BURDEN The image of a burden in a dream refers to everything that you carry around in real life. Dreaming about a physical burden placed on your shoulders indicates that you have to take on a responsibility. Watching others laboring under a burden implies that you are shying away from a responsibility. Groaning because the burden is heavy is a sign that you should be prepared for a difficult task. (See also "Luggage," "Camel," "Caravan," and "Suitcase.")

BUREAUCRACY Dreaming about entering an office and getting caught in the bureaucracy shows that you are annoyed, and dislike unfairness and being told what to do and where to go. (See also "Office.")

BURGLAR A burglar in a dream may indicate that someone is about to disrupt your peace, create chaos in your life, or take possession of something that you value. But a dream about a burglar breaking into a house could also simply be showing that you are thinking of straying from the straight and narrow. (See also "House" and "Thief.")

BURGLAR'S TOOLS Dreaming about the tools that are used to break into a house indicates violence. It could be that the unconscious is using the dream to protect the soul from harm. When a young woman in particular dreams about burglar's tools, they could be an expression of her secret (perhaps sexual) desires or anxieties.

BURNING Dreaming about burning something (pay attention to what was being burned in the dream, and check that symbol too) reflects a desire to remove something from your life. If the fire turns into a full-blown blaze, this indicates that some action will lead to an entirely new way of life. If you are getting burned, this could be a warning to be more careful with your comments that could "burn" someone else. When a pasture or a fertile field is burning, this could be a hint that there is profit in something on which you had given up. When the roof of a house is on fire, there may be a problem in the nerves above the neck, in the brain center, or in your mental attitude. (Also see "Fire" and "Blaze.")

BURRS Burrs tend to stick to each other, and in a dream they could stand for "sticking together," or having team spirit and solidarity. Because burrs stick to everything that comes along, they can also point to a person whom you can't get rid of. (See also "Glue.")

BURYING (SOMETHING)

Dreaming about burying something indicates that you are trying to bury the dark side of your soul, meaning your vices or your negative attitudes toward life. You may either be trying to forget them or to hide them out of shame. (See also "Grave.")

BUS Dreaming about a bus, a large vehicle that transports many people, can be a message that a worthwhile goal can only be reached by a community, because an individual doesn't have the necessary energy to reach it by him- or herself.

BUS/TRAIN STOP The image of a bus or a train stop is a message to stop and examine how you have lived or acted up until now, particularly when you dream about having been left behind and are alone at the stop. (See also "Harbor" and "Train Station.")

BUSH A bush in a dream stands for secrecy, because we can hide in a bush. It could be that you want to withdraw from the people around you. A green bush expresses the hope of being able to return to a full life (and love) again. A bush without leaves indicates conflicting emotions. (See also "Shrubs.")

BUSINESS Dreaming about business could be our inner voice telling us to pay attention to the advice being given by our unconscious. Young people seldom dream about business, because their life's struggle is just beginning. Older people are more likely to dream about "balancing the books," but this rarely has anything to do with financial matters.

BUSINESSPERSON (SEE "MERCHANT")

BUTCHERING The image of butchering something yourself points to your own negative behavior. Dreaming about butchering in general is a message to stop and consider whether or not what you have in mind could damage your reputation. A butcher in a dream is a warning to think twice before acting.

BUTTER Dreaming about butter being served is usually a good omen, because butter represents strength and a promise of success in a new venture. Spreading butter on a piece of bread, in folklore, means that the dreamer will be successful on the strength of his or her own power. Watching others spread butter is a warning sign that someone might be trying to "butter you up."

BUTTERFLY A butterfly in a dream could point to an emotional permutation that is similar to the changes taking place in the development of a butterfly (egg, caterpillar, cocoon). The Greeks depicted the psyche, the breath of life, or the soul as a delicate girl wearing butterfly wings (the girl, by the way, was thought to be the lover of Eros). In modern psychology, some interpret the image of a butterfly as the dreamer's soul; its fluttering wings represent the soul searching for some certainty. In ancient Egypt, dreaming about a butterfly with fluttering wings was seen as a symbol for the ever-changing luck that human beings experience. If you see yourself as the butterfly in a dream, this could mean that you are flitting about life thoughtlessly. Catching a butterfly may indicate that you will experience disloyalty within your circle of friends. Seeing only one butterfly could be a sign that you should watch out for carelessness.

BUTTOCKS (SEE "POSTERIOR")

BUTTON The button is a device that holds something together, and that is how this symbol is interpreted in dreams. A torn-off button refers to a broken relationship. Someone sewing on a button for you is a sign that you will receive protection. If you are the one sewing on a button, this means that you have nothing to fear on your job. Every now and then, buttons stand for coins that we receive but spend quickly on something useless. (See also "Needle" and "Sewing.")

BUYING (SOMETHING)

Dreaming about buying something refers to your determination to get

something that you don't possess yet, or to a determination that was lacking up till now. Sometimes other symbols in the dream point to things we didn't even know we were missing. (See also "Shopping," "Shop," and "Business.")

CABBAGE (SEE "VEGETABLES")

CABIN Dreaming about being in a dark cabin means that you want to leave a confined space and see daylight again. A cabin in a dream often announces a change in a location or of a job, ending a confining situation or condition. (See also "Ship.")

CABLE Dreaming about handling an electric cable indicates that in real life you are searching for contact. A damaged cable is a sign that you are lonely, or have difficulty making contact. (See also "Electrical Power Plant.")

CACTUS The characteristic thorns of the cactus represent assertive actions, and point to being ready to defend oneself. When a cactus appears in your dream, this could be a message not to hesitate in defending yourself against a ruthless person.

CADAVER To see or find an animal cadaver in a dream is a sign that a difficult or a less-than-successful period in your life is behind you, or that a plan or a task has either been accomplished or abandoned. If you see a cadaver of a specific animal, determine that animal's symbolic meaning to find a more specific message. (See also "Corpse" and "Vulture.")

CAGE A cage is a symbol for emotional inhibition. A caged animal in a dream means that the negative aspects of the caged animal are being dealt with successfully in real life. If the dreamer or another person is sitting in the cage, he or she may represent an imprisoned soul that wants the best for the dreamer but at this time is helpless against opposing forces; this image also points to an inferiority complex.

CAKE Dreaming about a cake usually has to do with the promise of something sweet in life. Getting a piece of cake means that love is just around the corner. Baking and eating cake point to warm and generous interpersonal relationships. (See also "Pastry Chef" and "Sweets.")

CALENDAR Dreaming about a calendar could mean that you dislike a particular assignment on your job because it is not in line with your expectations regarding advancement.

CALF A calf in a dream often represents the dreamer him- or herself. The dream might point to the dreamer's naive and ponderous personality. (See also "Youth," "Cow," and "Steer.")

CALL GIRL (SEE "PROSTITUTE")

CALLING CARD A calling card in a dream points to a secret admirer or to the possibility of making a new friend in real life. Additional conclusions about the meaning of the

dream can be reached if the card can be read in its entirety.

CAMEL Even the unconscious perceives the camel to be an animal that carries burdens. Dreaming about a camel means that either you or someone else is carrying a burden, which could be either emotional or physical. Dreaming about riding on a camel is a sign that you can count on life being rough and progress being slow. (See also "Caravan.")

CAMP Dreaming about living in a camp, without actually being a prisoner or a refugee, means that you are fighting problems or are hampered by prejudice. Only a vacation camp is considered a positive image, and means that you want to spend time in the company of happy people, are longing to be free of loneliness, or want to find harmony in a social setting.

CAN Dreaming about a closed can that can't be opened means that you want to keep certain emotions under wraps. An open can, on the other hand, is a sign that you have an abundance of feelings, and are willing to share them with others.

CANAL Dreaming about looking into a muddy canal implies a lack of progress in a particular situation to the point where you may fail altogether. A canal with very clear water is a sign that your problems will soon be solved. (See also "River" and "Water.")

CANARY The canary is the favorite bird of many lonely people. Like all creatures of the air, this bird can be seen in a spiritual or a psychological light, and describes the emotional isolation and the lack of inner freedom of the dreamer. (See also "Birds" and "Bird Cage.")

CANCER A dream about cancer does not point to a life-threatening disease in real life, even if you see yourself as the cancer patient. Rather, the dream stands for the fourth sign of the zodiac in astrology, which is represented by the crab, an animal that walks backward when faced with danger. So, it could be a suggestion to you to consider a course of action that you have used successfully in the past and that will work again.

CANDLE As far back as antiquity, the candle was considered a male sexual symbol. If the candle in your dream is burning with a bright flame, you can expect that your love in real life will be reciprocated. If the flame is going out, this means that your desire will not be fulfilled. (See also "Torch.")

CANE (SEE "SWITCH/CANE")

CANNIBAL Dreaming about human flesh means that you want to eliminate an opponent, or that you like someone so much that you could "eat him or her up." Other symbols in the dream can add to the interpretation. Freud considered a dream about cannibalism to be a sign of compulsive sadism.

CANNON Cannons in dreams often indicate a precarious situation in real life. In addition, the uncon-

scious uses this image, which strikes fear and terror in the soul, to remind us to be more assertive in life. (See also "Shotgun" and "Rifle.")

CAPTAIN The captain in a dream stands for that which guides your life through all trials, tribulations, and vicissitudes. Even though the outcome of such trials may not be known, you can always depend on having a faithful companion and trusted friend at your side. (See also "Ship.")

CAR (SEE "AUTOMOBILE")

CARAVAN Dreaming about a caravan is similar to dreaming about a camel, only here the burdens are shared. Although the journey may be risky, helpers are on hand to assist you in getting to your destination slowly but safely.

CARDS Dreaming about playing cards is a warning from the unconscious to be less frivolous, because in real life that could cost you a lot of money.

CARNATION Many garden flowers are like little elves who can help us get over something that could even rob us of sleep. Dreaming about receiving or giving a carnation usually indicates something pleasant is in store for us, such as the company of good friends, a fun get-together, or an unexpected change for the better at our jobs. (See also "Flowers.")

CARP The carp is a fish with many scales, and in folklore is considered to bring good luck. A carp in a dream often speaks like a human; it is believed to be the voice of the soul reminding us of something. (See also "Fish.")

CARPET Dreaming about unrolling a carpet means that you don't want to change anything in your life, but rather enjoy your present situation. Cleaning a carpet is a message to find a weak "spot" in real life and then do something about it.

CARRIAGE Dreaming about a carriage, a means of transportation, indicates that you will reach your goal slowly, or are afraid of an uncertain future. Getting out of a carriage is a sign that you are about to take your life into your own hands. (See also "Automobile" and "Coach.")

CART An overloaded cart in a dream could mean that you are taking on too many burdens in life. This image may also point to an illness that is sapping your strength, and be a message to make an appointment with a physician.

CASH REGISTER Dreaming about an empty cash register could mean that your life is empty right now. But it also could be a sign that you will receive some money. Dreaming about counting money in a cash register indicates that you are wondering how you will manage in the future or keep the money that you have; this could be a message to at least think twice before spending money. (See also "Money.")

CASTLE Dreaming about a castle, a building constructed for protection, may point to some kind of danger in your life. It could also mean that you are emotionally uneasy, and feel a need to restore some order. A castle in ruins implies that your emotional state is in ruins or your feelings are in turmoil, perhaps due to a relationship being in crisis. A castle can refer to a house, so you should also look up "House," which in modern dream analysis represents the human body. Sometimes people who dream of a castle live in fantasy, or are far removed from reality, in real life. Such a magnificent building could also be a warning that "pride cometh before a fall." Seeing a castle high on a hill could indicate that you are entertaining lofty ideas, which can only be realized with much hard work. (See also "Drawbridge.")

CASTRATION Casanova should have dreamt of castration. It would have reminded him to keep his sexual activities to a normal level, if for no other reason than to keep his virility intact. The positive side of such a dream is that the dreamer can't be harmed anymore by sexual temptation. (See also "Defloration.")

CAT A cat in a dream represents catlike independence and behavior. We know that cats try to get what they want (which in a dream usually refers to sexual desires) with velvet paws, but then pounce with sharp claws and hold on to what they have. The image of a wildcat may point to the personality of a woman who is too timid to express her urges in real life, only to live them out in her dreams. In a man's dream, a cat could represent a woman whom he wants to possess. In a woman's dream, it often stands for characteristics that describe her pronounced individuality, egocentrism, and fickle nature.

CATCHING A dream about things you catch and hold in your hands will tell you, together with other symbols, who or what in real life truly belongs to you. Dreaming about getting caught could be a sign of codependency in a love relationship, or indicate the degree of your enthusiasm by describing your preoccupation with a certain idea or emotion. (See also "Prison.")

CATERPILLAR The caterpillar, representing a developmental stage in the life of a butterfly, points to a developmental stage in your own life. It represents things unfinished, projects not fully thought through, and sometimes the state of being at a loss. However, the image of a caterpillar in a dream is a hopeful sign, meaning that things will turn out beautifully in the long run. (See also "Butterfly.")

CATTLE (SEE "COW")

CAVE A cave in a dream has to do with a dark place from which life comes into being, or a promise of maternal things, new beginnings, or renewal. Dreaming about stepping out of a cave indicates that you have successfully come through difficult times. Dreaming of taking refuge in a cave overnight means that you are at a loss about what to do in a doomed situation. Dreaming of living in a cave refers to your sense of isolation.

According to the Indian dream book *Jagaddeva,* fearfully stepping out of a cave is a sign of impending good fortune. But if the dreamer is running into a cave, a sad future is foretold. (See also "Grotto.")

CELLO Playing a cello in a dream means that you can hope for a happy union on an erotic or a spiritual level; however, it is possible to go too far, in the sense of pulling the strings too much. (See also "Stringed Instruments.")

CEMETERY A cemetery often appears in dreams when we are going through an actual crisis. We are, in a sense, looking for advice from those people who have passed away. From parents, we hope to find empathy for problems, which are being resolved unbeknownst to us. In fact, dreaming about coffins and graves usually indicates that we are dealing with problems that can be resolved. Visiting a grave may also mean that we are seeking a way out of a dark and dangerous situation. (See also "Funeral," "Burying," and "Coffin.")

CHAIN Even Artemidorus, the author of an ancient book on dreams, considered a chain to be a symbol for restriction. Dreaming about a chain breaking apart on its own implies that a separation is imminent. A chain broken in two by the dreamer indicates a new beginning with the promise of success. Feeling restricted by a chain means that you won't get very far in life, because you are unable to free yourself (from prejudice, for example). If the chain is a necklace, the interpretation depends on the material of which it is made (see also "Gold," "Diamond," or "Pearl").

CHAIR Dreaming about a chair or sitting on one suggests that you can only take short breaks at work, because chairs are not meant to be sat in for long periods. (See also "Armchair" and "Foot Stool.")

CHALICE (SEE "GOBLET/CHALICE")

CHAMBER POT The meaning is identical to that under "Toilet." In antiquity, people believed that dreaming about smashing a chamber pot foretold good luck or winning money.

CHAMBER/SMALL ROOM Dreaming about being in a narrow, cramped chamber or room points to physical discomfort that you are experiencing. (See also "Room.")

CHAMPAGNE Dreaming about drinking champagne means that you want to enjoy life without thinking about tomorrow. Or, this could point to wanting to bypass a moral barrier in the sexual arena. (See also "Alcohol.")

CHANGING A BABY'S DIAPERS A dream about changing a baby's diapers is a positive one, given that the contents are supposed to bring good luck to the dreamer. (See also "Feces.")

CHAOS Dreaming about a chaotic situation usually means that the dreamer is unable to deal with certain anxieties and feelings.

CHAPEL Dreaming about a chapel is a reminder to reflect on your behavior and actions, checking whether or not they have been proper.

CHASED/HOUNDED Being chased or hounded in a dream may take on many different forms, and the unconscious material that thus comes to light should be taken to heart by the dreamer. For instance, if you are being chased by someone of the opposite sex, it may be time to deal with a fear of erotic issues, to avoid falling prey to loneliness. In ancient Egypt, it was believed that dreaming about being chased meant that people were speaking ill of the dreamer.

CHAUFFEUR A chauffeur in a dream is usually steering our fate. When the chauffeur is listening to directions given to him, this means that you are reaching your goal in real life without any detours. Should the chauffeur refuse the directions given to him, this is a sign that you are unable to assert yourself. A chauffeur in a dream might also be a messenger in disguise. (See also "Messenger.")

CHECK Dreaming about a check has little to do with financial matters, but rather with promises to be kept and responsibilities to accept. Dreaming about writing a check implies making good on a promise in real life. Seeing a lot of checks in a dream is a sign that you are taking on too much in real life, and can barely follow through on what you have promised. Of course, the numbers on the check (and sometimes the name) are important too. (See also individual numbers.)

CHEEKS Dream experts in ancient Greece believed that dreaming about rosy, round cheeks was a sign of a "full cash register," whereas pale, sunken cheeks indicated financial difficulties. Putting rouge on your cheeks in a dream could mean that you have something to hide in real life. (See also "Makeup" and "Powder.")

CHERRY This sweet, red fruit stands for a cherry-shaped mouth. The cherry is a symbol for emotions and love. Picking cherries in a dream denotes meeting new friends or enriching a current relationship. Sweet cherries are like kisses, sour cherries signal disappointments, and black cherries sometimes point to a passionate, but painful, love relationship. Cherry blossoms represent eternal love, and also heartfelt warmth that promises a new beginning. In some Mediterranean countries, the cherry tree is considered to be the "tree of knowledge." (See also "Tree.")

CHESS Dreaming about playing chess and being in a favorable position indicates that you are working intelligently and with an alert mind, but are not taking sufficient advantage of your superior position. If you are playing poorly in the dream, this is a message to look for a partner in real life with better skills and to learn

from him or her. If the chess figures are thrown on the floor out of sheer frustration or angrily put away, this is a warning to act more restrained around your friends so that you don't lose them.

CHEST Dreaming about a chest is a sign of some kind of surprise. A locked chest refers to secrets that you need to keep to yourself. An open chest means that your curiosity is satisfied and good luck is promised; however, the latter has to be confirmed by other symbols. (See also "Wood.")

CHEWING Dreaming about chewing food may be an encouragement to use patience and hard work to solve a problem that is occupying you right now. (See also "Eating.")

CHICKENS Dreaming about cackling chickens can easily create a sense of panic in the dreamer. This image points to losing control over our thoughts. (See also "Feathered Animals" and "Hen.")

CHILD As a symbol, the image of a child is not always positive, because it has contemptuous undertones: "Only a child would act like that!" A child in a dream often refers to immaturity or to making yourself smaller than you really are. A child, however, is also a symbol for new possibilities and changed attitudes. If it is a pregnancy dream and you are carrying the child and give birth, this means that new things will develop in real life, or that a particular phase is over. When a child appears in the dreams of parents, this image could be making them aware of the difficulties that their own child is facing—even if the dream is very positive. The image of a child also points to a still unknown possibility, or something precious that you would like to possess. In a negative sense, a child in a dream might indicate your general state of neediness or distress; the child could also represent an animal that needs help. Several children in a dream point to turmoil in your life or a sense of being defenseless in your environment. Carrying a child indicates that you should find an answer to a present conflict; dropping a child is a warning of impending disaster. (See also "Baby," "Birth," "Youth," "Son," "Daughter," and "Pregnancy.")

CHIMNEY/FIREPLACE The image of a chimney is a symbol for needing to let off some steam, or free ourselves from pressure. According to Freud, a chimney stands for the female sexual organs. A fire burning bright in a fireplace means that you have nothing to fear in a love relationship or at the job, because you approach both with passion and tenacity. Soot expelled from a chimney, or smoke that escapes poorly or not at all, indicates that you are dealing with a difficult situation in your private life. (See also "Factory Chimney.")

CHIMNEY SWEEPER Dreaming about a chimney sweeper, in folklore considered to be a symbol of good luck, indicates a release from a burden, especially one that is emotional in nature. It could be that you have con-

quered something that has been particularly burdensome, such as an inferiority complex or a character defect that has made relationships difficult.

CHOCOLATE (SEE "SWEETS")

CHOIR If you are dreaming about listening to a choir, this means that you want to cultivate good relationships, or are grateful that you have harmonious relationships with friends and neighbors. (See also "Music.")

CHURCH For religious people as well as nonbelievers, the church represents a place of contemplation. If the entrance to the church is obstructed in your dream, this means that you need to deal with conflicts in real life. Dreaming about sitting in a church indicates a need for peace and harmony. A semi-dark church can be a reminder of the ambiguities of life, or an indication that you don't know which way to turn. Something obscene taking place in a church points to an increasing amount of internal stress or lack of control, and is a message that you need to take seriously. (See also "Priest," "Clergy," "Church Service," and "Temple.")

CHURCH SERVICE/WORSHIP Dreaming about worshiping is a message from the unconscious to look inward more, or to reflect on a higher purpose. A church service in a dream may represent an appeal to get your emotional affairs in order, to act on good intentions, or to deal with your anxieties or depression. According to ancient Egyptian books on dreams, attending a religious service meant that the dreamer will find sympathy. (See also "Priest," "Clergy," and "Church.")

CIGARETTE LIGHTER Flicking on a cigarette lighter in a dream indicates that you are a fiery person. Whether this is a positive or a negative trait can only be determined by looking at the other symbols in the dream.

CIRCLE A circle is a symbol for wholeness. In a dream, it may be represented by the shape itself, a group of people standing in a circle, or a round room or space. The message for you could be to draw a protective circle around your emotions, or to come to a final decision about something. The circle may also indicate that you are circling an object of your desires (this is usually meant in a positive sense). A circus arena where people are performing with and taming wild animals is also round, and could stand for uncontrolled passions. Walking into a circle indicates that you are pursuing a specific goal. (See also "Arena," "Globe," and "Circus.")

CIRCUS Watching a circus performer in a dream means that you are looking for someone who is mastering his or her life, and who could be a role model for you. Being the circus performer yourself is an indication that you want to give proof of your talents. (See also "Clown," "Circle," "Magician," and animals that perform in a circus.)

CITY The city is a maternal symbol,

and has to do with being embraced and protected. In a nightmare, the image of a city translates into a fear of unjustly losing the protection that we are used to. Many dreams with the image of a city also mirror our emotional state, and could be a hint for us to do something to reduce our worries and emotional unrest, in order to prevent a nervous breakdown. (See also "Nightmares" under Other Clues, and "Mother.")

CITY HALL (SEE "TOWN HALL/CITY HALL")

CLARINET (SEE "WIND INSTRUMENTS")

CLAWS Dreaming about being clawed and not getting away points to being stuck in real life. Perhaps this is a message to get out of a relationship that has become too oppressive for you.

CLAY Dreaming about building a house using clay means that you want to protect yourself from harmful substances, or make others think that you are unapproachable. Getting stuck in wet clay is a message from the unconscious to rely less on others, or have the courage to do something on your own. Because clay is also used for medicinal purposes, as in compresses and poultices, the dream could also be a warning that someone with less-than-honest intentions is after you. (See also "House.")

CLEANING (SEE "SWEEPING")

CLERGY When a woman dreams

about clergy, it is often a male figure who addresses intense emotions or admonishes. But this image could also refer to a memory of a priest or another caring person, whose advice you could use right now. (See also "Church Service" and "Church.")

CLIFF A cliff is similar to "Abyss" in meaning. Remember, the steeper the cliff, the farther you may fall. Dreaming about seeing a ship stranded on a cliff or a rock may be a message to change your course in real life. Even without the ship in the dream, a rock protruding above the surface of the water points to trouble in life, such as having difficulty actualizing a particular plan or job. (See also "Abyss," "Ocean," "Ship," and "Water.")

CLIMBING In climbing, your eyes are looking toward the future to improve your spiritual or material well-being. Climbing onto a roof shows that you are using your head in order to advance in life. Climbing a mountain indicates that improvement in your station in life can only be accomplished with effort. If the mountain is too steep, this is a sign that a plan may not work out, and it would be best to apply your energy to a different task that will be easier to accomplish. Climbing in a dream also points to an adventurous spirit and to determination. It shows that you won't spare any effort to get to a desired goal, even at the cost of losing a little skin. In addition, the image of climbing bears the message that you can never be totally sure of the outcome of anything, which might mean that in reality you don't feel all that secure.

(See also "Roof," "Stairs," "Ladder," "Crashing," and "Mountain.")

CLOCK/WATCH A clock or a watch in a dream often expresses our fear that life is moving along too fast. Or, either image could be a hint to watch how you manage time. For a more detailed interpretation, you need to remember the exact time on the clock. If the hour hand was almost at twelve, this could be a message from the unconscious that a task you are undertaking needs to be completed in a hurry. Of course, the dream could also refer to stages in your life. (See also "Morning," "Noon," "Evening," "Night" and any relevant numbers.)

CLOSET (SEE "CUPBOARD/CLOSET")

CLOTH The clothes that cover our bodies are made of cloth, so dreaming about cloth could mean that you have a secret to hide. This image could also point to wanting to get to the heart of a matter without many words. The color of the cloth conveys important additional information. Being together with someone under a piece of cloth indicates that you need a cohort in order to secretly plot against someone in real life.

CLOTHES (SEE "DRESS," "SHIRT," "RAGGED CLOTHES," "EVENING ATTIRE," AND "SHOPPING")

CLOUDS Clouds in a dream could be a curtain separating you from success in real life. Storm clouds, in particular, signify setbacks that could destroy your livelihood. Puffy, cotton-wool clouds, on the other hand, promise enjoyment. (See also "Lightning," "Thunderstorm," and "Sky.")

CLOVER Clover is not always interpreted as positive; it is often seen as a weed that points to emotional inconsistencies that need to be addressed.

CLOWN The clown is a figure who laughs as well as cries. Dreaming about a clown could be a sign of your sense of inadequacy (perhaps having to do with sex). The clown represents the happy side of the dreamer, but also is a reminder that there is a sad side, and an end to all things.

CLUB Dreaming about joining a social club may indicate that you wish your friends would be more open.

COACH A horse-drawn coach is a symbol of times past, which we associate with being quieter and more relaxed. Dreaming about a horse-drawn carriage is an expression of the dreamer's nostalgic idea of peace and relaxation.

COALS Coals are a symbol for energy. Dreaming about seeing coals burning with a bright flame indicates that a joyful event is about to take place in real life. Coals hidden under thick clouds of smoke indicate that future plans are in danger, or that sadness and grief will enter your home.

COAT Dreaming about a coat indicates that you are covering up some-thing, keeping a secret, or protecting a loved one. Putting on a new coat implies that you are trying to make a good impression. If the coat is either too wide or too short, this means that although you had the best intentions to keep a secret, you are letting it slip nonetheless. Spreading a coat over yourself or someone else is a sign that you are covering up something.

COFFEE Dreaming about a coffee bean supposedly has sexual connotations. Drinking coffee by yourself in a dream means that you are longing for a love relationship in real life; enjoying a cup of coffee in the company of others means that you are courting two different people, and might get neither one. In any event, dreaming about coffee always indicates involvement in something exciting.

COFFIN A dream about a coffin usually has little to do with death, although it does point to something that is ending. A closed coffin may represent someone in your life who is leaving and saying goodbye, or the loss of a position at work. Seeing a coffin float on water is a sign that something that you have been anxious about is being swept way. A coffin in a dream may also stand for the removal of prejudice. Seeing a corpse in the coffin means that you might be trying to put an end to a friend-ship or a love relationship; it could even be pointing to a divorce. Seeing yourself in the coffin means that you should put the past behind you, and put all your efforts toward the future. (See also "Corpse," "Funeral," and "Grave.")

COLD Dreaming about cold conditions may mean that you are truly physically cold. It could also be a message to pay attention to a possible illness, or to do something about being insensitive and lacking compassion. On the other hand, dreaming about having a cold indicates that you have a somewhat cold personality, or don't enjoy having contact with people. Reaching for a Kleenex in a dream has to do with people keeping their distance from you. Dreaming about having a cold may also indicate that something that you did is making you anxious; if you search for the reason that you did it, you might regain your inner peace.

COLLAR In psychoanalysis, anything round has sexual connotations, so a dream about a collar may be interpreted in that light. But dreaming about a clean collar can just as easily mean that you are preparing for an important (nonsexual) event in real life. A torn collar may mean that you are about to "wring somebody's neck" in real life.

COLORS Colors explain feelings that can provide important information about the dreamer's emotional state. According to some dream researchers, people who dream in color are more temperamental than those who dream in black-and-white. Working with colors in a dream may refer to covering up something that you don't like. (See also specific colors.)

COMB A comb is used to straighten out tangles in our hair. A comb in a dream stands for getting your

impulses under control, and thereby perhaps even winning the heart of your partner. Using a comb to make hair even messier than it was indicates that you are fairly careless in your relationships, or have sexual hang-ups that you hide behind extreme actions or behavior. (See also "Hair.")

COMMUNION (SEE "HOLY COMMUNION")

COMPANY Looking for company in a dream means that in real life you want to be less lonely, or to communicate with others to free yourself of an emotional burden. In ancient Egypt, being a guest at a party meant that the dreamer's situation will become confused. (See also "Guest.")

COMPASS Dreaming about a compass means that you are hoping to find a way out of a mishandled situation. (See also "Four Points of the Compass.")

COMPLAINING/COMPLAINT We know that constant complaining will not a get a sympathetic reaction from others, but perhaps bring forth a malicious joy and gloating. For this reason, some dream experts believe that complaining and lamenting in a dream translates into making oneself or others happy in real life. Filing a complaint before a court in a dream means that in real life you want your own opinion to prevail, regardless of the cost. (See also "Court.")

COMPOSING Dreaming about a reading, seeing, or working with clefs and notes indicates that you are searching for harmony and emotional equilibrium in your life. (See also "Music.")

CONCERT Dreaming about being at a concert attended by many people indicates that you are looking for harmonious surroundings and good company. (See also "Music.")

CONDOLENCE Expressing condolence always connotes some sadness. The unconscious, however, may be suggesting that the person expressing it is a hypocrite, and not really sympathetic to the fate of the dreamer.

CONDUCTOR A music conductor in a dream stands for someone who is in charge of all the instruments of the soul; he or she directs our emotions, and wants to bring them into harmony. The conductor also uncovers internal disharmony. (See also "Music.") A train conductor, on the other hand, stands for someone who has control over others. He or she pays attention to how our life journey is progressing, and makes sure that we travel in the right direction. The train conductor is also our friend, who will stand by us when we face a difficult situation. (See also "Traveling" and "Train.")

CONFESSION When this image appears in a dream, it could be a sign that in real life you want to unburden your soul of things that people don't generally talk about.

CONSTIPATION Dreaming about being constipated translates into being emotionally poisoned or hav-

ing the wrong attitude. For Freud, it was an expression of greed or the inability to give. (See also "Bowel Movement" and "Feces.")

CONTAINER Dreaming about an empty container is a sign that in real life your wallet is empty; a full container indicates that you are well off. But there is a warning involved, which is not to be careless. According to Freud, dreams about containers always have sexual connotations; in psychoanalysis, an empty container, for instance, points to impotence. (See also "Glass.")

CONVALESCENCE A dream about convalescence doesn't necessarily point to someone who is recovering from an illness in real life. Dreaming about convalescence is more likely a signal that difficult, trying times are about to come to an end. Or, this can be a message from the unconscious to reduce the stress in your life and stop working so hard. (See also "Hospital.")

COOK The image of a cook in a dream stands for the "cook of your soul." The cook may bring you distasteful food, or something that is "hard to swallow." But the cook could also bring a certain food that will renew your vitality. The saying "Too many cooks spoil the broth" could have a bearing on your dream as well. (See also "Hunger" and "Recipe.")

COOKING A family get-together might be in the making if you are doing the cooking in the dream; if other people are doing the cooking, you can expect an invitation. However, cooking might also refer to "boiling over," as with anger, or could have the connotation of having "cooked your own goose." (See also "Kitchen.")

CORNER Dreaming about bumping into a corner indicates that you are likely to feel put upon or criticized in real life. This image may also suggest that you are hiding in a corner, and too shy to speak your mind.

CORPSE Dreaming about a dead body refers to something that you have long taken care of, a certain feeling that you still are dragging around, or a relationship that should be ended. Dead people often appear in the dreams of people who are unhappy in their jobs. They want to do something about it, but all attempts have failed. In some dreams, dead people also stand for difficulties that have been overcome. If you dream frequently about corpses, this is something that should be taken seriously and might warrant consulting a psychotherapist. (See also "Grave," "Murderer," "Coffin," and "Cadaver.")

CORRIDOR (SEE "HALLWAY" AND "PASSAGE/ PASSAGEWAY")

CORSET The image of a corset in a dream refers to emotional and mental restrictions. A very tight corset means that you are emotionally tense, stuck mentally or emotionally, or "treading water" at the moment.

COTTAGE A cottage is a small house, and, as a dream image, may be suggesting that a small space is restricting your spirit. Or, the unconscious could be encouraging you to come out of your shell, or to free yourself from restrictions. On the other hand, a garden cottage might stand for the secrets that you want to hide, such as a secret love, or knowledge of somebody else's secrets. Other symbols in the dream will provide additional information. (See also "Garden" and "House.")

COURT Dreaming about standing in front of a court of justice as a defendant refers to being afraid of losing friends in real life. A conviction is a hint about a dark shadow clouding your soul. Simply seeing the court building means that you are worrying unnecessarily about something in your private life. (See also "Indictment" and "Judge.")

COURTYARD (SEE "YARD/COURTYARD")

COW A cow is a symbol for maternal qualities and unselfish giving. In the dream of an unmarried woman, however, it usually indicates that she is lacking warmth, patience, and kindness, and is too demanding. Dreaming about watching somebody milk a cow means that someone is trying to take advantage of you. Dreaming about milking a cow yourself means that you want to take advantage of a situation for financial gain. Surprisingly, men seldom dream about cows; when they do, it usually implies that they are a "momma's boy."

COWSLIP This is a flower that announces spring. Dreaming about it may connote a new sense of feeling alive, or hint at celebrating a new love.

CRADLE This dream image suggests that we can look forward to happy times. It also shows that, when faced with troublesome situations, we tend to "rock ourselves to sleep." (See also "Baby.")

CRASHING A dream about crashing is a signal that a drastic change will take place in your life. A crash interferes with any kind of forward movement, at least for a time, and always brings losses. (See also "Falling.")

CREAM (SEE "MILK")

CREVICE Dreaming about a deep crevice indicates that your interpersonal relationships are paralyzed, or points to loneliness and a lack of contact. Falling into a deep crevice is a sign that hopeless problems are on the horizon; if rescued, you will have a new beginning after a time of serious problems, or may trust that everything cannot but take a turn for the better. If you dream about climbing down into a crevice that has been created by tectonic activities, you have nothing to fear: The clear water that can usually be found at the bottom describes an alert mind and a competitive nature, whose strengths are only used for the good. Freud, however, viewed every type of crevice as a sexual symbol.

CRICKETS Crickets represent "stains" on the soul. Swarms of crickets in a dream suggest that something in your surroundings is in disarray. Sometimes a dream about crickets (and grasshoppers, who belong to the same family) points to having an erratic nature.

CRIMINALS (SEE "DREAMS ABOUT CRIMINALS" UNDER OTHER CLUES)

CRIPPLE Dreaming about being or seeing a cripple describes the dreamer's emotional helplessness, bordering on a sickness of the soul. (See also "Invalid.")

CROCODILE A crocodile is a symbol for negative hidden energies, and appears in the dreams of those who have yet to find a positive attitude toward life. A crocodile is also a symbol for a world without mercy, or for neighbors with bad intentions who can make life difficult for the dreamer. (See also "Dragon.")

CROSS The cross is a symbol for order. It often refers to a point in the dreamer's life where the future is being decided. Or, it may be a sign for the dreamer to come to terms with his or her present situation.

CROSSBOW Shooting with a crossbow in a dream means that you are hanging on to old ideas. This image also implies becoming discouraged because you cannot find a proper "weapon" that will give you an advantage.

CROSSING Crossing a river or a lake in a dream alludes to unconsciously moving to the bank on the other side. This could mean that you are searching for a different vantage point in life. Other symbols will determine if the change will be an improvement.

CROW Dreaming about noisy crows is a sign of an imminent loss. This image also foretells a serious incident with negative consequences in an intimate relationship. (See also "Raven" and "Birds.")

CROWD OF PEOPLE According to ancient Egyptian dream books, seeing a crowd of people in a dream is a promise of wealth and prosperity. But it so happens that people seldom dream about a crowd, because usually only a few individuals play a role in a dream.

CROWN A crown is a symbol of power, including power misused. A golden crown, for instance, indicates that you are feeling superior toward others, or forgetting your heart in pursuit of money and prestige. A crown of thorns indicates suffering, and a crown of myrrh an impending wedding (not necessarily yours) or the start of a new and happier time.

CRUTCHES Dreaming about crutches shows that you feel insecure and need help in real life. Leaning on crutches implies that you need to deal with your anger about something, perhaps something related to your job or your relationship. Watching somebody on crutches indicates that you are paying too much attention to others at the expense of your own needs. Throwing crutches away or destroying them means that a present emergency can be solved quickly.

CRYING Tears in a dream are usually tears of joy that brighten everyday existence. But if there seems to be no reason for the crying, the dream might refer to grief and worry in real life. The people in ancient Assyria believed that crying for a deceased person meant that the dreamer, if he was sick, would recover, or that he could start anew because the worst was behind him. ("See also "Laughter.")

CRYSTALS Crystals are considered objects that cultivated people own. Dreaming about crystals means that you believe that, in order for a relationship to be successful, you need to have what the well-to-do have. Light refracting in a crystal indicates that others see you in a less-than-favorable light. (See also "Glass.")

CUCUMBER Dreaming about cucumbers, particularly in the case of women, is usually seen as an expression of sexual lust. Biting into a pickle (a cucumber that has been preserved) in a dream indicates that present, real-life problems need to be solved quickly. Growing cucumbers in a vegetable garden indicates that you will have to wait a long time for results and success; harvesting cucumbers promises a better outcome for the issues that you are facing. (See also "Vegetables.")

CUP In psychoanalysis, a cup, like all other containers, stands for the female sexual organs. Drinking from a cup expresses a hope for an erotic experience; breaking a cup represents breaking someone's heart.

CUPBOARD/CLOSET The cupboard is a place where things are stored; in a dream, it translates into keeping something locked away that is precious to the dreamer. This could be a person whom the dreamer is in love with, but it could also be a habit that he or she wants to hold onto at any price. Opening a well-organized closet or cupboard means that everything in your life is also in order or that you are sociable and your heart is overflowing with love. A closet or cupboard in disarray indicates that your emotions are in turmoil. (See also "Key.")

CUPID Cupid as a dream motif points to a passionate, but fleeting, love affair, or one that is rather superficial. However, the image of the naked god of love in the form of a child appears mostly in the dreams of people who are familiar with mythology—in other words, Cupid is not an archetypal symbol.

CURLS Dreaming about messed-up curls means that your mind is also "messed up." Cutting off someone's curls indicates the end of a relationship that once was good and that you will remember with affection. (See also "Hair.")

CURTAIN A curtain in a dream points to secrets that we would rather keep to ourselves. Dreaming about closing or hiding behind a curtain indicates that you are afraid of something being exposed in real life. Opening a curtain, or looking through a window where the curtains are already open, means that you will soon have clarity about a certain subject or situation. Curtains in windows need to be examined in terms of which floor of the house the windows are located on—especially when the curtains are closed. This could be a sign of some kind of physical discomfort, and the floor of the house is the clue for discovering in which part of the body the problem lies. A theater curtain points to actions that we contemplate for the near future. (See also "House" and "Window.")

CUSTOMS The duty that is collected from us at a border is a symbol for the demands that life is making on us at the present time. Getting caught smuggling means that we feel too overburdened to resolve a certain matter in real life. (See also "Border" and "Border Gate.")

CUTTING Dreaming about cutting always stands for taking risks, regardless of what is being cut. Taking a risk could be to your advantage. But, in most cases, you will recognize that you have only hurt yourself if you believed you could get your own way either with bravado or brute force. Using your head would have gotten you much further. If a piece of bread or something else is being cut or sliced off, this indicates that a particular situation is not being resolved in your favor. (See also "Knife," "Nail," and "Scissors.")

DACHSHUND Dreaming about a dachshund indicates that your faithful companion is right by your side, but unable to help you. (See also "Dog.")

DAGGER Psychoanalysts believe that when a woman dreams about a being injured by a dagger, she wants to give herself totally to her lover. (See also "Sword," "Knife," and "Rapier.")

DANCING Dancing in a dream describes passions and desires, sexuality, or the whirl or the turmoil of life. A dance on a volcano in a dream can be a reminder of the mad rush of daily life. Sometimes dancing in a dream is a memory of a wonderful ball or party, and points to a hope that a desire in real life will be fulfilled. When the dreamer seems to dance through a fog, this reveals his or her feeling of insecurity. (See also "Volcano," "Fog," and "Waltz.")

DANGER A dream about danger should not be taken literally. Rather, the dream may be a warning of an impending conflict with which you will have to deal. It is equally possible that the dream is pointing to an inferiority complex, a problematic relationship, or a sexual crisis. However, all of these problems or issues can be remedied. A dream about danger could also simply be a hint to change your lifestyle.

DARKNESS Dreaming about darkness has to do with a shadow being cast over your soul, or could be a sign that you are not sure about something. Dreaming of something lurking in the dark is a message that in real life you should hurry and clear up an unsettled situation. (See also "Night.")

DARNING/MENDING People who darn socks or mend other pieces of clothing in a dream generally have difficulty taking care of their mistakes in real life. (See also "Sewing.")

DATES The date is a sweet fruit that can be interpreted in sexual terms, particularly if the dreamer is eating dates.

DAUGHTER It is possible that when parents are dreaming about their daughter, they are being made aware of her real-life problems, which are based on their own culpable actions and which they consciously decided to ignore. In a woman's dream, the (sometimes nonexistent) daughter serves as a signal that something is not right in the woman's private or emotional life. (See also "Child" and "Son.")

DAWN AND DUSK Dreaming about the dawn indicates that you are finding yourself in a confusing situation in real life, but there is hope of finding a solution. Dusk has a similar meaning, but implies finding no solution. (See also "Morning" and "Evening.") In addition, looking at the dawn in a dream is a signal that things in life will take a turn for

D the better. (See also "Red" and "Sun.")

DAY Dreaming about the dawning of a new day is a reminder from the unconscious to live with more purpose, to seize the day, or to let light sweep away the cobwebs in your head.

DEAD PERSON Seeing a dead person in a dream is often a symbol for the end of a difficult phase in our life, and perhaps one that was successfully resolved with the help of other people. (See also "Corpse.")

DEATH A dream about death rarely announces a physical demise. In most cases, it is a sign that we are holding onto something that should have been discarded long ago. In a way, it is a message from the unconscious to give our life new direction, or to avoid the dangers that are piling up in front of us. Dreaming about the death of someone close means, according to C.G. Jung, that we are severing the bond that we had with that person. Seeing someone die who in reality is already dead points to the deep bond we still have with that person. Death can also signal the end of a phase in the dreamer's life. A dream about one's own death shows a kind of emotional cleansing of the soul, a rebirth of a better self, or a change to a more positive approach to life's battles. (See also "Dying" and other symbols having to do with death.)

DEATH ANNOUNCEMENT A dream about a death announcement is usually the unconscious telling us something about the person whose death is announced. It could point to advice that person would give us if he or she were still alive. In other words, a death announcement can signify a healing, although in a frightening form.

DEATH, APPARENT When you appear to be dead in a dream, you are probably trying to make yourself invisible in real life, to secretly steal away from your friends or to avoid taking on a responsibility. Seeing others apparently dead suggests that you shouldn't get too worked up over things that only appear to be serious. (See also "Death.")

DEATH SENTENCE A dream that pronounces a death sentence for you indicates that you need to consciously make changes in your attitudes toward life. If the death sentence is given for someone else, you need to change your attitude toward that person. (See also "Court," "Judge," and "Scaffold.")

DECAPITATION Dreaming about being decapitated could mean that you are afraid of "losing your head," acting dishonorably, or being thought of as a weakling in a certain situation. But often the unconscious is trying to remind the dreamer that changed attitudes and new ideas are important for emotional survival, and can give life more meaning. (See also "Head" and "Amputation.")

DECEASED PERSON Dreaming about a deceased person suggests that you are expecting or looking for advice in real life. Or, the dream could be an indication that you are recovering from an illness, or being rescued from some kind of danger. (See also "Corpse" and "Urn.")

DECEPTION Dreaming about being deceptive is often an indication of a surprise or of a quick gain that is short-lived. Dreaming about being deceived by your partner is not something that should be taken too seriously; the person who is sleeping with your partner in the dream is often nothing more than support from an unexpected source in real life; sometimes the image may also be a hint to be less inhibited in matters of intimacy. (See also "Sexual Relations" and "Intercourse.")

DEER The deer is the animal that only comes out of the forest at dusk to graze. In a dream, the image of a deer stands for emotional desires, and encourages the dreamer to be more outgoing or less shy in the presence of others. A deer may also refer to a hidden bearer of good tidings. But a good fortune could be gone as fast as a deer disappearing into the woods. Since ancient times, a buck in a dream has been associated with a warning not to make hasty decisions. Dreaming about hunting deer but not killing any is a message to avoid making rash comments. (See also "Animals.")

DEFLORATION When a man dreams about defloration, he may be afraid that he is not competent sexually in real life. For a woman, such a dream may reflect a sense of insecurity in human relations. But often defloration is an indication that the

dreamer has lost something that is very dear to him or her. (See also "Virgin.")

DELAYS Dreaming about delays implies that you have no intention of changing your life. If a train is late in a dream, this means that you are angry that you have to wait for something that you want to achieve or get. A dream with delays often indicates a disruption of lifestyle. Dreaming about being delayed for a rendezvous means that your regard for your date is not all that great. (See also "Lateness.")

DELIVERY For men and women alike, dreaming about a delivery has to do with the recognition of new ideas that will become realities in a very short time. (See also "Birth" and "Giving Birth.")

DEMOLITION Dreaming of demolishing something together with others indicates that in real life you want to disregard something that is rotten or stale, or end an unhealthy relationship in order to find new and better ones. Watching the demolition of a house in a dream shows that you are afraid that your own character or good reputation is being damaged. Under-taking a demolition on your own is a sign that you are attempting to resolve emotional discomfort. Demolishing a dilapidated house points to overcoming a psychosomatic illness.

DEPARTMENT STORE Walking around a department store and looking at merchandise with indecision indicates that you are also not quite sure what you want in real life, and

D that others often take advantage of this. Should you buy something without the slightest hesitation, you will be envied in real life for your decisiveness. For an in-depth interpretation of the dream, you also need to pay attention to what you have bought and the price. (See also "Business," "Shop," "Shopping," and "Buying.")

DEPARTURE A very sudden departure in a dream indicates an avoidance of an unpleasant situation, or shows that you are fearful of taking on a responsibility. When another person is leaving, this could point to the end of a heated argument that you had wanted to win. (See also "Goodbye.")

DESERT Dreaming about the desert, a symbol for loneliness, is a reference to the isolation that we feel in real life, despite all the contact we have with other people. Riding or wandering through the desert means that we will reach our goal only through extreme deprivation or effort.

DETECTIVE Dreaming about a detective implies that the detective is uncovering your most secret thoughts, which could mean that you are afraid of being found out in real life. However, such a dream might just be a message from the unconscious to at last let go of all your secrecy.

DETOUR A detour in a dream stands for the detour that we take in life that costs us precious time. According to an ancient Egyptian interpretation, dreaming about making a detour meant that the dreamer should beware of bad advice. (See also "Street" and "Path.")

DEVIL The devil is considered a "fallen angel." If he appears in a dream, he is ruthlessly laying bare the defects and weak points in your character. Dreaming about the devil could also be an indication of your single-minded focus on profit. Seeing and speaking to the devil in a dream indicates that you need to be cautious in real life, because somebody is out to get you. Getting attacked by the devil means that you may lack self-control or good manners.

DIAMOND The diamond is the hardest of the precious stones, and is seen as a symbol for emotional wholeness. A diamond may indicate clear thinking, or point to the dreamer's concentration on creating a successful life, or his or her steadfast behavior toward certain people. (See also "Precious Stones.")

DICE A die in a dream is a reference to a square shape; only it is more dynamic in its meaning, because a die also has something to do with the game of dice, which implies an uncertainty with how the dice of fate might fall. If the dream is about the game, the numbers that are thrown are important. (See also the respective numbers.)

DICTATOR A dream about a dictator often refers to the dreamer's own ego, which is disregarding all caution and always wanting its own way. The unconscious is saying that it will go to any lengths to prevent any carelessness that may cause damage to the dreamer's psyche. (See also "Boss" and "Emperor.")

DIGGING UP Dreaming about digging up an object, maybe even a corpse, shows that you have a bad conscience, are out of sorts, or feel uneasy. Often this is also a way of expressing the fear that something has been unearthed that should have remained buried.

DILAPIDATED BUILDING
Dreaming about an unsafe, dilapidated building shows that you feel insecure in your environment. (See also "House" and "Facade.")

DINING CAR A dream about being in a dining car is often a reminder that the dreamer should not overindulge in real life. It is also a suggestion to choose a healthier lifestyle, particularly if the dreamer is eating too much. (See also "Train" and "Traveling.")

DINNER For older people, a sumptuous dinner might point to an especially happy old age, in which they will not want for anything. For younger people, this might mean that a particular job has been completed, and the fruits of their labor are about to be enjoyed. Generally, this image is a reference to our life reaching calmer waters, and means that we don't have to worry about what tomorrow will bring.

DINNER JACKET (SEE "EVENING ATTIRE")

DINOSAUR (SEE "DRAGON")

DIRT Dreaming about dirt is usually considered positive—a wagon, for example, can be pulled out of mud. Dreaming about getting dirt thrown at you or getting dirty means that you can expect to have a lucky streak in financial matters; after all, money has gone through many hands, and is therefore dirty. (See also "Mud.")

DISCOVERING (SEE "FINDING/DISCOVERING")

DISGUISE (SEE "MASK")

DISGUST Dreaming about feeling disgusted indicates that your soul is in some way critical of a comment you made or bad behavior you displayed, and is giving you a chance to seriously examine what you are doing. The unconscious uses disgust, because this is a feeling that we will likely remember. (See also "Vomiting.")

DISHES, BROKEN Dreaming about broken dishes sometimes indicates good luck. Buying new dishes, if the old ones were broken or discarded, suggests positive changes in familiar areas. (See also "Glass," "Porcelain, Broken," "Plate," and other breakable objects and containers.)

DISHES, DOING A dream about doing dishes implies that you want to get rid of guilt or imperfections. Dreaming about doing dishes specifically in the kitchen is a sign that you don't have a good grip on things (wet dishes are slippery and can easily fall and break).

DISSECTING Doing the dissecting, or observing a surgeon dissecting someone, means that you should make serious changes in your world or rid yourself of bad habits. (See also "Amputation" and "Physician.")

DITCH/TRENCH Dreaming about jumping over a ditch or a trench is a sign that you will be able to handle any obstacles that come up in life. Falling down while jumping means that it will be tough to get out of a present difficult situation. Digging for a treasure or other objects in a ditch makes it clear that a goal can only be reached with hard work. Digging deep into the soil indicates that you would like to explore your psyche more deeply. (See also "Abyss.")

DIVIDERS This instrument is used for measuring, and also makes circles. Therefore, dreaming about dividers could mean that you are "going in circles." (See also "Circle.")

DIVING Dreaming about diving in water shows that you are looking for intellectual ideas that would improve your life, and that all you need is a little imagination to find them. Seeing a diver is a sign to search your conscience to find out if you are envious of someone else's success.

DIVORCE Dreaming about a divorce doesn't point to the final dissolution of a marriage. Instead, it simply alludes to not having much luck with your partner. Or, the dream could be a message to be kinder and more friendly to your partner, in order to live in greater

harmony with him or her. (See also "Marriage" and "Adultery.")

DOCTOR (SEE "PHYSICIAN")

DOCUMENT A document in a dream expresses the hope of receiving something important in black-and-white, or of getting a promotion. The promotion could take the form of financial rewards, praise, and/or professional advancement. (See also "Seal.")

DOG The sexual implications of dogs in dreams are based on the sexual acts that they perform in public. Dreaming about being frightened of a dog, however, often only describes a bad conscience. A dog that is accompanying you indicates that your instincts are intact; a dog being chained or mishandled means that you unconsciously feel inferior. Large dogs accentuate the above; small dogs minimize it. The meaning of the saying "going to the dogs" can also play a role, but relies on additional symbols in the dream. Carrying a dog in your arms indicates that you have your urges under control. Seeing a dead dog means that something inside of you has died that needs to be resurrected. A dream about being bitten in the foot by a dog could point to your untamed passions, a fear of infection, or a fear of castration. Artemidorus believed the dreamer ought to be wary of swindlers if he sees a dog approaching with its tail wagging. Dogs that bark and bite in a dream may be a warning that somebody wants to do harm to you in real life. (See also "Barking Dog.")

DOLL A doll in a dream is a lifeless object that can only be played with, and represents your unfulfilled erotic desires. If the doll is a marionette, this is a warning from the unconscious not to "pull too many strings" in the hope that others will do what you want.

DONKEY An ornery donkey could be a message that the burden that you have saddled yourself with in real life will have to be endured a little longer. This can be a physical as well as an emotional burden. The donkey could also be telling you to be more patient and realize that better days are ahead. According to Artemidorus, a donkey carrying a burden points to a burden being taken away from the dreamer in real life.

DOOR As the opening to a house, a door in a dream could stand for an opening in the human body. But it could also indicate either looking out for, or getting out of, some kind of precarious situation, depending on whether the door in the dream is open or closed. In addition, a door is the entrance through which we reach the person whom we love. People who storm through a door in a dream might also do so in real life. Ancient Egyptian dream interpreters believed that an open door of a house meant that the dreamer could expect to receive company. (See also "House.")

DOOR LOCK Dreaming about the lock of a door is a good sign for the future (and an intimate relationship). Of course, we need to have the key

to unlock the door. Forcing the lock open in a dream doesn't put the character of the dreamer in a very good light, and such ruthlessness will not attract friends. If you are locking the door behind you in the dream, this shows that you are depriving yourself of opportunities that would have opened up for you in the future. If you are unable to unlock the door in spite of great effort, this is a signal to get out of a present situation the best way that you can.

DOORMAN If a doorman in a dream stands at the entrance of a building, he can be seen as keeping bad influences away. The doorman can also be a warning that you may not be watching carefully enough, or that you sometimes confuse good with evil. (See also "Bellhop," "House," and "Hotel.")

DOUBLE BASS The double bass is the largest and the lowest-pitched of the stringed instruments. A dream about a double bass, as with all other stringed instruments, has strong erotic connotations. The deep, strong sound of a double bass could stand for the intense lovemaking that you want to experience, although you are unsure of how your partner would react to it. The double bass in this sense expresses your own lust.

DOVE The dove, a symbol for peace, also has erotic connotations, which are related to gentleness and an amorous embrace. In addition, the dove stands for the sensibility that allows creativity to flourish. A flying dove in a dream implies that good news is on its way in real life. Catching a dove is a sign that you will act unfairly toward a close friend; killing a dove points to squandering the friendship of a well-meaning person. A well-stocked dovecote implies that you are fond of having guests; an empty dovecote points to loneliness. Hearing doves coo in a dream, unless there are actually doves outside making this sound, indicates that you have a disturbed relationship in real life.

DRAGON The dragon is an archetypal symbol for a cold-blooded vitality, from which the soul seems to have been banished. The positive side of this symbol when it occurs in a dream is that the monster within us is being conquered. Fighting a dragon in a dream often describes the fight that we have with ourselves, particularly with our emotions. The female dragon is usually the "bad mother" who is turning away from her child. According to Artemidorus, the image of the dragon is connected to wealth and treasures, or stands for a person who occupies a high position and is expected to promote the dreamer. Others believe that if we are repulsed by a dragon in a dream, a serious danger may lie ahead in real life, and if a dragon is turning away from us in a dream, life may take a turn for the worse. (See also "Lizard" and "Monster.")

DRAWBRIDGE A dream about a drawbridge being lowered over a moat, so that you can walk into a castle, is a sign that you will find a responsive ear for an impending

project. A drawbridge that remains pulled up indicates difficulty in a present situation. (See also "Ditch/Trench" and "Castle.")

DRAWER Like a closet or a cupboard, a drawer in a dream is a place where you want to keep something from other people, and can imply that you are reserved. An open drawer indicates that you are too trusting of the people around you. A closed drawer is a sign that you should examine whether or not you are being too quick in dismissing the advice of others. (See also "Cupboard/Closet.")

DRAWING The subject or object that has been drawn in a dream, either by you or by others, will be the key to the meaning of the dream. If the picture is faint and difficult to make out, this can be a message to look back to see if you have made some kind of mistake in the past; a faint picture can also point to something in your life right now that needs to be quickly cleaned up. (See also "Painting.")

DRAWING BOARD Dreaming about working on a drawing board implies that in real life you are making plans that are easy to carry out. (See also "Drawing.")

DRESS A dress in a dream stands for the way that we cover ourselves both internally and externally. Putting on a shabby dress in a dream indicates an emotional state in disarray; this may also imply that the dress needs to be changed, so that the dreamer can be more him- or herself. Wearing a dress from one's grandmother—a frequent dream of older women—means that the dreamer wants to age gracefully or to dismiss remarks from unfriendly people. Undressing in front of other people implies that we want to show that we disdain traditional morals and standards; however, this image could also be revealing our ignorance. Pay attention to the color of the dress in the dream and to other symbols, in order to get the best possible interpretation. (See also "Nakedness" and the respective colors.)

DRESSING Getting dressed or changing clothes in a dream means that you are determined to convey self-confidence when in public, you don't want to appear ignorant (be naked), or you want to be seen in society in a favorable light. Dressing somebody else in a dream indicates that someone in your life needs support. (See also "Dress.")

DRESSMAKER (SEE "TAILOR/DRESSMAKER")

DRINKING Hard liquor is seen by the unconscious as an addictive substance that can do harm to the dreamer's body. Clear water, on the other hand, indicates the dreamer's desire for profit and insight. Sharing a glass with someone else means that you will also have to share the profit. If you dislike the person with whom you are drinking, this is a warning that someone wants to do you harm. Drinking from a clean, clear spring points to good luck and good health,

or to a quick recovery. (See also "Alcohol," "Spring," "Water," and other liquids.)

DROWNING Dreaming about drowning, or seeing others drown, is usually a sign that something in real life that is very precious is being lost. It is also a hint to be more careful in the future and avoid making mistakes. Dreaming about being rescued from drowning is a message from the unconscious that not all is lost.

DRUGS (SEE "NARCOTICS")

DRUGSTORE A drugstore in a dream could be a warning to pay more attention to your mental, spiritual, and physical health. Or, it could point to a "prescription" promising advice and help. In another sense, this image could be a reminder of something that has long been forgotten.

DRUM A drum, usually beaten continuously, often appears in nightmares from which we wake up totally exhausted. When asked, we usually have no answer as to why the drumbeat was so frightening. Few people take the sound of the drum into the wakened state; they only know that it grated on their nerves. According to the latest research, repeated dreams about drums point to distress in the dreamer's nervous system.

DRUNKENNESS Dreaming about others being drunk indicates that you are disappointed in the people around you. Dreaming about being drunk yourself could mean that the unconscious wants to remove your inhibitions so that you can deal with your problems better; this could also be an indication that you do not take reality seriously enough. (See also "Alcohol.")

DUCK Dreaming about a waddling duck could mean that you are having difficulty getting ahead on your job. Dreaming about a duck swimming indicates that you can expect your plans to proceed "swimmingly," with very little chance of being stifled. (See also "Feathered Animals" and "Goose.")

DWARF A dwarf in a dream often stands for the dreamer's inferiority complex. If you see yourself smaller in a dream than you are in real life, this means that you believe you are at a disadvantage and cannot compete. Sometimes a dwarf in a dream is the "friend in need." (See also "Reducing.")

DYING Dreaming about dying, according to some psychoanalysts, has to do with a desire to get revenge on a person whom the dreamer hates and wants to eliminate from his or her life. Freud and his followers believed that the hated person is a rival at whom the jealous dreamer wants to strike. However, we believe that a dream about dying refers to an emotional maturation process that will have a positive influence on the dreamer's character and his or her relationship with the surrounding world. (See also "Corpse," "Death," and other symbols related to dying.)

DYNAMITE Dreaming about dynamite is a signal that you might "blow up" and violate the social norms of your community. It is possible for any number of things to blow up, so this could also be a message to exercise "hands off" in certain areas of life. (See also "Explosion.")

EAGLE The "king" of birds, the eagle is a positive image, suggesting freedom from earthly matters. It stands for grandiose thoughts but also for all-consuming passion and spirit. Seeing an eagle high in the sky in a dream shows that you hope that high-flying plans in real life will be successful. Catching this bird of prey means that you want to savor success without sharing it with anyone else. An eagle diving from high above to catch a prey indicates that you are quick and courageous. This image also has negative connotations, as expressed in the saying "High rollers often fall hard." A caged eagle suggests that you feel inhibited by others. Freud saw the eagle as a powerful sexual symbol, because, he argued, it is unable to temper its urges and insists on having its prey.

EAR The ear is a symbol for femininity; thus, ear piercing could represent defloration. Dreaming about having your ear pulled is a message from the unconscious to pay more attention to a particular person or situation in your life. Dreaming about cleaning your ears is a hint to free yourself from a certain prejudice.

EAR OF CORN The ear of corn is a phallic symbol, and says something about the dreamer's vitality and love-making.

EARTH The earth is an archetypal symbol for the maternal womb, which is represented by the Greek goddess Gaia, who emerged full-bosomed from chaos, promising new life. Dreaming about turning over soil means that in real life you want to reinforce and strengthen your viewpoints or delve deeper into a particular subject. Eating dirt in a dream means that you should pay more attention to earthbound matters instead of living in the clouds and having unrealistic hopes. Looking at the planet Earth in a book, or seeing it as a globe suspended in space, indicates that you want to escape from some situation or travel to foreign countries.

EARTHQUAKE A dream about an earthquake may be a sign of deep, unconscious fear; a warning of sudden changes that could throw your life into turmoil; or a reminder to rely on your skills and to persevere and rebuild, brick by brick, what has been lost. In the case of the latter, attend to what needs correction, and perhaps even consider starting all over again. However, sometimes dreaming about an earthquake is only a signal that something in one's personality has shifted and needs to be straightened out.

EAST (SEE "FOUR POINTS OF THE COMPASS")

EASY CHAIR Dreaming about sitting in an easy chair means that you are waiting for others to create a comfortable life for you. Another interpretation is that you want to have peace and quiet, but have little, because you aren't doing much to create this yourself. (See also "Armchair.")

EATING Try to remember what it was that you were eating in the dream. This will give you additional information, because the food may indicate some kind of intellectual nourishment that is missing in your life and for which you have a real yearning. If you are refusing food, this means that you have an aversion to something in your life with which you need to come to terms. (See also "Disgust," "Hunger," "Chewing," and "Meal.")

ECHO Dreaming about hearing your own echo, or that of someone else, means that someone is trying to take your ideas and make them his or her own or to get you to accept his or her ideas.

ECZEMA Dreaming about suffering from eczema is a message from the unconscious that something in your life needs to be attended to; this could be either personal problems or actual physical symptoms.

EDELWEISS Dreaming of picking edelweiss in the mountains shows that you have too high an opinion of yourself. This could also be a message to be more like this flower—in other words, to be strong and self-assured, and not to shy away from an argument.

EDUCATION The level of education that is presented in the dream reflects an unconscious discovery of a lack of education in real life, which should be remedied. Here, education refers to emotional education, meaning maturity.

EEL The eel suggests something slippery, perhaps some type of intrigue that is threatening you. If the eel is caught or dragged on dry land in your dream, this means that problems in real life can be solved. If it escapes or slips out of your hands, difficulties are on the horizon or money is slipping through your fingers. We do not think much of the psychoanalytical interpretation, which suggests that the eel, because of its shape, symbolizes the male sex organ, and which therefore views women's dreams about eels as sexual. (If this image is more like a serpent, check that entry; if it is more like a fish, check that one.)

EGG An egg is a symbol for rebirth, for something new that is germinating, or for change. As is the case with the image of a child in a dream, an egg in a dream announces a new development, the successful completion of a new task, or the beginning of a new phase in life. An egg also indicates that worries will leave you or that success is assured; if you see more than one egg in the dream, your success will even be greater. Breaking or dropping an egg means that losses are in the making, or points to an emotional debacle. If the eggs are colored (and are not Easter eggs), it's important to make note of the colors. (See also "Child.")

EGG TIMER (SEE "HOURGLASS")

EIGHT Eight represents law and justice or cause and effect. A horizontal eight is the symbol for infinity and thus for conquering death. (See also "Number.")

ELECTRICAL POWER PLANT A power plant creates electricity—in other words, energy. Dreaming about a power plant shows that the unconscious is giving you more power, so that you can tackle your problems with more energy. Only occasionally in a dream is there the implication that electric currents can kill. Then, it would be a warning to use your emotional energies more carefully, in order to avoid a nervous breakdown.

ELEPHANT This animal often represents a mother figure whose powerful protection we seek. Dreaming about an elephant indicates that you can count on no harm coming to you in real life. Riding an elephant means that, metaphorically, you are planning to move up to higher ground. (See also "Elephant Trunk.")

ELEPHANT TRUNK According to many psychoanalysts, dreaming about the trunk of an elephant refers to a huge penis, and so is an expression of a man's exceptional virility. However, we tend to agree with the interpretation of modern psychology, which maintains that the dreamer who is embraced by the elephant's trunk is protected from harm. (See also "Elephant.")

ELEVATOR An elevator gets people to the next "level." Dreaming about going up implies that in real life you will get ahead with the help of others; dreaming about going down means that you can expect disappointments. Ending up in the basement is a message to check your emotions—you could be shocked by what they reveal. (See also "Stairs" and "Basement.")

ELEVEN Dreaming about the number eleven indicates hard work, many tribulations, or a difficult beginning. But the two 1's (in 11) can also point to the interrelation of two people or to a lack of understanding in their relationship. Not by chance is the number eleven interpreted by some dream experts as a symbol of an unsolvable conflict; after all, eleven is a prime number and therefore indivisible.

EMBARKING Dreaming about embarking on a trip—say, aboard a ship—is a sign that you are breaking with the past or that your life's journey is shifting direction. There is also a degree of uncertainty involved in boarding a ship, especially when the dream doesn't reveal its destiny. (See also "Traveling," "Boat," and "Ship.")

EMBRACE Freud considered an embrace in a dream as a desire for sexual union. It's important to pay attention to whom you are embracing in the dream. Is this the person with whom you are in love in real

life? Or, the dream could be a message that someone loves you. Either way, you can rest assured: Lady Luck will shine on you in matters of love. However, if the person you are embracing is someone you don't like very much, you need to be wary of false friends.

EMBRASURE An embrasure, meaning a recess of a door or a window, refers to obstacles that you have to face and remove on your journey through life. But an embrasure is also the opening through which a gun is fired and, in this case, seeing one in a dream could mean that you are focused on a task in real life; however, this could also be a reference to sexual matters.

EMBROIDERING Dreaming about embroidering, an activity that calms the nerves, indicates that you are involved in stressful activities in life. Watching someone else embroider means that you will have to face a tiring job. It is also possible for embroidery to refer to "needling," and could point to someone in your life teasing you. (See also "Sewing.")

EMERALD Getting an emerald as a gift in a dream points to having an affectionate friendship that might provide true emotional harmony in your life. Along with the diamond, the emerald is one of the hardest of the precious stones, and promises success in all intellectual endeavors. (See also "Diamond.")

EMPEROR The image of an emperor in a dream represents the ruler of the soul, whose inspiration you should follow without question. If the emperor who appears in the dream is a historical personality, you need to find out what is or was special about this person and explore whether or not you can make these attributes your own. (See also "King.")

END OF THE WORLD This dream image characteristically appears when we entertain apocalyptic thoughts or when we are afraid because life is asking too much of us.

ENEMIES Dreaming about enemies usually shows us the two sides of ourselves that often fight with each other, in order to remove the shortcomings that distort our character. Dreaming about recognizing and killing an adversary is a message from the unconscious that existing hostility can only hurt us. (See also "War.")

ENGINE (SEE "TRAIN ENGINE")

ENTERING Dreaming about entering somewhere usually indicates that we are entering a strange terrain, which could imply an illegal means of gaining something that could not be accomplished legally. For entering any means of transport, see "Embarking."

ESCORT When you dream about being escorted, it's important to identify who is escorting you. Often it is only a shadow (see "Shadow"). However, the escort may represent your inner self, which has discovered a problem that needs to be solved.

EVENING In the case of an older person, the evening in a dream usually suggests the end of life. For a younger person, it points to the end of a particular phase in life. Dreaming about dusk sometimes is a sign that the dreamer is entertaining secret desires. (See also "Night.")

EVENING ATTIRE If you are wearing evening attire and a social occasion has been arranged, pay attention to the color of the attire in order to determine if the occasion is a happy or a sad one. Sometimes evening attire is an indication that the dreamer wants to raise his or her social status. If others are elegantly dressed, you may be fearful of being left behind and of a rival taking over.

EXAM (SEE "TEST" AND "TEACHER")

EXCAVATING MACHINE This image replaces, as do the bulldozer and similar earth-moving equipment, the archetypal dragon. (See also "Dragon.")

EXCREMENT (SEE "FECES")

EXECUTION Dreaming about an execution usually is a message that we should think of something new or change our lifestyle, in order to join the race for success with renewed motivation. Dreaming about an execution is never life-threatening, but only points to an emotional or a spiritual shift. (See also "Executioner" and "Hangman.")

EXECUTIONER The executioner in a dream represents easily putting an end to a period of oppression or depression. Seeing an executioner in a dream means that you can count on a happy future that is free of worry because you don't need to be concerned about the past. (See also "Hangman.")

EXITING This image implies that you are looking for a new way to self-realization. Exiting a vehicle may point to leaving old habits behind, or trying to find a new mindset that would provide fresh energy in order to radically change your life. Less often, exiting from somewhere implies having reached a goal or completed a phase of one's life.

EXPLOSION Dreaming about an explosion is often a warning that something in our nervous system is out of kilter. Pay attention to what it is that is exploding in your dream. This could be a way to determine whether or not your well-being, on either a psychological or a physical level, is in jeopardy. Sometimes actual noises from the world outside become part of a dream and awaken us. Then, correct interpretation is only possible when other dream symbols are examined as well. (See also "Lightning," "Thunder," "Thunderstorm," and "Dynamite.")

EYE The eye is considered the mirror of the soul. Freud saw the eye, because of its shape, as a symbol of the female sexual organs. In his view, dreaming about eyes also has to do with castration; he based this theory on the story of Oedipus, who lost his eyesight because he had committed incest (Oedipus complex). Rubbing one's eyes is seen as a substitute for masturbation. According to modern dream interpretation, seeing eyes in a dream has more to do with one's overall emotional state or one's attitude toward future events. Emotions can be read by looking into the eyes, making an erotic interpretation plausible. A dream about eyes may indicate looking at your existence from an inner perspective. Going blind could mean being intellectually blind, or being unable to see reality clearly. It's also important to try to identify the color of the eyes. (See also "Mother," "Glasses," and the respective colors.)

FACADE The facade of a house in a dream reflects the impression that you make on the world around you. Dreaming about a house in which the inside is in need of repair, although the outside is beautiful, shows that you are pretending that everything is just fine in a deteriorating relationship. If the facade is crumbling, this is a sign to pay more attention to your appearance, for, according to folklore, the way you look is the way that you will be received. (See also "House.")

FACE Even in a dream one can "lose face," and this is always a warning about a real-life situation. Seeing a face in a dream may imply that either something internal is out of control, or that you should concentrate on being more productive and start "making a mark" in life. The dream often serves as a mirror, holding up to us our weaknesses. Dream interpreters in the past have suggested that a pale face indicates bad news, rosy cheeks imply that nothing is standing in the way of love, a beautiful face promises joy, and an ugly one points to sorrow. Putting on makeup in a dream indicates that you want to hide your character defects, or have made the decision to mislead somebody. Washing your face could mean that you want to wash away guilt. (See also "Mirror.")

FACTORY The factory—the place where our unconscious does all the "dirty" work for us—describes our emotional capacity and our resistance against outside influences. Try to remember what was being produced in the factory, because this would enable you to determine the source of your emotional difficulties, which the unconscious wants you to remove. (See also "Factory Chimney" and "House.")

FACTORY CHIMNEY Dreaming about a factory chimney has something to do with exaggerated sexual needs that seem out of control. A factory chimney emitting thick smoke most likely means that you want to hide some character weakness. (See also "Factory" and "Chimney/Fireplace.")

FAILING Dreaming about failing an exam that in real life you have passed long ago is an indication that you are afraid of an impending appointment

or negotiation. This fear, however, is unfounded, because you have everything at your command that will help you be successful. (See also "Test.")

FAINTING Dreaming about fainting is a clue that something is happening in real life without your having any part in it. If you are fainting, this means that you might get a present, perhaps even an inheritance or an unexpected declaration of love. If others are fainting, the unconscious is warning you to be wary of people who are trying to curry a favor in a rather cunning way.

FAIR Dreaming about a fair may point to a "vanity fair," a place characterized by frivolity and ostentation, and be a mirror of yourself that the unconscious is using. The loud hustle and bustle of a fair could be a reminder of either the discomfort that you feel in the company of certain people, or what you don't have control over in your life. Strolling alone around a fair shows that you feel treated carelessly in life.

FAIRY The good fairy often appears in a dream at the precise moment when we are fulfilling our most secret desires. In the case of a woman, the fairy could represent something that needs to be emotionally "polished up"; in the case of a man, it might symbolize his wife, girlfriend, or anima (the female side of him), which he wants to see more willing. (See also "Witch.")

FAKIR A fakir in a dream is you yourself, and suggests that your life is difficult but that you can handle it. Or, this image could be a message that you must put up with hardship on the road to success.

FALL Fall is the time of harvest, but also when things come to an end. When older people dream about fall, this indicates that they are at the height of their creative powers, but are already contemplating retirement, so that they will still have time to enjoy the fruits of their labors. Men dreaming about fall often are afraid of losing their virility. In the case of younger people, it usually indicates the end of a successful phase in their lives. Sometimes such a dream also describes the end of an intimate relationship, to which the dreamer is still holding on. Fall then symbolizes a cooling off or a fading away of emotions. (See also "Harvest" and the three other seasons.)

FALLING Falling in a dream often signals loss, either for the dreamer or another person. Such a dream indicates that you are giving up without having a valid reason to do so. A fall from great heights implies that you have removed yourself from reality and are now returning to solid ground. If others are crashing, this could indicate the source from which a loss is threatening. According to Freud, dreaming about falling has sexual connotations (he might have made an association with the "fallen woman"). However, we believe that such a dream could be pointing to inhibition or difficulty in an intimate relationship. Falling into a bottomless pit means that you are afraid to

make social contact, but in the dream you can let go and needn't be considerate of others around you. A severe fall denotes "Pride cometh before a fall." Occasionally, people experience falling and flying together in a dream. (See also "Abyss," "Crashing," and "Flying.")

FAMILY Dreaming about one's own family is usually considered positive, unless the dream involves fighting. But sometimes family members stand for people in our lives who mean us harm. (See also "Parents.")

FAN Fanning yourself in a dream indicates that you want to hide your true intentions, or perhaps create a stir so that people will pay attention to you. In a woman's dream, when the dreamer is fanning herself, this often describes the coquetry with which she approaches the opposite sex.

FARMER Dreaming about a farmer, when we are living in the city, means that we have the desire and the determination to live more in tune with nature and to simplify our life. (See also "Field," "Harvest," "Garden," "Sowing," and "Barn.")

FARMHOUSE The living room in a farmhouse is a symbol of home. Dreaming about it means that in real life you are looking for comfort and warmth, or need peace and quiet. (See also "Room.")

FASTING Dreaming about fasting is a sign that in real life you don't have enough energy to persevere.

Sometimes it also points to emotional deprivation that needs to be addressed. (See also "Hunger" and "Eating.")

FATHER The father is the archetypal symbol for logic, conscious functioning, and willpower. A father figure in a dream is usually the advocate for life's purposes and traditions. If you have or had a good relationship with your own father, he will be the one who reduces unconscious conflicts. He will lead you by the hand and guide you in the right direction. In the dream of a girl, the father usually substitutes for her first lover. In the dream of a woman, the father may represent her husband or—if her marriage is in trouble—her hope for a new relationship. The father in a boy's dream is more of an authority figure as well as a rival: the husband of the mother whom he loves (which led Freud to formulate the Oedipus complex, because Oedipus killed his father and married his mother). If the dreamer had a trusting relationship with his or her deceased father when he was alive, in the dream the father will lend advice and help in difficult situations. If you yourself are the father in the dream—even if you are not a father in reality—this means that you may have a brilliant idea that is worth actively pursuing. (See also "Boss," "Teacher," "King," and other father figures.)

FEAR Fear plays a prominent role in dreams, particularly in nightmares. In ancient Egypt, being fearful in a dream meant that the dreamer was not satisfied with him- or herself in real life. According to modern psychology, fear points to a mistake that the dreamer would like to undo. Screaming during a dream means that the dreamer is dealing with a particularly severe mistake, which requires a great deal of his or her own initiative to remedy.

FEATHERED ANIMALS A dream in which feathered animals are cackling loudly indicates that in real life people who are envious of you, or want ill for you, are spreading rumors about you. Killing feathered animals in a dream means that you want to protect yourself from bad gossip. (See also "Goose" and "Chickens.")

FEATHERS Feathers blow about in the wind, which describes the wavering personality that the dream is mirroring for you. It is a warning from the unconscious that some indecisiveness will rob you of your "feathers."

FECES A dream about feces, like all other anal-related images, has nothing to do with the foul-smelling substance that the body discharges. Dreaming about feces is seen as positive, especially in the form of manure, which is used in agriculture as a fertilizer for a better harvest. In many instances, a dream about feces is related to financial matters or to evaluating the worth of someone's character. It points to the dreamer's sense of order and generosity (constipation refers to holding back, meaning that the dreamer is stingy, pedantic, or controlling). But it can also indicate a fear of losing something, perhaps money. In the past, some psychoanalysts believed that dreaming about passing feces had to do with castration. Freud said that, in a child's dream, this indicated that the child had experienced a loss. But the main reason for the dream in adulthood, he claimed, was too much emphasis on cleanliness in childhood, which he saw as the root of neuroses and sexual inhibitions in later years. Modern psychoanalysis maintains a similar view: that such a dream is due to an overly strict upbringing, and is an expression of the loss experienced in childhood. (See also "Bowel Movement" and "Toilet.")

FEEDING ANIMALS Feeding animals in a dream could be a sign that you are feeling lonely, and are searching for someone whom you can love or who loves you.

FENCE A fence in a dream stands for an obstacle that has been put in your way in real life. Climbing the fence means that you can remove the obstacle. Getting stuck or tearing a hole in your clothing in the process is a warning to be careful so that you don't get hung up and suffer setbacks. (See also "Gate.")

FENCING If either you or others are fencing in a dream, this means that to persevere in real life you need to engage in battle. But your soul is resisting such advice.

FERRY If you see yourself or others on a ferry in a dream, you can expect changes to take place in the near future that involve setting new goals.

The ferry also implies that you are about to "throw overboard" something that is old. (See also "Boat" and "Ship.")

FERTILIZER Fertilizer is a substance that helps things grow. Dreaming about a big heap of fertilizer is a sign that money and prestige will greatly increase for you. Fertilizer being hauled off shows that you have some unpaid bills. (See also "Manure.")

FESTIVE CLOTHES (SEE "EVENING ATTIRE")

FEVER A dream about a fever could be a message to try to cool down a passion that has you at fever-pitch. However, such a dream might also point to symptoms of a real illness. (See also "Thermometer.")

FIELD An agricultural field is a symbol for fertility, Mother Earth, and a connection to nature. Dreaming of a field in full bloom, or one with a crop that is ready to be harvested, means that you are about to enter a particularly fruitful phase in real life (the sowing of seeds has been successful). An empty field, or one that has been plowed, points to a problem that you can overcome only with persistent work, or to impending danger due to your self-created misfortune. Working a field with enthusiasm connotes success in love. Seeing a field is a reminder of your responsibilities.

FIGHT Dreaming about being in a fight alludes to a conflict in real life,

F with which you don't have the courage yet to deal. Taking part forcefully in a fight involving several people indicates that you are bearing down and dealing with a seemingly hopeless situation successfully in real life. (See also "War.")

FIGS Dreaming about figs usually has erotic connotations; their sweetness may be an expression of hope for a happy union. (During the Dionysian feast, Greek women carried baskets in the shape of a phallus that were made from the wood of fig trees.) Generally speaking, the fig represents the creative, male power that invigorates the eternal feminine. In certain countries, the fig has the same meaning as the plum (see also "Plum").

FILING Dreaming about filing, or seeing someone else filing, is a message from the unconscious not to let yourself go in real life, but to strive to become more orderly and strong enough to withstand external influences.

FILM/MOVIE In the semi-darkness of a movie theater, many things become clear to us and trigger dreams. It is not uncommon to dream about parts of a movie that we have just seen a few days before. However, the content has changed somewhat in the dream, and what we see are actually aspects of our own life. Our unconscious presents us with a situation that is similar to what is happening in our life.

FINDING/DISCOVERING (SOMETHING) Dreaming about finding or discovering something is an indication of a hope, no matter how futile, for a lucky break or a coincidence. This dream is a message from the unconscious to rely more on our own skills.

FINGER Fingers are related to our sense of touch. As part of the hand, they represent a desire for a greater freedom of action. We often use our fingers in a dream—for example, to identify an object. Losing a finger in a dream means that you might have misjudged a situation in real life. Seeing your fingers larger than they are in real life means that you are trying to reach for something that is difficult to grasp. Dirty fingers either mean that you are having a lot of trouble completing a difficult task or that people are asking the impossible of you. Very long fingers don't imply that you are a thief, but rather that you want to grab a good opportunity. Dreaming about cutting your nails, according to Indian dream researchers, suggests that you will soon go through a difficult time in your life. (See also "Arm," "Thumb," and "Hand.")

FIRE Fire is an archetypal symbol for spirit and love. It is also a symbol for the libido, and thus for sensuality as well as an all-consuming, fierce passion. Jung saw fire as a symbol for cleansing or for getting rid of what is old and useless. At the hearth, fire allows us to be warm and comfortable. When the fire burns bright, either inside (the fireplace) or out, this means that something new is being created, or that ideas are being realized. Flames reaching high into the sky indicate that a burning problem is being solved. A fire that is being extinguished shows that some plans may be thwarted. Occasionally, a fire can turn into something that is dangerous. (See also "Putting Out a Fire.")

FIRE DEPARTMENT A dream about a fire that the fire department is putting out may mean that burgeoning wild passions are threatening to consume you. In a completely different interpretation, the jet of water from the fire hose could mean that the germs that threaten your body will be destroyed. (See also "Putting Out a Fire.")

FIREPLACE (SEE "CHIMNEY/FIREPLACE")

FIRED Dreaming about being fired, usually from a job, often has to do with a fear of having made a mistake in real life. Such a worry usually dissolves into nothing, because the dreamer is not only doing everything right but he or she may even be promoted. If the dreamer is the one who is terminating either a job or a friendship, this usually points to a loss of trust in real life.

FIREWORKS Watching fireworks in a dream means that you want to achieve great things in life. If you ignite the fireworks, you have flashy or spectacular goals for your life. This also implies that you want to present yourself to the world in the magnificent light of success, and that success is quite likely. (See also "Rocket.")

FIRST, OR GROUND, FLOOR (SEE "FLOORS")

FISH Psychoanalysts consider fish to be synonymous with male sexuality; in fact, as far back as Babylonian times, a fish was considered a phallic symbol. However, we believe that fish describe the depths of the human soul. A fish is a positive symbol, because it provides healthy nutrition and represents emotional energy. Dreaming about fish can also be a warning, especially when they are huge and look vicious, or appear suddenly from deep below (our unconscious). Dreaming about being a fish, according to C.G. Jung, is a message that we can rejuvenate ourselves at the "Fountain of Youth." When fish are lying about, this is a sign of diminished vitality. When they are swimming in clear water, this connotes a happy, carefree state. According to Artemidorus, seeing dead fish indicated a sense of hopelessness or a recognition of failure in spite of serious effort; catching a live fish, on the other hand, implied great success. (See also "Fishing," "Net," "Spring," and "Water.")

FISHERMAN A fisherman in a dream is searching for the content of our psyche. Dreaming about a fisherman who is too lazy to take his catch off the hook or out of the net indicates that you allow yourself to be cheated out of the fruits of your labor. Dreaming about scaling a fish before preparing to cook it is a sign that you will see suddenly and clearly (as if scales have fallen away from your eyes) how to handle a situation in order to profit from it.

FISHING A dream about fishing is a message not to lose patience. A fish getting hooked is an indication of a positive turn that is underway. Fishing where there is no water means that you are wasting time attempting something that is of no use. (See also "Fish" and "Net.")

FIST A fist is a symbol for fighting. Dreaming about a fist is a sign that you lack a necessary argument in real life. (See also "Hand.")

FIVE According to Chinese philosophy, the number five represents the center where the feminine (Yin) and the masculine (Yang) are united. Here, the feminine stands for earthbound and softness, and the masculine for heavenward and strength. Besides this unifying center, the number five connotes natural vitality. In addition, dreaming about the number five indicates that good fortune is just around the corner. (See also "Number.")

FLAG The flag is an archetypal symbol for joy, and often alludes to sensuality, which, however, is fueled less by emotions than by physical urges. In psychoanalysis, the flag is sometimes seen as a stick with a fluttering piece of cloth, the stick being a phallic symbol, the cloth having maternal and female connotations, and the fluttering standing for a uniting of the two. Here, the color of the cloth is also important.

FLAILING Dreaming about flailing back and forth may be a warning not to act hastily; this could also be an indication that you are being hit or that you are hitting someone.

FLAME Dreaming about a flame being extinguished means—if you consider the flame to be a male sexual symbol—that you fear you will lose your libido. More plausible to us is the interpretation that a flame is a sign of inner cleansing. A flickering flame points to an all-consuming passion. Flames are considered a warning when they are leaping around a house (translated to your own body); they then refer to physical and emotional problems. In Egypt, people believe that dreaming about flames means that you can count on a huge increase in your finances. (See also "House," "Blaze," and "Fire.")

FLASHLIGHT A flashlight in a dream is seen as a deceptive device because it only illuminates a small area (or small matters), leaving the dreamer completely in the dark about the rest. A flashlight that fails to turn on when the switch is flicked implies that the dreamer will have another dashed hope. (See also "Lamp" and "Light.")

FLAT FEET People dreaming about having flat feet might have difficulty getting ahead in life. (See also "Foot.")

FLAX Dreaming about a field of flax in bloom indicates that you will have plenty of good luck and happiness. (See also "Field" and "Yellow.")

FLEA Dreaming about this unpleasant pest points to disagreeable thoughts or stressed nerves in real life. (See also "Pests.")

FLEEING Dreaming about fleeing suggests a flight from yourself or a fear that you are unable to persevere in the battle called life. If you are successful in fleeing, you have every reason to finally trust your own skills and talents.

FLOOD Because the water flooding the banks of a river deposits all kinds of debris, a flood can describe a fear of unfavorable circumstances causing you pain. When a flood approaches and the dam is holding, you know that you are able to deal with almost anything that life will send your way. Dreaming about a flood also points to the danger of being overwhelmed by illusions or of totally overestimating your own capacities. Ocean waters flooding the shore are a sign that you have completely lost your equilibrium and may require medical attention to help you regain your emotional balance. (See also "Low Tide," "Stream," "Ocean," "River," and "Water.")

FLOORS As a part of the house, which symbolizes the human body, a floor represents a specific area of the dreamer's body. For instance, the ground floor depicts the pelvic area, and the roof the upper part of the head. Walking up to the ground floor indicates that the dreamer wants to make a conquest. For the proper interpretation of the dream, it's important to recall what was happening on the floor. (See also "House," "Roof," and "Basement.")

FLOWER BUD Dreaming about flower buds points to a "budding" love affair. A bud being cut off the stem is a sign that a warm, sincere relationship is falling apart. (See also "Flowers.")

FLOWER PISTIL A flower pistil can be seen as a phallic symbol, and together with a beautiful flower can describe a successful sexual relationship.

FLOWERS A dream about flowers is an expression of pleasant thoughts and emotions, and therefore is considered positive. It's important, however, to note the color of the flowers (see also "Colors"). Dreaming about wilted flowers implies that something in your life is also wilting. Picking flowers suggests that you are hoping for your sexual desire to be fulfilled. A bouquet of fresh flowers means that love is right around the corner. Stomping on flowers suggests that you are stomping on the emotions of your lover while pretending to love him or her. In the Indian dream book *Jagaddeva,* it is stated that dreaming about flowers is a sign that the highest form of happiness will come your way. (See also "Flower Bud.")

FLUTE As with all wind instruments, dreaming about a flute has sexual connotations. Dreaming about hearing a flute playing in the distance means that you are longing for a lover in real life. If you dream about playing the flute yourself, this is an indication that you are lovesick.

FLY Being bothered by a fly in a dream is a message to try to be more relaxed in real life. Flies may also represent people or things that bother you, and that you would rather forget. (See also "Insects.")

FLYING Dreaming about flying occurs fairly often. Generally, it should be taken as a warning, especially if we ourselves are flying like a bird—in other words, without any aid. Freud considered dreams about flying as expressions of erotic desires. It's true that flying in a dream creates a kind of euphoria, which people as far back as antiquity interpreted as ecstatic love. Modern dream research, on the other hand, judges flying in a dream as a sign of exaggerated self-confidence. In addition, flying at great heights entails the possibility that the dreamer will fall later. It's easy to fall into a void when flying too high. However, the soul of the dreamer could sprout wings and be released from all earthly burdens. Flying without the aid of some kind of vehicle across an imaginary landscape could mean that the dreamer is too far removed from the realities of life. In Egypt, people believe a dream about flying is a sign that the dreamer will find a way out of a difficult situation. (See also "Airplane," "Traveling," and "Falling.")

FOAM Foam in a dream refers to a person who is putting on airs in order to deceive others. A person walking out of the ocean where the waves are white-capped is starting a new phase in life that promises to be successful. (Here, the dream is taking on an image from mythology: Aphrodite, emerging from the ocean waves.)

FOG Fog in a dream represents inhibition and not seeing clearly in real life; it also implies a lack of focus that keeps us from accomplishing our tasks. When the fog is so dense that you can't see anything, this means that it is time in real life to depend on others. This can also be an indication that you don't have enough energy to get through life. (See also "Steam," "Smoke," "Landscape," and "Water.")

FOOD (SEE "EATING")

FOOL If you see yourself or someone else as a fool in a dream, this means that, just this once, you want to be different from what convention dictates and to discard some of what you show the world.

FOOT Dreaming about a foot indicates your point of view, or the progress you are making as you pursue life's journey—which will be hindered if the foot is injured. If you are unable to see your own feet or legs in the dream, you are in danger of losing your way or your objectivity in real life. Seeing your feet exaggeratedly large implies that, to your own detriment, you are living the high life. Freud considered a dream about a foot to be sexual (or phallic) in nature, because a foot is slipped into a shoe (meaning the vagina). (See also "Leg.")

FOOT STOOL A foot stool is a practical device that provides comfort. Dreaming about resting your feet on a foot stool implies that you are well taken care of in real life. Sitting down on a foot stool alludes to groveling in your own home. (See also "Chair.")

FOREST The forest is a symbol for the mystery of life, in which we throw ourselves from one adventure into the next. For older people, a dream about a forest stands for the search for lost values. For younger people, it is related to the path into the "jungle of life," which can lead to success, unless ferocious monsters, wild beasts, or other obstacles appear on the scene and make getting ahead difficult.

FORK Dreaming about pushing food around on your plate with a fork indicates that you are bored or perhaps looking for a fight. On the other hand, a pitchfork will bring good luck, because it is a symbol of work that promises to be successful.

FORTRESS (SEE "CASTLE")

FOUNTAIN A fountain is an archetypal symbol for youth and rejuvenation. It connotes emotional rebirth, and calls forth the image of the effervescent "spring of life." Pregnant women often dream about fountains. However, seeing a fountain in a dream may also be an indication of sexual problems that you need to address. Dreaming about drinking from a fountain (the "water of life") means that, wanting to rebuild something in your life, you are reaching for inner strength, of which you are not yet conscious. If the water in the fountain is clear and effervescent, this means that you can expect your emotional strength to be renewed or that you will find joy and happiness in good company. A fountain without water describes the envy that others might feel toward you in real life. Falling into a fountain implies that your bad habits have resurfaced, and will surely bring you no joy. (See also "Water" and "Spring.")

FOUR The number four is almost always a positive symbol; it stands for security, stability, power, and preserving what we have. It also represents orderliness in nature—as there are the four seasons, the four points of the compass, and the four phases of the moon. (See also "Square.")

FOUR POINTS OF THE COMPASS The south—in the Western Hemisphere—represents emotions and a good heart. The north stands for emotional coldness but also sober thoughts. The west, where the sun sets, denotes the night and lurking dangers. The east, where the sun rises, is related to the radiance that lights up our journey through life. (See also "Night," "Sun," and "Wind.")

FOX The fox in a dream stands for a false friend or for cunning and shrewdness that you want to use in order to fulfill your desires (including sexual desires). Catching a fox implies that you have yourself, and particularly your temper, under control and that people can't easily take advantage of you. Killing a fox indicates that you have discovered somebody's else's deviousness, or that somebody wants to harm you. Encountering two or more foxes is a sign to be cautious around certain people in your environment. According to Artemidorus, when the dreamer sees a fox, he is the subject of gossip. Dreaming about a fox, an animal that can transmit rabbis, may also indicate that you are afraid of acquiring an illness.

FRAME Dreaming about a frame that holds your own picture stands for vanity and suggests that you always need to be in the limelight. A frame without a picture represents your powerlessness in achieving anything, because you lack the necessary funds. (See also "Painting" and "Photography.")

FRECKLES A dream about freckles connotes points of view or attitudes that you would do well to adopt. Only if you are the one with the freckles should this dream be seen as a message to come to terms with your inferiority complex.

FREEZING A fear of freezing in a dream translates into a general fear of trouble in real life. Dreaming of freezing might mean that a longstanding friendship in real life has cooled down to the point of being frozen. Or, the unconscious could be pointing out that something inside of you that needs your warmth and understanding is about to turn to ice. If the feeling of being cold in the dream is a reflection of external low temperatures, the interpretations above would not apply, unless other symbols point you in those directions. (See also "Ice.")

FRENCH HORN As with other wind instruments, the French horn is usually considered a male sexual symbol. Hearing the sound of a French horn in a dream could mean that you are longing for a person whose temptations you cannot refuse.

FRIEND A friend in a dream is usually the shadow of our own ego, our constant companion on life's journey. If a friend shows up at the wrong moment in a dream, this puts us in a bad light. A friend in a dream often seems to be like the real person, but then turns into an arch-enemy who wants to do us harm. If we have a fight with a special friend in real life, it may be he or she who wishes us ill, but it could also be the all-powerful stranger or our double, which could be a warning from the unconscious. People in antiquity believed that dreaming about a friend meant that the dreamer would receive very important and useful news. (See also "Acquaintance.")

FROG Women generally dream about frogs (men seem to dream more about toads). Although some people think that the frog is ugly, a dream about it is seen as positive because of the way that the frog develops. The stages of growth from a spawned egg into its final form can be compared to a spiritual transformation that we are undergoing. The frog may also represent the "good soul" in an "ugly body," or be a sign of overcoming an aversion. A frog hopping about happily indicates that your heart is "skipping a beat" for joy because of a job well done. A frog jumping away from you points to having been careless and paying for it dearly. Stepping on a frog (or a toad) means that you want to demonstrate power over someone who is weaker than you. Hearing frogs croak means that you can expect good news.

FROZEN FOOD Dreaming about eating frozen food usually expresses the hope that a relationship will "thaw out" soon and be harmonious. (See also "Ice.")

FRUIT Depending on its shape, a fruit is usually considered a male or a female sexual symbol. In this sense, dreaming about picking fruit points to success in matters of love. If, on the other hand, the fruit is full of worms, trouble might lie ahead. According to ancient Egyptian dream interpretation, the dreamer will meet someone agreeable when he is offering fruit to somebody. Fruit can also represent intellectual wealth, success, and a favorable change in everyday life. The Indian dream book *Jagaddeva* says that gathering or enjoying eating fruit connotes personal good fortune. (See also specific types of fruit.)

FRYING PAN According to Freud, like everything else that can be put on a stove, a frying pan is a sexual symbol.

FUNERAL Dreaming about a funeral is rarely connected to a death. Often it is an indication that the dreamer ought to bury some-

thing—a conflict with the person who is being buried, a relationship, a useless object, or something that he or she was planning to do. Dreaming about being buried yourself means that you may be feeling inferior, apprehensive, or sorry for yourself, or that something inside of you may have died and should be buried. (See also "Grave," "Corpse," "Coffin," and "Death.")

FUNERAL PROCESSION The image of a funeral procession in a dream indicates that something in real life is being buried, but perhaps only your fear of failure. A funeral procession can also show that one phase in your life has come to an end. Or, this image may suggest that, while anticipating a new beginning, you are still nostalgic about the past.

FUR Sometimes fur—the garment of an animal—symbolizes its personality. Dreaming about wearing a fur (pay attention to which animal the fur came from) means that you need something that will protect you from the adversities of life, which could include being ill or just having a cold. Dreaming about wearing an expensive fur implies that you are trying to find your way around inhospitable (cold) surrounding or that you are asserting your skills. (See also individual furry animals.)

FURNITURE Dreaming about new furniture is an expression of everyday aspirations that have a good chance of coming to pass. This image might also point to a longing for a beautiful home.

GAGGED Dreaming about being gagged means that in real life you are unable to find the right words to express your feelings.

GAITERS Gaiters are overshoes that we use to protect our feet, enabling us to walk through difficult terrain unharmed. Dreaming about gaiters means that you are afraid of a difficult situation looming ahead in real life, or of a person who is about to "heap dirt" upon you. Sometimes dreaming about gaiters is a hint that our perfectionism is causing us difficulties in life.

GALLERY Dreaming of walking through an exhibition in a gallery indicates that you are looking for direction in your life's journey. It would be easier to interpret the dream if you are able to remember a particular picture or painting. Dreaming about a gallery often alludes to the state of our schooling or our desire for further education. A dream about wandering through a gallery occasionally implies the laborious manner in which we are handling our life. (See also "Painting.")

GALLOWS Gallows in a dream are a place where we "hang" burdensome real-life problems. Dreaming about yourself hanging on the gallows can be a positive sign, indicating that the worst is over. It's been said that should you see somebody else hanging on the gallows in a dream, you should use your charm in real life to win over an unpopular person. (See also "Hanging.")

GARBAGE If you are dreaming about throwing out garbage, this can be seen as an attempt to be relieved of emotional (or other) problems. Every now and then, such a dream might indicate that the dreamer should have kept something that was useful but has been carelessly discarded. If you are looking at garbage in a dream, you are trying to get rid of unpleasant thoughts. (See also "Rubbish.")

GARDEN A garden is an area in a dream that only a few people are allowed to enter. It is often surrounded by a fence, and frequently the gate is narrow and small, indicating that we don't want people in real life to see inside us. The state of the garden—either well cared for or left unattended—is an indication of your emotional state. If everything is growing and the garden is in full bloom, this shows that you are enjoying life, and that your love life and family life are intact. If a man has an erotic dream about a garden, the garden probably represents the womb of women or the paradise that he hopes to rediscover. According to ancient Egyptian dream interpretation, if a person dreamt about walking through a beautiful garden, his entire life would be lived well. (See also "Field," "Flowers," and other plants.)

GARDENER The gardener in a dream is pulling the weeds from the garden beds of the soul, which otherwise would turn into a tangled wilderness. Dreaming about a gardener is usually considered to be an indication that something in our psyche is off kilter. If the dreamer is the one who is gardening, many dream experts believe that his or her real-life problems will be solved without any outside help. (See also "Farmer" and "Garden.")

GAS STATION Dreaming about stopping at a gas station means that you ought to take a break in real life. You need to "refill" your energy.

GATE Dreaming about a gate that prevents you from entering a meadow or a garden in full bloom means that your wishes won't come true for a while, and that you have to be satisfied with what you have right now. A gate is usually a symbol for problems. Those who open the gate must deal with whatever is behind it. (See also "Door" and "Meadow.")

GEM Dreaming about seeing a gem, either a rare mineral or a piece of precious jewelry, is a reflection of yourself or your ego, and means that you want to shine. A true gem has very specific characteristics (clarity, brilliance, and a certain fire), which could be pointing to the ideals that you want to project in life. Losing a precious stone means that your image is diminished. (See also "Jewelry" and specific stones.)

GENITALIA Dreaming about genitalia has less to do with the organs involved in sexual activity than with the vitality of the dreamer. Other symbols in the dream will indicate if it is a matter of too much or too little vitality. (See also "Phallus" and "Vagina.")

GETTING UP Dreaming about getting up implies that you want to straighten up, stand tall, or be free of small-mindedness. Getting up also symbolizes your vitality.

GHOSTS Dreaming about ghosts usually points to the dreamer's confused state of mind. Ghosts might also indicate that we easily fall prey to temptation or that we are vacillating too much.

GIANT The giant in a dream, a figure from fairy tales and mythology, is the larger-than-life father (or "wise man") whose size makes us cower and feel powerless. Some giants are not to be tangled with; they serve as a warning to keep our urges in check. Giants who are perceived in a dream only as a shadow might refer to a big business enterprise in the making that promises large financial rewards.

GIFTS Dreams about gifts often have something to do with a lifestyle change, or may indicate that up until now nothing has been given to us. Receiving gifts may mean that we can count on being accommodated in life; the type of gift and its symbolism are also important. Dream interpreters in ancient Egypt thought that receiving gifts pointed to an improvement in one's circumstances. (See also "Birthday" and those symbols that could generally be considered gifts.)

GIRDLE A girdle compresses, and thus often restricts breathing. In a man's dream, a girdle could represent a beautiful woman who "takes his breath away"; this may mean that he will fall head over heels in love in real life. In a woman's dream, a girdle might represent the "breathlessness" with which she or someone else is plunging into an adventure (possibly a love affair).

GIRL When a female who is not an adult yet appears in a man's dream, this alludes to a sexual appetite that society considers immoral. However, dreaming about flirting with a girl has less to do with amorous desires than with spending money unnecessarily. When an adult woman sees herself as a girl in a dream, this could point to her fear of becoming a spinster or of not being attractive enough to the man she loves or to men in general. (See also "Women" and "Virgin.")

GIVING BIRTH Dreaming about giving birth always refers to some kind of rebirth or new beginning. In a woman's dream, giving birth could be a sign of her evolving personality. Or, this may mean that she can expect a new and happy relationship to develop, or that she will be able to discard something from her life that is old and broken. In a man's dream, this image points to the birth of a new idea or a change that will be an advancement personally. A problem-free birth is a signal that almost everything that is undertaken will be successful. A difficult birth, on the other hand, implies a loss, failure in business, or the separation from someone. (See also "Birth" and "Pregnancy.")

GIVING BIRTH TO A DEFORMED CHILD When you are the deformed child in the dream, this means that you are harboring thoughts about something illegal that can lead to disaster. Or, such a dream may be based on envy: You believe that others are better off than you are. (See also "Cripple.")

GLACIER Dreaming of a landscape covered with a large body of ice points to frozen emotions or to relationships that have turned to ice. Conquering a glacier in a dream is a sign that you will soon have new love and affection in your life. (See also "Ice," "Freezing," and "Snow.")

GLASS Dreaming about glass points to a frail relationship, but also to the transparency of the dreamer's thoughts, which are obvious to others. Dull glass means that you lack a clear understanding in certain areas. Looking through a glass window points to seeing something that you can accomplish. A glass container that is breaking alludes to either a final separation or a frail condition. A glass filled to the brim promises happy times spent in good company, and when you drink it down to the bottom, good health. One can, however, also dream of sitting in a glass house, which indicates weak nerves, or that we would like to blame others for our failings. Freud considered a glass container to be a symbol for the female sexual organs. (See also

"Glasses," "Window," "Container," and "Crystals.")

GLASSES Dreaming about glasses alludes to being made aware of certain flaws in your ego. Ill-fitting glasses indicate that your view of something is distorted. Putting on a pair of glasses that belongs to somebody else implies that you ought to rely more on your own strength and stop paying so much attention to misleading advice from the people around you. Looking through clean glasses shows that you are clear-sighted in real life. Of course, rose-colored glasses mean that you are overly optimistic and naive. Similarly, fogged-up glasses mean that you should start seeing things more realistically. Broken glasses are a symbol for good luck that can easily crumble. It's also important to pay attention to the color of the frame. (See also "Frame" and "Glass.")

GLASSES CASE A case for glasses is generally considered to be a sexual symbol. If the case is empty in your dream, this might indicate that you are at a loss concerning a love relationship.

GLOBE A globe has the same symbolism as a circle—namely, whole-ness—but is more dynamic. It often describes our emotional balance or core value, and our relationship to the surrounding world. (See also "Circle.")

GLOVES Gloves cover hands, and in a sense make them invisible, which could mean that you want to keep other people in the dark as to your

actions or are possibly trying to hush something up. Dreaming about dropping a glove could be a substitute for wanting to "throw down the gauntlet," for instance, at your competition.

GLUE Dreaming about glue points to your conservative side. This image indicates being "glued" to something old, or to a job or a position that is keeping you from advancing.

GOAT Goats make bleating, complaining sounds. Dreaming about them therefore suggests that you can't do anything right for someone in your life, and that his or her criticism might be justified. Watching goats playing and jumping happily about means that your spirits are a bit too high, perhaps to the point of foolishness.

GOBLET/CHALICE (SEE "MUG," "CUP," AND "CONTAINER")

GOBLIN Like the good fairy, goblins can also appear in our dreams. They usually help us to brighten our emotions. In the form of forest spirits, they can also make us aware of the darker side of our personality. (See also "Nymph.")

GOD'S HOUSE (SEE "CHURCH")

GODMOTHER/GODFATHER Godparents, often parent figures in a dream, are the helpers in difficult situations. If you are the godparent in the dream, you should think about being a bit more generous to people, which would not only cost you money but also real effort. The godchild whom you don't like in a dream is your own shadow, with which you need to deal. (See also "Parents," "Mother," and "Father.")

GOLD Gold withstands any and all weather conditions, so in the past it was a symbol for immortality. Gold is also the archetypal male symbol, comparable to the sun, and stands for freeing new mental and spiritual energy. Dreaming about finding gold means that you will receive an unexpected financial windfall; losing gold means that you need to be careful and not show others what you have. Giving gold as a gift is a sign to be more careful with your finances. Wearing a lot of gold jewelry points to being too frivolous. (See also "Money" and "Jewelry.")

GOLF Dreaming about golf, a game originally that only the well-to-do could afford, indicates that you love parties and company, but also that boredom will set in soon. Sometimes dreaming about a successful shot foretells having good luck.

GONDOLA Dreaming about this somewhat swaying mode of transportation often describes an adventure from which the dreamer won't come away unscathed.

GOODBYE Saying goodbye in a dream alludes to a change in the dreamer's own life or lifestyle. If the dreamer is young and his or her parents are saying goodbye, this could be a message to become more self-

sufficient. Saying goodbye to a girlfriend or a boyfriend usually indicates that the dreamer has questions about the faithfulness of his or her partner; but this could also mean that the dreamer is trying to get away from everyday boredom. Saying goodbye to an older person can imply a permanent parting or be a message that it's high time to let go of bad habits. (See also "Departure.")

GOOSE A goose in a dream—if we accept the premise that this animal is not very smart—points to a person in your life who is naive in sexual matters or has sexual inhibitions. A plucked goose is a sign that people are taking advantage of you, or that money is being handled carelessly. Quacking geese indicate that you can expect unpleasant company who will try to take advantage of you, or spread nasty, potentially harmful gossip about you.

GORILLA In contrast to other apes, the gorilla conveys a certain brutality. Thus, dreaming about a gorilla points to using this brutality for overcoming an opponent, or to an opponent using it to defeat you. Although the gorilla is a scary animal, it looks worse than it really is.

GOUT Dreaming about suffering from gout indicates that you are worried about not being able to keep up with other people. Seeing another person with gout implies that your own spiritual side or your contact with others is in disarray. Dreaming about gout also suggests a fear that someone close to you could become sick, or is weakened due to an accident. (See also "Illness.")

GRAIN Dreaming about grain alludes to using it to strengthen your ego. Grain is also a symbol for the idea that if we want to be successful, hard work comes before pleasure. The same interpretation is given if you see the wind gently moving across a wheat field that is ready to be harvested. Dreaming about a wheat field destroyed by a thunderstorm is a message not to fret about lost time, but rather to apply your efforts to a different area. A dream about a field of grain swaying in the summer breeze points to maturity and to being able to let go of bad or unhealthy habits. Also what is implied is that with new and healthy attitudes, you will be able to make new friends. An empty kernel of grain connotes an emptiness on an emotional level that is causing you pain. (See also "Harvest.")

GRANDPARENTS Dreaming about one's grandparents doesn't only refer to childhood memories. Even if the grandparents are long dead, they appear in a dream as protectors, who might want to save us from some foolishness in a real-life situation. Of course, the dreamer would need to have or have had a good relationship with them, or at least his or her parents would need to have said good things about them. A grandfather, like one's father (see also "Father"), often appears in a dream to give advice (such as in financial matters). The image of the grandmother serves more like that of a super mom (see also "Mother"), who wants to put everything right that is bothering the dreamer. Only seldom do grandparents appear in a dream to point out one's weaknesses.

GRAPE The grape represents enduring vitality and alludes to changing spirits. Eating sweet grapes in a dream promises romance in real life, whereas eating sour grapes points to jealousy. (See also "Wine.")

GRAPE HARVEST Dreaming about taking part in a grape harvest, which happens in the fall, means that you are at the threshold of a new period in your life that promises to be pleasant. For older people, this image conveys the message that they can look forward to an old age in which many of their wishes will come true.

GRAPEVINE Since ancient times, the image of a vine heavy with grapes has been a symbol for a happy home. However, a grapevine without any grapes is a sign of impending trouble. (See also "Grapes" and "Wine.")

GRASS Dreaming about beautiful, green grass is a promise of well-being and wealth in real life. Parched grass, on the other hand, indicates worry. Sometimes a dream about grass is a message to "let grass grow" over a certain matter or affair. (See also "Green," "Lawn," and "Meadow.")

GRASSHOPPER (SEE "CRICKETS")

GRAVE Dreaming about a grave (your own or that of someone else) implies that certain hopes have been dashed. But you could also be burying a problem that has caused you a great deal of stress. The image of a grave also points to helplessness. When older people dream about a grave, this can be a sign that they tend to live in the past. Their unconscious could be telling them that they still have a future to look forward to, and one that is worthy of being enjoyed. (See also "Funeral," "Monument," "Cemetery," and "Burying.")

GRAVEDIGGER A gravedigger represents emotional disturbances that you need to let go of or bury. This image may also be a hint to let go of a worn-out relationship so that you can start anew. When a gravedigger appears in a nightmare, emotional problems are indicated. (See also "Nightmares" under Other Clues.)

GREEN Green is the color of springtime, hope, and emotions. It stands for your relationship to reality and for a simpler life, and in seeing green in a dream you are being encouraged to pay more attention to both. Green also points to love, wealth, and joy. Only a garishly green color is seen as negative, as it is considered the color of the devil. (See also "Colors," "Grass," and "Devil.")

GRENADE A grenade going off suddenly in a dream indicates that a situation very dear to your heart is changing. (See also "Explosion" and "War.")

GRINDING Here, grinding refers to a process of producing something edible. Dreaming about grinding

wheat into flour has to do with producing mental nourishment, which in real life can be used to the dreamer's advantage. The image is always positive. (See also "Mill.")

GROTTO A grotto is a cave where nymphs live. It represents the problems that we have living with others. A spring originating from a grotto indicates a renewal of life's energies or of our own vitality, but this image could just as well be suggesting that it is time to change to a more natural lifestyle. Many dream analysts equate a grotto with the female sexual organs, because it is dark and damp. (See also "Cave" and "Spring.")

GUEST Dreaming about guests usually translates into the dreamer's desire for more social activities. A guest who is a stranger represents the alter ego of the dreamer that wants a life of leisure. In ancient Egypt, dreaming about a guest indicated that great expenditures were about to pile up.

GUEST HOUSE The house stands for the body. Dreaming about a guest house is a sign to pay more attention to your body in order to improve its potential. This could point to a vacation, a visit to a spa, or time spent in a hospital. (See also "Guest" and "House.")

GUITAR The guitar, like most stringed instruments, has something to do with Eros, the Greek god of erotic love, and implies complete devotion in matters of lust and love. If you are the one who is playing the guitar in the dream, this could indicate that you have sexual desires that have remained unfulfilled. Listening to guitar music, however, points to getting together agreeably with good friends. (See also "Stringed Instruments.")

GUN To determine the meaning of a dream about a gun, you need to know if the magazine is full or if the bullets have already been fired, because both reflect on your virility and your capacity to perform. (See also "Pistol.")

GUN POWDER Dreaming about using gun powder aimlessly or indiscriminately means that you are also wasting your energies in real life, or will soon complain about having weak nerves.

HAIL Dreaming about hail, which is rain having turned to ice, might be a warning that in real life things will come down hard on you. This could also be a prediction of an argument in which words will fall hard like a hailstorm.

HAIR Hair stands for natural or essential energies. According to Freud, hair has the meaning of a secondary sexual characteristic. Artemidorus believed that going bald in a dream pointed to a loss of relatives or of possessions; an extravagant, flowing headdress implied a protection or an increase of possessions; and uncombed hair indicated impending worry and grief. Phaldor said that hair represented intellectual and material assets, and loss of hair pointed to failure and humiliation. Modern dream interpretation sees loss of hair as a warning about losses or as a fear of losing in real life. In dreaming about hair, examine your urges as well as your thinking, because often hair represents our spiritual state of affairs. Try to recall if you saw a full head of hair or thin hair, or whether it was well cared for or messy. The color of the hair may also be important. The Indian dream manual *Jagaddeva* states that hair that has been cut off foretells poverty and misery for the dreamer. (See also "Beard," "Baldness," "Head," and "Wig.")

HAIRDRESSER/BARBER The beauty salon and barbershop are the places where we get our hair cut and shaped. The dream is a hint that we need to look at our physical well-being.

HAIR-STYLING PRODUCT
Dreaming about smoothing out your hair with a conditioner or a mousse is an acknowledgment that something that is bothering you in real life needs to be straightened out. The dream may also indicate that you are trying to ignore something in your life (possibly something having to do with an intimate relationship). (See also "Hair.")

HALL Dreaming about a hall describes the dreamer's sense of community. A person can also hide or get lost in a roomful of people, which could mean that the dreamer sees him- or herself only as a "fellow traveler." Dreaming about being the only person in a big hall is a sign to seek contact with others, unless you don't mind being completely without friends. (See also "Room.")

HALLWAY A long hallway is a symbol for a narrow passageway approaching an as-yet-unknown destination. Thus, dreaming about a long hallway can be a message to try to free yourself from a rather narrow point of view, or to work on overcoming some kind of emotional misery, even if you don't yet know where the journey will take you. Walking through a dark hallway implies that you are trying to rid your soul of its shadows or that you are afraid that somebody will force you into becoming his or her accomplice. (See also "Darkness" and "Narrow Space.")

HAMMER The hammer is a symbol of power. Using a hammer in a dream is a message that very little can be accomplished with force alone.

HAMSTER The hamster is a rodent capable of stashing up to 50 grams of grain in its cheeks. Dreaming about a hamster therefore points to gluttony, or can be a message to take on less in life.

HAND A hand reaches out, is used for work, holds on to things or people, or lets go. In other words, it is the physical instrument of action. Dreaming about hands doing something is a message from the unconscious, and their actions can relate to real-life situations. Dreaming about an injured hand, or a hand bitten by a dog, means that in real life at this moment you are unable to act. Dirty hands indicate that in real life you are acting less than honorably. Some psychoanalysts believe that the left hand has female connotations and the right hand male. (See also "Arm," "Finger," "Left," and "Right.")

HANDS (ON THE CLOCK) Hands on the clock show the hour, minutes, and seconds—the time of day. To interpret a dream in which this image appears, you need to remember where the hands were, and to check the symbolic meaning of the respective numbers and that of "Clock." (See also "Clock/Watch.")

HANGING This image means that the dreamer is left "high and dry" or is slandered or deceived in some way. If the dreamer is being hanged, this means that a goal can only be accomplished with a lot of tedious work. If others are hanged, this is a warning to watch out for vicious people. On the other hand, wash hanging outside in front of a neighbor's window points to conflict and being exposed. (See also "Gallows" and "Laundry, Doing.")

HANGMAN Dreaming about a hangman preparing for an execution is a message that you need to deal with and eliminate various shortcomings of your own. The hangman in the dream may also be passing judgment on a specific matter. (See also "Hanging," "Gallows," and "Execution.")

HARBOR Dreaming about reaching a harbor means that you have reached your goals or that a new phase in your life is beginning. The harbor—like the train station—also often shows that wishes have come true. (See also "Ocean" and "Ship.")

HARBOR PILOT The harbor pilot is a positive dream image, because he or she is the one who guides ships safely to their destinations. A harbor pilot in a dream also means that you will have help in getting through a difficult situation. (See also "Ship.")

HARE According to mythology, the hare represents the fertile powers of the moon (see also "Moon"), which rules over plants and water, and is also a symbol of woman. In modern dream interpretation, the hare is a symbol of animalistic fertility; therefore, dreaming about a hare implies that the dreamer thinks about intimacy more in terms of quantity than quality. The hare, even though it has a considerable appetite, is considered less harmful than the rat or the mouse (see also "Rats," "Mouse," and "Rodents"). The image is more of a mirror of the dreamer's timidity, which he or she should try to overcome. Because of the hare's speed and the way it darts from side to side when running, it is difficult to catch, and it is this quickness that is at the core of the message of a dream about a hare: The dreamer is being told not to vacillate, but to be quick, in thought as well as action. Men dreaming about shooting a rabbit are hoping that the pursuit of their sexual interest will be successful.

HARP It is well known that the harp is a difficult instrument to master, so dreaming that you or someone else is playing this instrument could mean that you should have low expectations concerning a certain matter. (See also "Music" and "Musical Instruments.")

HARROW Dreaming about working a field with a harrow means that you must work hard in real life to achieve your goal. (See also "Field.")

HARVEST Dreaming about a harvest is a favorable sign. This image points to strength of character and to a desire to finish successfully something that you have started. Hard work will get you there. Often a dream about a harvest is connected to the image of fall, a season when life is winding down. For older people, the fall represents a time when life, they hope, will be free of worry. If the harvest is poor in your dream, expect lean times in real life. New seeds, however, are a sign of hope. (See also "Fall" and "Seeds.")

HASTE Dreaming about being in a hurry, but never arriving, might be a message from the unconscious to slow down; the turtle gets to where it needs to go.

HAT Dreaming about wearing a hat may allude to swift ideas darting through your head. Many psychoanalysts see the hat purely as a sexual symbol, which refers to the male sexual organ, virility or impotence, or certain devices to prevent conception. Dreaming about an oversized lady's hat points to emotional cravings and compulsive fantasies. (See also "Helmet.")

HAWK A dream about a hawk diving from great heights to capture its prey means that the unconscious is asking you to get going and tackle some predicament. A bird flying in sweeping circles high in the sky implies that you are pursuing high ideals. (See also "Birds.")

HAY Dreaming about lying down in hay implies that in real life you must get used to a more modest lifestyle. Bringing in hay, on the other hand, means that you can count on having a full wallet soon—that is, if you "make hay while the getting is good." A dream about bails of hay in a field indicates that hard work lies ahead for you, or that the fruits of your labor belong to someone else.

HEAD The head is the part of the body that guides all senses and mental processes. Dreaming about an injury to the head suggests that in real life you should seek medical attention, whereas decapitation is a sign that you might be "losing your head" over a certain situation. In China, people believe that the head is the seat of heavenly light. Artemidorus saw it as a symbol for the father or a male relative. For Freud, the head symbolized masculinity; for Jung, it was an archetypal symbol for the self, and the upper part of the head also had phallic meaning. The Indian dream book *Jagaddeva* says the dreamer makes a claim to power if he splits his own

head open in the dream; another interpretation is that the dreamer can count on having many descendants. (See also "Body" and "Decapitation.")

HEADLIGHTS (SEE "SPOTLIGHT")

HEART Dreaming about the heart is often a warning, usually of an illness (sometimes of a close relative). It may point to heart problems with psychosomatic undertones, which may result from interpersonal conflicts. In some cultures, people believe that the heart is the seat of the soul, so dreaming about heart problems would be related to emotional problems or lovesickness, such as having a "broken heart."

HEATHER Heather is a plant of the fall, and although dreaming about it promises older people a time of rest, for younger people it might imply the conclusion of a pleasant development. Often, however, a dream about heather describes the perseverance with which the dreamer is confronting an opponent. Wilted, dried heather is a sign that the dreamer might have to end a close relationship. (See also "Flowers.")

HEDGEHOG For the unconscious, the hedgehog with its spines is equated with being prepared for defensive action. This means that in real life you shouldn't hesitate to "show your spines" toward those who want to do you harm. Dreaming about a hedgehog that is curling itself into a ball shows that you insist on being left alone and in peace.

HEEL The heel is the part of the foot that is injured easily, and describes our "Achilles heel." Dreaming about an injury to the heel indicates that in real life your point of view is shifting or that something is interfering with your getting ahead.

HEEL OF A SHOE If you are losing a heel off your shoe, this is a message to try to avoid unnecessary expenses. This could also mean that you are "losing ground." If the heel is replaced, expect that a tolerable compromise is in the making. (See also "Shoemaker.")

HELL Dreaming about hell implies that you have a bad conscience that causes you great anguish. (See also "Devil.")

HELMET Dreaming about wearing a helmet indicates that in real life you want to protect your head. This image could also be a message to act only when there is no chance of making a mistake. (See also "Head.")

HEN A hen protects her eggs. Dreaming about a hen means that in real life you have nothing to worry about. Slaughtering a hen in a dream is a sign that you are being careless. In antiquity, people believed that dreaming about a hen with many small chicks meant that the dreamer would have many children. (See also "Egg" and "Feathered Animals.")

HERBS Dreaming about looking for or finding herbs indicates that you want to do something for your health, in order to be more successful in life.

HERD A herd walks ahead of the person tending it. Dreaming about a herd might mean that the dreamer always deals with his or her responsibilities later. However, this image could also refer to a herd instinct on the part of the dreamer, and therefore indicate co-dependency. (See also "Animals.")

HERDSMAN Dreaming about a herdsman tending a large herd promises the dreamer great wealth that will increase over time. Older people dreaming about a herdsman can look forward to an enjoyable retirement, because they are protected by the "Good Shepherd." (See also "Shepherd.")

HERMIT/RECLUSE Dreaming of being a hermit can be seen as a message from the soul telling you how lonely you really feel, even while you pretend to enjoy contact in pleasant company. The loneliness is deep inside. Such a dream could also be an expression of your search for a person who will understand you and accept you the way you are.

HIDE Hide is what covers the body of an animal and is exposed to the outside world. In a dream, it often is a symbol for a "soft hide" that is hidden under rough skin.

HIGH SCHOOL GRADUATION Dreaming about going through a high school graduation, even if you received your diploma a long time ago, means that you are undergoing changes in your personality or lifestyle. Dreaming about not graduat-

Hing means that you are afraid of changes that you think you can't handle, or that you are resisting changes because you would rather hold on to what is familiar. (See also "Test.")

HIKING Dreaming about hiking implies that in real life you have the will to get ahead, one step at a time, without getting impatient. If the path is challenging and the hiker is wearing a backpack, or if he or she is demanding too much of him- or herself, this means that your goal can only be reached with difficulty. (See also "Backpack" and "Walking.")

HILL Dreaming about a hill points to problems lying ahead in real life. A difficult climb up a steep hill indicates that you could be facing an insurmountable situation. Not reaching the top implies that you are setting your sights too high. Reaching the top, on the other hand, means that you can look forward to success. A moderate climb suggests that you can count on getting ahead in life. Coming down a hill connotes that an important part of your life is coming to an end; however, this could also imply that you have finally reached you goal, and can look forward to easier times. The ancient Egyptians believed that dreaming about climbing a very steep mountain indicated that the dreamer would have to face many obstacles in life, which could only be overcome with a great deal of effort. (See also "Abyss," "Falling," "Crashing," "Climbing," and "Wall.")

HIP The hip, the area between heart and the sexual organs, describes the connection between the emotions and the physical urges. Dreaming about pain in the hip area indicates that you can expect to have a painful experience in a love relationship.

HITTING Hitting someone may refer to your determination to stick to your own opinion.

HOARSE Dreaming about having a rasping voice, or someone else having a rasping voice, usually means that we are unable to defend ourselves against ugly accusations or schemes. It could also be a message from the unconscious that we talk too much and should only speak up when we are sure that we have something important to say. (See also "Stuttering.")

HOBO (SEE "VAGABOND")

HOLE According to Freud, dreaming about holes refers to sexual matters. But a hole that is opening up in front of the dreamer may also be a warning of impending danger. Falling into a hole could mean that the dreamer will be taken advantage of by friends or the competition; this could also mean that he or she is unable to handle a sexual problem. Only a small hole is seen as positive, because there is little danger of falling into a small hole.

HOLY COMMUNION Taking part in holy communion in a dream implies that you want to be free of feelings of guilt. Here, the unconscious is asking you to check your conscience to see whether or not something has been handled honestly.

HOME One's home also plays a role in dreams. If you feel comfortable in your home in the dream, you needn't be concerned about your emotional well-being. But if the home is in disarray or without the normal furniture in place, you are probably emotionally out of sorts. Painting your home in a dream is a sign that you need a vacation. (See also "House" and "Apartment.")

HOMESICK Dreaming about being homesick indicates that the dreamer is hurting from an irrevocable loss or is longing to recapture a sense of security.

HOMETOWN We can dream about our hometown without having left it. Such a dream could indicate that we feel uprooted, or lack contact with the people around us. This could also be a message from the unconscious to adapt to our surroundings better in order to feel less isolated.

HONEY In India, honey symbolizes the fire that is burning in all of us and alludes to the unveiling of the inner self. In many indigenous cultures, honey is a symbol of rebirth. Dreaming about honey can be translated into the sweet life for which we all long.

HONEYCOMB A honeycomb full of honey in a dream is a sign of hope that your life will be full of love and happiness. (See also "Bee.")

HOOKER (SEE "PROSTITUTE")

HOOP A hoop in a dream is similar in its meaning to a circle and a wheel. Dreaming about attaching a hoop around a barrel means that you will meet a new friend soon or find a new circle of friends. (See also "Circle" and "Wheel.")

HORN The horn as a wind instrument refers to sexual matters. In reference to antlers, see the description under "Antlers." (See also "Wind Instruments.")

HORSE The horse symbolizes the essential vitality of human beings. It is also the archetype of the feminine mother and the male intellect. When in motion, the horse symbolizes untamed freedom and an impetuous temperament are not limited to sexual matters. When the horse and the rider are one, this implies that you will rarely encounter emotional or sexual difficulties. A horse that is well cared for and handled kindly indicates that your life will be undisturbed, or that you have reined in your temper. If the horse is neglected, the dream will probably be a nightmare, with the horse alluding to the ghost of untamed impulses, and will show that your urges are out of control. Horses that shy away from, or take off with, their riders indicate a fear of a loss of vitality or virility. Horses have even talked in people's dreams, telling them to stay calm in a certain situation. The color of the horse also plays a role. A fiery, black stallion indicates that you are repressing your vitality at the expense of your soul. There is something eerie about a white horse; appearing in a dream, it points to isolation, a lack of community, or something destructive. In a dream where horses appear in specific colors, check those colors. According to Artemidorus, a man mounting a beautiful horse in a dream can expect good luck in love. However, Phaldor believed that when a horse is being mounted by a man, the horse represents a beautiful woman whom he wants to possess physically. (See also "Reins," "Saddle," and "Horseback Riding.")

HORSEBACK RIDING Dreaming about riding a horse in an even, comfortable gait indicates that you are in control of your urges. Should the horse move in a excited canter, or even take off in a full gallop, this means that you need to reign in your preoccupation with sex. In addition to the allusion to sexual matters, a dream about horseback riding refers to traveling or to the ups and downs of life's journey. (See also "Traveling," "Reins," "Saddle," and "Horse.")

HORSESHOE A horseshoe pointed at you in a dream means that you need to be wary of people misleading you in life. (See also "Magnet.")

HOSPITAL Dreaming about being in the hospital shows that you are facing problems that can't be solved without outside help; such dreams usually have nothing to do with an illness, but point to an emotional issue. Pay attention to the diagnosis, for it could indicate the kind of emo-

tional problem with which you are dealing. Waiting for the results of an operation implies that you are faced with an important event in real life. In addition, the floor of the hospital on which you are staying can provide information about which part of your body needs attention. (See also "House," "Physician," "Invalid," and "Operation.")

HOST/HOSTESS Dreaming about being the host or hostess implies that you have a healthy constitution and a love for food, with a tendency to overindulge. (See also "Guest House.")

HOSTEL/INN Dreaming about a hostel or an inn, a place where strangers often talk to one another, points to loneliness in real life, which can be overcome by being more open-minded. Dreaming about being alone in a hostel is a sign that your emotions might be causing a physical illness. (See also "Guest House," "House," and "Hotel.")

HOT-AIR BALLOON (SEE "BALLOON")

HOTEL Dreaming about signing into a hotel means that you may be searching unconsciously for something. Entering a hotel room describes a transition that you may be experiencing, especially when the room seems like a strange and somewhat dubious place. Other hotel guests represent obscure shadows of yourself. Try to recall the name of the hotel, and see if it symbolizes anything that would shed further light on the meaning of the dream. (See also "Guest House," "Hostel/Inn," "Bellhop," and "Doorman.")

HOUNDED (SEE "CHASED/HOUNDED")

HOURGLASS An hourglass in a dream points to time wasted that is irretrievable. Dreaming about an hourglass indicates that you feel time is passing too quickly, or that you want time to stand still. Sometimes such a dream points to a separation from a loved one or the loss of a close friend.

HOUSE Dreaming about a house is an indication of our internal and external states. Even Artemidorus thought that a house in a dream stood for the human body. According to modern dream interpretation, dreaming about the outside of a house refers to the impression that we want to create of ourselves in society, or to our public face and personality. The different floors of a house can be compared to the different parts of the body or different emotional levels, to which the unconscious wants us to pay attention. The roof as well as the upper floors represent the head, with its various functions. The basement, a dark space with assorted entrances or openings, is usually considered to be a reference to the sexual parts of the body. A dream about a house may describe the condition of the individual parts of the house and what, if anything, needs to be improved or repaired. An old, dilapidated house is a reminder about

what you need to rebuild or correct in yourself. Dreaming about a luxurious villa often indicates that we pretend to be more than we really are. Dreaming about working inside the house is a reference to your professional life or job, and what you need to change in this area. Dreaming about building or buying a new house is a sign to attend to your emotional well-being. Such a dream can also indicate the end of a weak condition. (See also "Guest House" and specific parts of a house.)

HOWLING Hearing a wolf or a dog howling in a dream is an indication that there is something unsettling in the dreamer's environment. (See also "Dog," "Barking Dog," "Wolf," and "Crying.")

HUNCHBACKED Dreaming of being hunchbacked has nothing to do with a physical deformity. In fact, it may show that you are hoping to bring home a sack full of money. Seeing somebody else with a hunched back can be a message to examine yourself and to be less critical of the mistakes of others.

HUNGER Dreaming about being hungry expresses a longing for food and vitality. Feeling hungry is often part of a nightmare and a warning of impending emotional damage. (See also "Nightmares" under Other Clues, and "Thirst," "Chewing," "Cook," and "Meal.")

HUNTING Dreaming about going hunting implies that in real life you

H are searching for a friend or a boss who will understand you. Coming home empty-handed from a hunt means that in real life you have doubts as to whether your search will ever be successful. Try to recall which animal in your dream was being hunted (see also that animal).

HURRICANE (SEE "STORM" AND "WIND")

I **ICE** Dreaming about ice could be a sign that your emotional state is frozen, and that loneliness and worries are in store for you. This image also points to angst, a fear of a close relationship becoming frozen, as well as a breakdown in financial matters. (See also "Breakdown," "Breaking Through," and "Freezing.")

ICE SKATES Ice skates are the means by which we can move on ice, and this image translates into overcoming a personal problem. (See also "Ice.")

ICE SKATING Dreaming about having fun ice skating shows that in real life you needn't be afraid of falling down. But breaking through the ice while ice skating is a sign that you should expect problems, especially in interpersonal relationships. (See also "Breakdown," "Breaking Through," and "Ice.")

ICICLE Sometimes when women dream about icicles, this indicates that a sexual relationship is cooling off.

ILLNESS Dreaming about being sick indicates that you are emotionally deprived. Suffering from a heart disease shows that you lack empathy. Eye problems suggest that you are being asked to look at a certain person "with different eyes." Stomach and intestinal problems imply that you need to digest something before it can be put right. (See also "Physician.")

INCEST Surprisingly, dreaming about incest with a close relative or even one's own mother or father usually doesn't refer to sex. On the contrary, such a dream could be a sign that your relationship with your parent, child, or sibling is lacking warmth, which you secretly crave. Sometimes incestuous activities with a relative are a sign that this person is in trouble and in need of our help. In this case, the dream could be a message to look after the person more consistently. Dreaming about incest with a parent may also simply indicate that you are homesick. (See also "Mother Complex" and "Sexual Dreams" under Other Clues.)

INDICTMENT This image alludes to having done something wrong. Appearing in front of a judge as a defendant could be a message to consider changing the way you live, improving your life, or creating a more positive environment for yourself. A dream in which another person is the defendant implies that you have done, or are about to do, an injustice to somebody. (See also "Judge" and "Court.")

INFANT (SEE "BABY")

INFLATION Dreaming about inflation has little to do with monetary matters, but rather with your fear of exhausting yourself physically and emotionally.

INHERITANCE Dreaming about an inheritance usually has nothing to do with finances. More likely it is the unconscious pointing out to you how much emotional strength you have, and that if you use this strength you could improve your private life considerably. Dreaming about an inheritance alludes to receiving a gift that can reduce your emotional burdens, or that requires a change in your attitudes.

INJURY A dream about an injury that doesn't cause pain implies that you feel injured in real life because of the emotional pain that someone has inflicted on you, or that you have created yourself. (See also "Blood," "Scar," and "Wound.")

INK Dreaming about using ink for writing is a sign that you would do well to rely on written documents rather than on verbal agreements. The latter are often misinterpreted. Spilling ink shows that you are unconsciously putting a big period after an agreement that will be to your benefit. A blot of ink, in contrast to other stains, is a positive sign. (See also "Stain" and "Blot.")

INN (SEE "HOSTEL/INN")

INSANE ASYLUM Completely normal people dream that they have been committed to an insane asylum from which they are never released.

Such a dream usually indicates that the dreamer is jittery, and needs to bring more order into his or her life. The dream could also point to feeling despondent about a certain situation in real life. This situation could be health-related, or have something to do with an insult you received at your job with which you are unable to come to terms.

INSECTS Dreaming about a swarm of insects surrounding you may reflect the state of your nerves, as they are reacting to the myriad influences with which you are constantly bombarded. Being stung by those insects indicates that your nerves are truly overtaxed. (See also specific insects.)

INTERCOURSE Dreams about intercourse may not have that much to do with sex. As a symbol, intercourse often points to creation or birth, discovering new intellectual concepts, or the rebirth of the soul. (See also "Sexual Dreams" under Other Clues, and "Sexual Relations.")

INTERSECTION Dreaming about standing at an intersection indicates that you are lost, and don't know how to proceed in life to be successful. Often it connotes angst, which might refer to an emotional illness or a state of indecision. Sometimes such a dream gives a hint of how to proceed; pay attention to the direction that is suggested. (See also "Four Points of the Compass.")

INTOXICATION A dream about intoxication could be the unconscious making you aware of having acted confused or as if you had "lost your mind."

INVALID Dreaming about being an invalid could mean that you shouldn't give up but should continue to fight with courage even in the face of seemingly overwhelming opposition. Dreaming about someone else as the invalid can be a message not to ignore a person in real life who is in need of your help. But it is also possible that an invalid in a dream is an expression of yourself, and may point to having lost a sense of emotional stability or to having emotional problems. Dreaming about visiting an invalid in the hospital could mean that you are trying to make contact with people who can help you with your emotional problems. Caring for an invalid may imply that you are at an emotional low point in your life. (See also "Cripple.")

INVISIBLE, BECOMING A dream in which you become invisible is a message from the unconscious to stop trying to be "at the head of the line." According to an ancient Egyptian belief, those people who made themselves invisible in a dream we should avoid speaking badly of in real life.

IRONING Dreaming about ironing indicates that you want to "iron out" something or bring a certain project to an end.

ISLAND Dreaming about an island may refer to loneliness in real life. Because islands are often surrounded by a turbulent ocean, an island could also stand for a safe place to which you should retreat in order to gain new strength.

ITCHING Dreaming about itching might simply mean that you are being tickled by a rough blanket or a feather from your pillow. However, if the itching has no external source, it could stand for some type of emotional distress in real life, such as a fear of a test or jealousy toward an rival. Such a dream could also imply that you are "itching" to do something (perhaps spend some money).

IVORY The tusks of an elephant are generally seen as a sexual symbol and indicate male aggressiveness. Dreaming about handling ivory may possibly be a suggestion to look for a different job.

IVY A dream about ivy mirrors your ambition. Your thoughts are like ivy growing up a post; they revolve around the issue of how to get ahead in life.

JAIL Dreaming about jail has to do with being the prisoner of your emotions, or not being able to make decisions freely. This image could also mean that you somehow feel limited in your actions or possibly are misjudging your true circumstances. In the case of the latter, the dream could be a message from the unconscious to start being more realistic. (See also "Gate" and "Fence.")

JASMINE Dreaming about this aromatic flower can be translated into your desire for pure, true love. Wilted jasmine flowers, on the other hand, might indicate the end of a relationship.

JEALOUSY A dream about being jealous is like a mirror reflecting your hidden fear of losing what you love the most.

JEWELRY A dream about jewelry could be an expression of your hope for a better station in life, or your desire to shine in good company or be successful. Dreaming about wearing jewelry implies that you like to embellish yourself or points to diverting attention from mistakes you have made. Dreaming about wearing jewelry without owning it implies that you may not get very far in life, because your attention is always directed toward your appearance. Giving jewelry as a gift alludes to communicating sincerely with the people around you. (See also "Gold" and "Pearl.")

JUDGE A judge in a dream may be the person who ascribes different meanings to what you have said. The dream could also be a warning, telling you not to speak too carelessly or to sign any contracts whose content, including the fine print, you have not read at least twice. (See also "Court" and "Lawyer.")

JUGGLER Dreaming about admiring a juggler at work indicates that in real life you are trying to take advantage of others doing the work instead of working yourself. Dreaming about being a juggler yourself implies that

you are trying to keep everything in balance without dropping or destroying something. (See also "Circus.")

JUMPING Dreaming about jumping a hurdle successfully implies that you are able to deal well with an important situation in real life. Jumping into something (water or a pit, for example) shows that you will encounter a dangerous situation, from which you will be able to extricate yourself only with difficulty.

KETTLE As is the case with other containers, dreaming about a kettle may not necessarily have a positive meaning. According to folklore, a full kettle points to doing a lot of work for many guests or a large party, and an empty kettle implies quarrels and strife. A kettle boiling over in a dream shows that we are stumbling from one frenzied situation to another. (See also "Container.")

KETTLEDRUM Playing the kettledrum in a dream implies that you are making an announcement in real life that will not reflect well on you. Or, this could mean that you are making too much noise, so people are annoyed with you.

KEY Dreams about keys often allude to a mysterious matter or a secret for which we are trying to find the key; by the same token, if we have lost the key, we will never be able to unravel the secret. Dreaming about losing a key is also seen as a message to stop being so secretive. According to Artemidorus, the image of a key in a dream points to the dreamer's having found the key to the heart of the person whom he or she loves. In addition, a key in a dream could be a warning not to go on a trip or someplace else, because this change in location would be contrary to the lifestyle with which the dreamer is familiar. (See also "Locksmith" and "Door Lock.")

KEY RING Dreaming about holding a key ring without choosing a key implies that you are frittering away energy and time, and having difficulty making decisions. This also may mean that the key to lasting good luck has yet to be found.

KINDLING
The meaning of kindling, easily combustible wood for starting a fire, is similar to that of a "Cigarette Lighter." However, kindling may also point to your attachment to traditions or leaning toward simplicity—in other words, you are not all that "fired up" about modern life.

KING The king is the archetypal symbol for a father who lends support in a difficult situation. Dreaming about a king often highlights the father-child relationship and the dependency that the dreamer might have on a father figure. (See also "Emperor.")

KISS A kiss is a symbol for great happiness. It promises recovery in

real life if the dreamer is sick. Kissing in the context of an erotic dream indicates that all is well in a relationship, even if the dreamer kissed someone other than his or her partner. Sometimes a kiss refers to intellectual communication. Watch out if others kiss you in a dream, because it might be the kiss of Judas. (See also "Lips," "Mouth," and "Tongue.")

KITCHEN The kitchen is a symbol for your maternal self, and is the place in dreams where emotions change and vitality is nourished. Dreams about kitchens have a great deal to do with emotional digestion. According to Freud, many items in the kitchen (frying pan, hearth, potato masher, and so forth) point to sexual desires that the dreamer hopes will come to pass. Working in the kitchen means that you won't shy away from hard work in real life. (See also "House," "Stove," and "Cooking.")

KNAPSACK A dream about a knapsack being carried on the back of a soldier naturally has more connotations to do with combat than does a satchel being carried by a student. However, both suggest that we are carrying what life has dealt us. (See also "Soldier," "Student," and "Backpack.")

KNEE This joint in the leg is a symbol for connections that make everything work well. Dreaming about a stiff knee refers to people in real life who won't "bend" to your wishes. Dreaming of pain in the knee implies that things aren't going well or that business is slow. Dreaming of being on bended knee means that you are properly humble in real life. A dream in which you are working on your "hands and knees" means that you have been humiliated by your own actions or behavior. (See also "Leg.")

KNIFE A knife is a tool used for cutting and dividing. Therefore, dreaming about a knife could mean that you want to cut someone out of your life or you want to divide something—perhaps a responsibility that is too difficult to carry alone. In addition, in the language of dreams, cutting and dividing can be translated into analyzing and differentiating. According to Freud, as with all cutting or piercing objects, a knife has a phallic or a sexual meaning. He believed that seeing a cutting or piercing tool in a dream indicated that the dreamer would plunge headlong into wanton sexual activities, and that sharpening a knife in a dream implied that the dreamer was tempted to betray his or her partner. (See also "Rapier.")

KNIGHT Some people believe that dreaming of a knight in full regalia bursting onto the scene and taking the castle without showing any mercy could be describing the arrogance of certain men, because they believe they can have any woman they desire. However, sometimes such a dream is only an expression of a longing for an adventure. In a woman's dream, the knight often changes from an archetypal patriarch to the gentleman she would like to have by her side.

KNOCKING DOWN Who or what is being knocked down in the dream is important. Nevertheless, dreaming of knocking something or somebody down points to feelings of hatred that the dreamer is carrying, or that are knocking him or her down. Such emotions ought to be looked at closely, so that they can be discarded.

KNOT A knot in a dream usually stands for problems that are difficult to solve or situations in which we are unsure of what to do. It is also possible for the unconscious to be using the image in the sense of the Gordian knot, the knot that Alexander the Great cut with his sword; imitating the great conqueror means that the dreamer will have great success in carrying out brilliant ideas or practical plans. (See also "Ball of Wool or Yarn.")

LABORATORY The laboratory is the place where the soul experiments. Other symbols in the dream will indicate whether or not the experiment will be emotionally manageable or successful.

LABYRINTH Dreaming about being in a labyrinth indicates that you are emotionally lost and do not know which way to turn. Navigating a labyrinth successfully shows that you have come through a difficult time. Dreams about labyrinths are not as rare as people might think. Sometimes they point to an emotional or a spiritual problem, or a secret love for someone whom others believe is not deserving. A labyrinth can also stand for a dark, mysterious place, in which we are trying to find the exit without knowing where it will take us.

LADDER Dreaming about a ladder means that you are not sure about your chances for advancement or that your life is at a precarious stage. Climbing with great effort, one rung after the other, indicates that getting to the top will be difficult, and falling off will be like falling into an abyss. Freud believed that climbing up and down a ladder represented the sex act; however, in our opinion, this is a little far-fetched. (See also "Rung," "Stairs," and "Falling.")

LADY Dreaming about a lady with whom you want to become socially or sexually involved implies that you are looking for "better" company or a sexual adventure that is also stimulating intellectually. Hidden behind the lady is often the dreamer's own mother (see also "Mother"), an authority figure who wants to admonish the dreamer to change his or her lifestyle. It's important to make sure that it is truly a lady about whom you are dreaming.

LAKE Like the ocean, a lake describes our collective unconscious, only here the waters at the shoreline are much calmer. These waters don't know the expanse of the ocean or its turmoil. Dreaming about a lake may refer to the saying "Still waters run deep," or could be a sign that more tranquil times are ahead. It's possible that you have just come out of a stage in your life that was extremely tense, and now you are relishing peace and quiet. However, you can't relax completely, because a storm could whip up the surface of the lake and drench you to the bone. (See also "Ocean.")

LAMP To properly interpret a dream about a lamp, you need to remember how bright or how dim the light was. A lamp dispersing bright light promises emotional tranquility; a dull light implies being emotionally uptight. A lamp whose light goes out indicates that the dreamer feels helpless in a precarious situation. A broken lamp is a message to be careful; perhaps something inside is fragile or possibly already broken. Turning the light on implies having come through a bewildering situation. (See also "Streetlight" and "Light.")

LANDSCAPE A landscape in a dream where the sun is shining brightly means that we can expect a life free of worry. A foggy landscape or one with dark clouds in the sky represents our gloomy thoughts, which prevent us from getting ahead in life. (See also different types of landscapes and natural occurrences.)

LANE (SEE "TRACKS," "TRAIL," AND "STREET")

LARK Dreaming of a lark soaring up into the sky implies that in real life you can expect to get to the top quickly, or that you are in high spirits. (See also "Birds.")

LARVAE Dreaming about insect larvae indicates that in real life you are standing on the threshold of a new development; only seldom does this image imply a temporary state of helplessness.

LATENESS A dream about being late is a message from the unconscious not to miss out on a great opportunity that life is presenting to you right now. Similarly, people in ancient Egypt interpreted such a dream as a prediction of missing a great opportunity. Dreaming of being late usually refers to an obstacle on life's journey. Sometimes the dream is in the form of a fear that we will oversleep and miss our train or be late for work. (See also "Delays.")

LAUGHTER Laughter is somewhat like a sigh of relief when we have found a way out of a difficult situation. In the past, dreaming about laughing was believed to be crying in disguise, and vice versa. The dreamer, by the way, usually wakes up while laughing, and often continues without knowing why.

LAUNDRY, DOING Dirty laundry represents inner uncleanness or guilt feelings. According to Artemidorus, doing laundry meant that the dreamer wants to shake off some kind of unpopular notion.

LAUNDRY ROOM A laundry room in a dream is an interesting place. All kinds of things come together there, because the laundry room is usually in the basement, which represents the unconscious.

Dreaming about going to the laundry room means that you need to clean up some emotional matter. (See also "Basement" and "Soap Bubbles.")

LAUREL The evergreen laurel tree has been a symbol for splendor since ancient times. A laurel wreath was a promise that the hero would receive glory and honor. Being decorated with a laurel wreath in a dream points to many good things happening in the future. The leaves of the evergreen laurel tree stand for a promise of wealth. (See also "Tree," "Leaves," "Green," and "Wreath.")

LAWN A well-cared-for green lawn in a dream is a sign that all is well in your life. An uncared-for lawn that is full of weeds could represent the darker side of your life, a relationship handled carelessly, or an untidy home. (See also "Garden," "Grass," "Park," and "Meadow.")

LAWN MOWER A lawn mower in a dream may have something to do with the proverb "Pride cometh before a fall." If you are operating the lawn mower in the dream yourself, this may mean that you are trying to keep the competition in real life from growing too big. Listening to somebody else mowing the lawn indicates that you are nervous or that your mind is racing. (See also "Grass," "Machine," "Lawn," and "Meadow.")

LAWYER The lawyer is the person in a dream who makes things right, which alludes to something in your life being in disarray. Pay attention to whether or not issues were resolved in the dream.

LAXATIVES Dreaming about laxatives is the unconscious giving you a hint to rid your body of unhealthy things, to let go of emotional baggage, or to improve a muddled situation.

LAZINESS Dreaming about being lazy is the unconscious telling you to slow down and not use up all your energy. Such a dream might also point to a state of real exhaustion.

LEAD Dreaming about pouring heated lead shows that you are taking great pains to accomplish something that is useful, but that the result is still somewhat bizarre or confusing. In a German New Year's tradition, lead is heated and poured into a basin of cold water; according to the shape that the lead takes on, either a good or a bad omen is seen for the coming year.

LEASE Dreaming about leasing something implies that in real life you are becoming dependent and might have to pay for it dearly. Looking for a tenant, or leasing something to somebody, indicates that you want to enforce your will on others.

LEASH Dreams about leashes are usually about dogs on leashes. But it is also possible that the dreamer is the dog in the dream, and somebody is leading him or her around in real life. Therefore, who is at the other end of the leach in the dream is important. However, regardless of who is holding the leash, such a dream could mean that we want to keep somebody on our side or even force our will on someone.

LEATHER Many dream experts consider dreams about leather garments a sign of sadomasochistic tendencies. However, we believe that such dreams have more to do with the quality of the material: Wearing a leather garment will protect the dreamer from many dangers. (See also "Dress.")

LEAVES Usually a leaf is considered part of the "tree of life." Fresh leaves in a dream are a sign of good health. Dreaming about wilted leaves could be the unconscious bringing to the dreamer's attention the presence of an emotional weak spot, or indicating a disappointment that needs to be overcome. Falling leaves show that we need to reestablish our emotional equilibrium. According to a dream book from the Middle Ages, green leaves are supposed to mean good luck, whereas wilted leaves foretell misery. (See also "Branch," "Tree," and "Fall.")

LEFT Dreams about left and right refer to places in the body. The heart, located on the left side of the body, pertains to emotions or psychic energy, and is generally also seen to be the seat of the unconscious. The left also refers to the dreamer's feminine side. (See also "Right.")

LEG In a way, the leg is seen as the "motor" of the foot, so it has something to do with forward motion as well as going backward. The sexual interpretations made by Sigmund Freud seem less convincing. Freud believed that dreaming about beautiful legs implied that the dreamer was satisfying his or her sexual urges, and that breaking a leg indicated adultery. (See also "Amputation" and "Foot.")

LEGUMES Dreaming about eating peas or beans is a message from the unconscious not to be so puffed up (full of air) and arrogant toward the people around you. (See also "Beans.")

LEMON A dream about a squeezed-out lemon indicates that the dreamer feels used by someone in real life.

LENTILS Dreaming about cooking lentils is supposed to be a sign of frustration (because Esau sold his firstborn for a meal of lentils). Eating lentils indicates that you want to enrich yourself at the expense of somebody else. (See also "Beans.")

LETTER Dreaming about a letter implies that you are preoccupied with a subject, and had expected more than the end result shows. A letter may also indicate that you feel emotionally distant from the people around you. (See also "Mailman" and "Telegram.")

LETTUCE (SEE ALSO "SALAD GREENS/LETTUCE")

LICE Lice crawl around constantly and cause the skin to itch. Dreaming about lice could stand for the state of your nerves in real life. Lice may also indicate that you are restless and lack

focus, and that this may sabotage everything you do. Dreaming about killing lice, according to Artemidorus, meant that we were eliminating something nerve-racking from our mind or our life; when we can't get rid of these pesky little creatures, we are unable to eliminate something that is making our life difficult. (See also "Pests.")

LIGHT The image of a light in a dream represents freed-up intellectual energy—everything is illuminated and can be seen clearly. An age-old symbol of hope, light indicates a new beginning or a rebirth, or means that the dreamer has no need to worry about health or money. A light being turned on shows that you have a sudden bright idea. A light shining in the distance indicates the awakening of new passions. A light suddenly being turned off implies that you are in the dark, or that emotional trauma or at least bad news is likely. Bright light, to the point of hurting the eyes, is a negative sign, the meaning of which can be determined by other symbols in the dream. (See also "Darkness" and other symbols having to do with light.)

LIGHTHOUSE Dreaming about a lighthouse implies that we have "seen the light"; this image is also like a marker that we encounter along life's journey, showing the way. The lighthouse is always a positive image. (See also "Lamp," "Streetlight," and "Light.")

LIGHTNING Dreaming about lightning is a sign that uncontrollable

L powers are influencing your emotions. Dreaming about a bolt of lightning implies that you have a sudden insight about how to get your life in order. For Freud, lightning had phallic meaning. According to Artemidorus, getting hit by lightning was a good omen; he also equated fire created by lightning with gold, which can be easily obtained but just as easily lost. When lightning strikes close by, this means that you will probably move to another location. For people in love, lightning shows that love is striking them "like lightning"; for a married couple, however, this image points to separation. People in India believe that dreaming about lightning means that an illness will strike. A storm with lightning alludes to difficulties and tension in your personal life. (See also "Blaze" and "Fire.")

LILAC Dreaming about lilacs alludes to a desire for love and tenderness. For a more precise interpretation, pay attention to the color of the blossoms. (See also "Violet" and "White.")

LILY Unlike other flowers that have erotic connotations, the lily is a symbol for power. If you are holding a lily in a dream, this may mean that in real life you are very successful and have achieved a position of authority. If the lily is wilted, or you are throwing the lily away, you may be abusing the power that you have over others. Giving a lily as a gift shows that your emotions are pure. (See also "Flowers.")

LILY OF THE VALLEY This is the flower that announces spring.

However, seeing it in a dream may indicate that a love affair will end painfully, because the flower is poisonous.

LIMPING Dreaming about limping indicates that you will not reach your goal easily and could be complaining about it. Another message behind such a dream is to roll up your sleeves, muster some courage, and try to conquer your fear. In addition, dreaming about limping often points to the dreamer's sense of superiority over handicapped people. (See also "Leg" and "Foot.")

LION Since antiquity, the lion has been a symbol for the sun's unlimited energy. Today, we equate the image of a lion with unbridled emotional energy, passion, and strength, even though it is often frightening when a lion appears in a dream. Dreaming of a lion may mean that your passions will overpower you and cause you pain. If the lion in the dream appears as the legendary "king of the jungle," this means that you can't be fooled easily in life, but are self-assured and walk through life without looking over your shoulder. In addition, this image points to being very successful, but also difficult to live with because you often have little regard for others. It also may mean that your passions are under control. Dreaming about being attacked by a lion indicates that you are threatened by someone with an aggressive personality. A lion in a dream can point to the release of creative and intellectual energies as well as destructive aggressions.

LIPS Dreaming about red lips usually means that secret sexual desires will be fulfilled. Only pinched lips foretell sorrow in love. (See also "Kiss" and "Red.")

LIVER A dream involving the liver usually occurs when there is some kind of physical irritation in real life. Most of the time, we can't locate the source of the irritation when we wake up. However, if the dream appears with any frequency, it's a good idea to try to find the source of the sensation and seek medical advice. (See also "Abdominal Pain.")

LIZARD The lizard is the small version of the dragon, which means that the dreamer wants to be larger than he or she really is. (See also "Dragon.")

LOCKSMITH Dreaming about a locksmith implies that a door that used to be locked is opening, which could mean that someone's heart is opening to you. Dreaming about being the locksmith yourself suggests that you feel you are a (often unwelcome) mediator.

LOG Dreaming about stubbing a toe on a log means that in real life someone wants to set a trap for you. Splitting a log indicates that you can expect something positive from people who used to be indifferent to you, but are now on your side because of your convincing ideas. (See also "Wood.")

LOOKING OVER YOUR SHOULDER Dreaming about looking over your shoulder shows that someone in real life means you harm.

The dream is a reminder from the unconscious to keep your eyes open and look straight ahead to your goal.

LOOM (SEE "WEAVING LOOM")

LOOP A loop conveys the image of something being enfolded. Dreaming about making or seeing a loop means that in your job or other areas of your life you are counting on what you have instead of what you might get in the future.

LOST When you have lost something in a dream, it is important to determine what it was, and then to find its symbolic meaning. Such a dream usually points to an emotional weakness. On the other hand, a dream in which you yourself are lost may refer to your inability to find your way in emotional and spiritual matters.

LOTTERY TICKET A lottery ticket in a dream is similar to one that we hold in real life, in which winning or losing depends on the numbers drawn, except that here it may not have anything to do with monetary gains or having good or bad luck. The numbers on the lottery ticket are important because of their symbolic meaning. If the ticket has no (visible) numbers, this is a message that it is far better to rely on hard work and stop chasing Lady Luck. (See also "Winning," "Number," and specific numbers.)

LOVER Dreaming about a new lover usually indicates that in real life the dreamer might be too dependent on another person, maybe even enslaved. The unconscious uses this powerful image in order to make the dreamer aware of this dependency. In the case of married people, dreaming of a new lover often indicates a lack of sexual gratification in their marriage.

LOW TIDE Low tide symbolizes relaxation. But dreaming about low tide may also connote a meager wallet. However, this situation will change at some point, because high tide comes eventually. Dreaming about low tide is also a sign that land is near.

LUGGAGE A dream about luggage is a reference to your energy and skill in traveling successfully. Losing pieces of luggage implies losing energy, and may even refer to an illness with which you are dealing. (See also "Suitcase.")

LUTE (SEE "GUITAR")

LYING Dreaming about lying is a sign that you are not being honest with yourself or that you are denying something that needs attention. When other people are lying to you in a dream, this indicates that someone in real life wants to hide information or his or her true self from you.

MACHINE Dreaming about machines that roar and move shows that life is humming, or that you can expect a venture to be successful.

However, a rusty machine points to emotional problems that need to be addressed. (See also "Train Engine.")

MAGGOT (SEE "WORM")

MAGICIAN A magician spreads magic; watching a magician in action in a dream alludes to getting back what we have lost in the hustle and bustle of everyday life. We are reminded of the magic of a beautiful time and given the hope of possibly re-creating it in the future. When we are the magician in the dream, this indicates that we want a certain situation to go away "like magic." (See also "Circus" and "Clown.")

MAGNET A magnet in a dream attracts. Perhaps you are longing for a partner who could help you gain a better standard of living. If you are reaching for a magnet, this means that a new partnership can be used to your advantage. Watching someone else using a magnet may indicate that somebody is unfaithful.

MAGNIFYING GLASS People who dream about a magnifying glass want to be more than they really are in real life. This image also points to being petty or a perfectionist. (See also "Microscope.")

MAGPIE The magpie is a bird related to the jays, and appears in dreams more often than is generally believed. Dreaming about magpies in the sky is a sign that you are confused and need to find out what you are confused about. Or, this image could point to a fear, perhaps of an impending test or of someone who wants to hurt you. The magpie is known to collect things indiscriminately, and is often seen as a thief; therefore, a dream about this bird could be a message to be more careful with your intellectual "possessions."

MAILMAN The mailman stands for someone who comes to our home to bring us something that we have been waiting for, perhaps with great expectation. Whether the mailman brings good or bad news depends on other symbols in the dream. If the mailman is eagerly awaited, but then only walks past the house, this means that we might be in for disappointment in real life. Dreaming about a mailman also means that our hopes or fears may come to pass. (See also "Letter" and "Postage Stamp.")

MAKEUP Putting on makeup in a dream indicates that you are hiding something in real life or covering up your insecurities with arrogance. Seeing people with makeup in a dream is a signal to be careful when choosing new friends. (See also "Cheeks.")

MAN According to C.G. Jung, a strange man appearing in a man's dream always represents the unconscious shadow of the dreamer himself. The shadow is trying to force the dreamer to face his shortcomings. In the dream of a woman, a man is the animus, which is the unconscious masculine side of her psyche. If the woman talks to the man in the dream, she can expect to find diversion from the worries in her life. In the dream of a girl, a man usually stands for a teacher, father, or favorite person. When dreaming of getting and following advice from an old man, the dreamer can expect a happy turn in real life. According to ancient Egyptian interpretation, a man appearing as a shadowy figure in a dream was a warning of danger in real life. (See also "Teacher," "Father," and other male symbols.)

MANURE In antiquity, people believed that dreaming about a pile of manure foretold good luck and well-being, because manure helps plants to thrive and produce fruit. Today, such a dream often refers to money. Dreaming about manure could also be our unconscious reminding us how something that seems foul and negative can be turned into something positive. (See also "Fertilizer" and "Feces.")

MAP A map in a dream is not unlike a map in real life. By consulting a map in a dream, you will find out how to get to your destination. When such a dream is translated, it will tell you how to successfully reach the goal you have set for yourself in real life. If you can see the map clearly, the dream could show you the way. But if the map is blurred or you are unable to find your destination, this could be a sign that something important or serious is blocking all your efforts.

MARIONETTE (SEE "DOLL")

MARKETPLACE People meet and communicate with one another at a marketplace. Sometimes the marketplace is so large and offers so much that it is easy to get lost there. Dreaming about not being able to decide what to buy indicates that in real life you are being confronted with an uncertain, difficult situation or that you won't get something that you want. (See also "Plaza.")

MARRIAGE Dreaming about getting married indicates that in real life you are lonely or sexually unsatisfied. Dreaming about being forced into marriage shows that you feel a constraint that makes life at the job or at home difficult. (See also "Divorce.")

MASK A mask points to dishonesty, or means that the dreamer wants to hide or not show his or her true face. Many people who dream about a mask feel inferior or suffer from some type of sexual dysfunction. Dreaming about wearing a mask at a carnival is less severe in its meaning: The dreamer wants to be with happy people and slip into a different personality. (See also "Carnival" and "Beard.")

MASKED BALL Dreaming about being at a masked ball indicates that you can expect a happy, but possibly short, love affair. However, when you dream of being at a masked ball and it isn't even carnival time, this could imply that you are pretending and that others around you are somewhat fed up. (See also "Carnival.")

MASSAGE In most cases, dreaming about a massage has sexual connotations. Getting a massage may indicate that the dreamer wants to take the easy route in lovemaking. But sometimes dreaming about a massage points to someone in real life who wants to squeeze us somehow and do us harm.

MASTIFF Dreaming about being bitten by a mastiff or any other large dog implies that you are being "stabbed in the back" by someone who you thought was a true and honest friend. (See also "Dog.")

MATTRESS Even in a dream, a mattress is only a part of a bed. Lying on just a mattress implies that in real life you have let something pass you by, and for now must be satisfied with what you have. (See also "Bed.")

MAZE (SEE "LABYRINTH")

MEADOW Walking across a meadow in a dream where flowers are growing in abundance means that life is showing you its best side. As far back as Babylonian times, people believed that walking across a meadow in a dream meant that they always took the shortest route to success. (See also "Green" and "Lawn.")

MEAL Dreaming about eating a meal implies that you are emotionally well nourished. Dreaming about sharing a meal with others is a sign that you need more emotional and spiritual connections. Eating and watching others eat is a hint to check your ego. Serving a meal to others implies that you make contact easily because of your generosity. (See also "Hunger.")

MEASURING (SOMETHING)

In a dream about measuring, it's important to remember the numbers and check their symbolism. Such a dream could also be a sign that you feel insecure or are too much of a perfectionist. When others are doing the measuring in the dream, this could mean that your productivity on the job is being measured.

MEAT Eating meat in a dream may point to a lack of emotional nourishment. But such a dream could also be a sign of a nutritional deficiency that should be corrected. Sexual connotations should be dismissed, even though one could think of "desires of the flesh." The Indian dream book *Jagaddeva* interprets eating one's own flesh or that of someone else as a longing for power being granted or a promise of many descendants.

MEDAL Dreaming about wearing a medal indicates that you are concerned about external appearances and are arrogant, and that this could be why people don't look kindly upon you. Seeing other people wearing medals in a dream shows that you admire the efforts and successes of others.

MEDICINE The bitter medicine that we have to take in a dream is a reminder that we have to swallow many things in real life. But the ordeal helps us grow and shows us how we can do better. Medicine that tastes good might go down more easily, but generally is not very helpful; translated, this could mean that you are not taking enough risks in order

to get ahead in life. (See also "Hospital" and "Physician.")

MEETING Speaking at a meeting in a dream could be a message to talk less in real life. You could be labeled a chatterbox or not regarded as a very trustworthy person. (See also "Speech.")

MENDING (SEE "DARNING/MENDING")

MERCHANT A merchant in a dream could be the broker who directs your emotional "purchasing" power to the proper merchandise that would correct your lack of emotions. A merchant in a dream may also encourage you to act. Often the dreamer is the merchant, because he or she wants to initiate needed actions him- or herself. (See also "Shop.")

MERRY-GO-ROUND Dreaming about a merry-go-round indicates that the dreamer's life will soon become lively or turbulent.

MESSENGER Whether the messenger in a dream is bringing good or bad luck depends on other symbols in the dream. (See also "Mailman.")

METEOR As with shooting stars, a meteor appearing in a dream stands for a flash of inspiration or an understanding that sets us free. Both point to our intellect, which we may be determined to activate when confronted by a grave situation.

MICROPHONE When a microphone appears in a dream, this could be a message to record something that could be useful. This image may also be a sign that you need help in communicating better with the people in your life.

MICROSCOPE A microscope in a dream is a signal not to dismiss the small things in life, for they could be very important. (See also "Magnifying Glass.")

MIDGET (SEE "REDUCING")

MIDNIGHT Dreaming about midnight, the time of deepest darkness, often indicates that difficult problems loom ahead. Midnight also conveys an image of ghosts.

MIDWIFE Dreaming about a midwife is a sign that unexpected help is on the way, or may even point to the discovery of a secret. (See also "Birth.")

MILE MARKER Dreaming about a mile marker, when it is also a border sign, shows that you are facing a change in your life. The normal mile marker is more like a signpost, indicating the number of miles you have covered on your life's journey or how many you have yet to travel to reach the next stage in your life.

MILESTONE A milestone is a symbol for the beginning of a new phase in your life. Other symbols will indicate how you are to proceed. (See also "Street" and "Mile Marker.")

MILITARY Dreaming about being in the military and told to stand at attention means that in real life you are letting yourself go physically and should have more discipline. People who dream about the military and were actually soldiers in the past may have to face a situation in real life where they must show assertiveness. By the way, people who have been in the service for many years usually don't dream about the military, perhaps because it is so much a part of their daily routine and would therefore have little symbolic significance. We find the following interpretation of psychoanalysis terribly far-fetched: If a woman dreams about the military, this means that she harbors secret desires to be raped, and suppresses such desires only because of her moral principles. (See also "Mobilization" and "Soldier.")

MILK Dreaming about milk is always seen as positive. It is a symbol of selflessness, a characteristic that attracts not only people but also money, which generous people want to give to the dreamer. Milk can be equated with spiritual and emotional nourishment that the unconscious is providing, with the message that it is now time to increase your awareness. People who dream about drinking milk are generally well liked by everybody. Spilling or burning milk means that the dreamer is worrying too much about a certain problem. (See also "Cow.")

MILKING A COW (SEE "COW")

MILL Dreaming about the wheel of a mill in constant motion indicates that you have the enthusiasm to achieve something; a wheel standing still, on the other hand, connotes a lack of energy. A windmill with the wind turning the wheel at full speed is a sign that you can look forward to accomplishments that are the result of your own efforts. (See also "Grinding," "Machine," "Water," and "Wind.")

MILLER The miller is the person who keeps the wheel of a mill in motion. He or she is a symbol for keeping everything going. Dreaming about a miller means that in real life you are the one who sets things in motion, from which the community will profit. Only occasionally does such a dream refer to the dreamer's pattern of "watching how the wind blows" in order to remain popular and liked by others. (See also "Wind.")

MILLIONAIRE Anyone can dream about being a millionaire, even if he or she lives from hand to mouth in real life. This dream image could be a message from the unconscious reminding the dreamer that the rich are no better than the poor, and that even the rich can't take their money with them to the grave. For people with financial problems, dreaming of a millionaire may be a sign of hope, suggesting that things can only get better. By the way, dreaming about winning millions rarely means that this will happen in real life.

MIRROR Mirrors in dreams are rare, because dreams themselves are often the mirror of real life and real-life experiences. When they do appear, their meaning is usually serious. In Egypt, people believed that a mirror in a dream stood for death or an accident, because the image in the mirror was outside the person and the person's soul had slipped into the mirror image. Modern dream interpretation sees it this way: The mirror image of a person is his or her real self that is being recaptured. But, as with touching up a photograph, we often try to improve on the image we see in the mirror, with the intention of making a better impression on the people around us. (See also "Painting" and "Photography.")

MISCARRIAGE Dreaming about a miscarriage expresses insecurity and impending changes in real life. When a woman dreams of a miscarriage, this could be a fear that she will not get what she wants. In case of a man, the image points to his own mishandling of, or misbehaving in, a certain situation.

MOBILIZATION Mobilization is not necessarily an image having to do with war, even if other images in the dream allude to war. The unconscious may be using it to pull the dreamer out of a lethargic mood and to encourage action. (See also "Soldier" and "Military.")

MODEL Seeing yourself in a dream as a fashion model, or as a model for a painter or a photographer, indicates that you would like to be seen in a more favorable light in real life. But this also may show that you have given all of your life over to somebody else. Dreaming about seeing a model and being the artist implies that your ambition doesn't match your everyday existence, or that you want something out of life beyond that.

MOLE Dreaming about a mole or a molehill implies that you feel at a loss because you can't see what the future holds. Some people who dream about this burrowing creature with tiny eyes and concealed ears continue to be preoccupied with the past.

MONASTERY Dreaming about being in a monastery indicates that you need time for contemplation, or more peace and quiet in your life. (See also "Hermit/Recluse," "Church," "Monk," and "Nun.")

MONEY Both paper money and coins represent emotional energies. Dreaming about finding money indicates that your emotional battery needs recharging; losing money shows that you are lamenting the loss of a particular habit or emotional vitality. Money in dreams refers to emotional strengths or a lack thereof, but it may also allude to winning or losing and to wealth or poverty. It is important to pay attention to where the money came from, as well as its color and denomination. According to some psychoanalysts, in a man's dream money in the form of gold coins refers to virility and vitality, whereas silver coins are seen as turning to nurturing; in a woman's dream money almost always has to do with erotic specula-

tion. Dreaming about counting money is a hint to be more generous with the people who are closest to you. (See also "Number.")

MONK A monk evokes the image of a life of poverty and renunciation. If you are the monk in the dream, it is likely that there is something precious to you that you have to forgo in real life. Meeting a monk in a dream could be a sign that you are searching for advice or help from a selfless person. (See also "Clergy.")

MONSTER Dreaming about a monster often points to exaggerated feelings of lust or untamed sexual urges. But this image can just as well refer to an emotional state or stored-up psychic energy. Dreaming about being in a fight with a monster indicates that your emotions are in conflict or that you are fighting an illness. In the case of the latter, healing is foretold if the monster is defeated or suddenly disappears from the scene. If you are afraid of the monster, this means that you should not expect very much from those people who feel superior to you. (See also "Dragon" and "Crocodile.")

MONUMENT Dreaming about a monument may be the unconscious telling us to do some thinking. If you are the monument in the dream, you have a greatly exaggerated view of yourself. Only occasionally does a monument in a dream indicate that the dreamer will be successful in real life. A monument in the form of a tombstone supposedly predicts a long life.

MOON The moon represents the primeval female as well as the light of the unconscious. The individual phases of the moon point to a change to another position in real life, and therefore may have positive meaning. A crescent moon indicates that you will gain in prestige and respect. If the moon is shining brightly, you can expect wealth and good luck; people in antiquity also believed this to be so. A full moon indicates that you are in a very lucky phase in your life. Dreaming about a waning moon is a message to take any necessary precautions in order to hold on to what you have worked so hard for. A new moon stands for the preparation of an important event. According to Phaldor, if a man is dreaming of holding the moon in his hand, he will have good luck with a beautiful woman. In the case of a woman, the moon is a reminder to use her sexual powers to her advantage. In Indian mythology, the moon is seen as a drinking vessel, which is a maternal symbol for the renewal of energy, and into which a person meditating should immerse himself. (See also "Sun" and "Stars.")

MOON ECLIPSE Dreaming about the eclipse of the moon might reverse everything that has been discussed under "Moon."

MOOR A moor is a boggy area, and may symbolize the unconscious. If you see yourself or someone else walking on a moor in a dream, this could point to an uncertain future in real life. Being in danger of sinking on a moor shows that a real-life situ-

ation could be truly desperate. However, if you see yourself floating above the moor, this is a good sign, and means that you are above all everyday worries. (See also "Swamp" and "Water.")

MORNING Dreaming about morning announces the end of darkness, dissolves uncertainties, and reveals new possibilities. The time when the sun rises is the moment when everything is revealed, and when decisions are made that may develop into something good or ill. Sometimes this time of day in a dream refers to the dreamer's youth. (See also "Sun" and the other times of the day.)

MORTAR Dreaming about a mortar—a vessel in which something is ground with a pestle—or any other kitchen appliance that is used for grinding or crushing is a signal that in real life you are about to repudiate someone to whom you were very close.

MOSAIC Dreaming about a mosaic, either seeing one or putting one together, indicates that you may face complicated problems in real life that have to be solved one step at a time if you want to get ahead.

MOSQUITOES (SEE "INSECTS")

MOTH Dreaming about moth-eaten clothes indicates that you have difficulty making contact and feel insecure. (See also "Pests.")

MOTHER According to C.G. Jung, the mother can be an archetypal

M symbol for what is secretive, hidden, and dark; for the abyss, the unconscious, and the inescapable; for seduction and poison; as well as for female authority, loving-kindness, caring, and rebirth. Often when a man dreams about his mother, she is a stand-in for a woman he wants to get close to in real life; but this may also mean that he lacks self-sufficiency. When a woman dreams about a mother figure, this could be a sign that she is becoming aware of her femininity; in the case of a man, a mother figure represents the ideal of the opposite sex. Dreaming about one's deceased mother is a warning, the meaning of which depends on other symbols in the dream. Losing one's mother in a dream means that in real life the dreamer has a bad conscience. When trying to understand the meaning of a dream about a mother, you need to be clear about what your relationship is or was with your own mother. If the relationship is or was less than ideal, the interpretations above might mean the reverse. (See also "Parents" and "Father.")

MOTHER-IN-LAW People who dream about a mean mother-in-law might have problems in their own immediate family. The unconscious often brings up the image of a mother-in-law as a stand-in for one's own mother, from whom one seeks advise.

MOTOR (SEE "MACHINE")

MOTORCYCLE Similar to an automobile, a motorcycle in a dream is a symbol for the dreamer's ego, which is in need of discipline. At the same time, the image of a motorcycle can be a warning not to waste too much emotional or physical energy. If you have a passenger on board who is holding on to you tightly, this indicates that there is someone whom you want to tie to yourself.

MOUNTAIN GUIDE This is a positive dream symbol. The mountain guide helps the dreamer overcome obstacles and reach the summit. The mountain guide could actually be a mentor in real life who provides support for the dreamer on the road to success.

MOUNTAIN PASS A mountain pass in a dream is the equivalent of a difficult juncture in your life, which gives rise to the hope for a new beginning. Other symbols in the dream will show if you have reached a high point in your life or career that can't be "topped," and so now the descent will begin. (See also "Ascent" and "Mountains.")

MOUNTAINS Large mountains looming in a dream imply having to overcome a lot of difficulties in real life. Dreaming about searching for a hidden path to the summit indicates that you want to embark on something new without help from others. Sometimes dreaming about mountains expresses the dreamer's desire for a simpler way of life, regardless of how difficult such a change might be. (See also "Hill" and "Mountain Guide.")

MOUSE In addition to what is discussed under "Rodent," a little mouse in a man's dream can refer to the female sexual organs. A red mouse then would allude to deviant sexual desires. A mouse also stands for the dreamer's bad habit of sticking his or her nose in everyone's business. Mice who turn up in a dream in great numbers indicate that something is bothering or worrying the dreamer. Fear and disgust are common feelings associated with such a dream. (See also "Rodent" and "Rats.")

MOUSETRAP A mouse caught in a trap is usually the dreamer him- or herself, and could mean that the dreamer can't let go of a relationship that should have ended long ago.

MOUTH The mouth is usually an erotic symbol describing the dreamer's virility, but it can only be interpreted by also looking at other symbols in the dream. (See also "Lips" and "Kiss.")

MOVIE (SEE "FILM/MOVIE" AND "THEATER")

MOVING Dreaming about moving without doing so in real life indicates that you don't feel very comfortable anymore where you are living. Therefore, this could be a message to do something about changing your living arrangements. Moving from a small apartment to a bigger one or even into a house in a dream shows that you want to escape a sense of confinement. (See also "Narrow Space" and "House.")

MUD Dreaming about drudging through mud indicates that you

might not be very concerned about the company that you are keeping, or that there might be someone who wants to drag you down to his or her reckless lifestyle. (See also "Moor," "Reeds," and "Swamp.")

MUG When a mug appears in a dream, it is important to determine what it was that you were drinking. An empty mug indicates that your wallet is empty; a mug filled to the brim means that you can expect to make lots of money. (See also "Container" and "Cup.")

MULTIPLICATION TABLE When children dream about the multiplication table, this indicates that they are counting on getting good marks in school and that they will usually get them. In the case of adults, this image points to demonstrating knowledge at the wrong time, which makes them seem like a know-it-all.

MUMMY Dreaming about a mummy is not all that uncommon, even today. According to an ancient Egyptian dream book, dreaming about a mummy indicated that the dreamer could expect a long life. (See also "Cadaver.")

MUMS Mums are the flower of fall, which can be translated into the fall of one's life. White mums often allude to a grave; colorful mums have to do with love in later years.

MURDERER When a murderer appears in a dream, it is like a shadow, and kills love, emotions, and ambitions that were precious to us. A murderer in a dream can also be an indication that a phase in our life has come to an end. Or, it can point to an impending difficult situation that we, the members of our family, or our friends might have to face. (See also "Cadaver.")

MUSEUM A museum in a dream is a building with many rooms where our need for contact with beauty is nurtured. For a complete interpretation, try to remember the pictures or objects that were on display, and then look up their symbolic meaning. (See also "Painting.")

MUSHROOM When experts dream about collecting mushrooms, this means that they will take advantage of knowing their weaknesses as well as those of other people. Dreaming about eating mushrooms is a message to be satisfied with small successes. Because some mushrooms can produce hallucinations and some have the shape of a penis, psychoanalysts have been known to interpret dreams of mushrooms sexually.

MUSIC Dreams about music address the emotions. In ancient Egypt, dreaming about listening to beautiful music meant that the dreamer would have a happy heart; shrill music, on the other hand, indicated disharmony in the dreamer's personal life. It is also possible for the melody in the dream to be a subject for further interpretation. However, people who are not musically talented rarely have dreams about music. (See also "Concert,"

"Song," and specific musical instruments.)

MUSICAL INSTRUMENTS Musical instruments have various sexual meanings. Stringed instruments are considered female (the person moving the bow, of course, is male). Wind instruments are viewed as male. Dreams about musical instruments may imply a range of activities, from crude sexual acts to those related to spiritual eroticism. (See also "Conductor," "Orchestra," and specific musical instruments.)

MUSSEL A female sexual symbol, a mussel is shaped like the vulva. A mussel is surrounded by a hard shell, and it may represent a treasure that a man wants to possess for the rest of his life. For both men and women, dreaming about mussels is usually a positive sign. A closed mussel refers to virginity; sometimes, however, this image can indicate a lack of emotional maturity. (See also "Snail.")

MUZZLE Even if it is a dog in the dream who is wearing a muzzle, the muzzle still refers to the dreamer and his or her inferiority complex, which prevents the dreamer from speaking up when it is warranted. Dreaming about putting a muzzle on somebody else or a dog indicates that the dreamer wants to stop someone from gossiping. (See also "Dog.")

**NAIL** A nail can be seen as a device to prevent things from falling apart. Using a nail in a dream can stand for an act of last resort, rescuing us from a desperate situation. According to ancient Egyptian dream interpretation, dreaming about nails pointed to the fulfillment of hopes. Nailing down something in a dream means that in real life you are "nailing down" an opinion or a point of view that supports your conviction. A bent nail indicates that you are thinking of manipulative ways of reaching a goal. In contrast, dreaming of cutting your fingernails or toenails points to a loss of something in real life. (See also "Cutting" and "Hammer.")

NAKEDNESS Dreaming about being naked usually happens in a nightmare. If you are walking on a crowded street naked or sparsely clothed, this means that in real life you have revealed your ignorance, or are afraid to be yourself, because people might find your behavior immoral or see that you have an inferiority complex. However, those dreams where being naked feels positive point to our wish to be independent or to state our opinions freely, even if the topic is a delicate one; with such dreams, it's also important to pay attention to other symbols. (See also "Dress.")

NAME Hearing your name called out in a dream is a warning about imminent danger in real life. If your name is simply seen (perhaps written down somewhere), it carries more of a feeling of praise, or may allude to receiving an award. Dreaming about writing your name in a document denotes a contract in real life that you need to look over very carefully and read more than once, especially the fine print.

NARCISSUS In Greek mythology, a beautiful youth pined away for love of his own reflection, and was then turned into the narcissus flower. This flower therefore points to the dreamer's egotism and caring for no one but him- or herself. A similar interpretation is mentioned in the dream book written by Artemidorus in the second century. (See also "Flowers.")

NARCOTICS Dreaming about narcotics, even if you never took any drugs yourself, could point to having had a euphoric experience in real life.

NARROW SPACE Dreaming about squeezing through a narrow space might mean that you have memories of your birth, or that you feel like a new person. Usually, however, this image is a message that in real life we are looking for a way out of a difficult situation and that we should persevere. Should you be facing changes in your job or private life, the narrow space could represent the difficulties that you must face before you can feel comfortable again. (See also "Hallway," "Crevice," and "Ravine.")

NAUSEA (SEE "DISGUST" AND "VOMITING")

NAVEL Dreaming about the navel points to "contemplating your own navel." The unconscious is trying to make you aware that being a human being doesn't mean you have to be self-centered, self-absorbed, or egotistical. The opinion of some psychoanalysts, that the navel stands for a mother complex, is not tenable, because the cutting of the umbilical cord represents the child's *separation* from the mother. The idea that the navel in a woman's dream points to lesbian tendencies seems just as unlikely. (See also "Mother Complex" under Other Clues.)

NECK The neck is the connection between the head and the body. Dreaming about washing your neck in clear water thus points to physical and emotional health. However, a swollen neck doesn't indicate illness, but rather a bulging wallet. Wounds or boils on the neck suggest some type of physical or emotional affliction. (See also "Head.")

NEEDLE A crocheting or knitting needle in a dream represents the "needling" we often have to endure in real life. It represents the "small stuff" that can lead to strife.

NEIGHBORS When neighbors appear in our dreams, they are not always the good people whom we know in real life; often they are rather "bad" people who want to start a fight with us. A dream about neighbors could be a warning from the unconscious to be careful in choosing friends.

NERVOUSNESS Feeling nervous in a dream usually indicates a restless soul, which could mean that in real life the dreamer's defenses are low. Often nervousness in a dream is a sign of being unnecessarily agitated about everyday events to the point of causing a headache.

NEST Dreaming about a bird's nest with birds inside means that you can expect a happy family life or are ready to establish your own household. An empty nest suggests that you have been left alone. Dreaming about a destroyed bird's nest indicates that someone of whom you thought highly is turning his or her back on you. If you are the one in the dream who is destroying the bird's nest, this indicates that you are disregarding all conventions or trying to separate yourself from your environment. (See also "Birds.")

NET Dreaming about going fishing with a net shows that you want to achieve success in sexual matters. How successful you will be depends on the number of fish you catch. If you yourself are captured in a net, this means that you want to "get caught" by someone you love. The image of a net occasionally describes uncertainty, either in private life or on the job, to the degree that the dreamer feels fidgety.

NETTLES Dreaming about sitting in a bunch of nettles means that in real life you have carelessly put yourself in danger, and it is up to you to extricate yourself. If you are reaching into a nettle bush in the dream, you could be suffering from an underlying psychological problem and may need to seek professional attention.

NEWSPAPER Reading the newspaper in a dream provides us with important information about our personal life. If we can read the words clearly, we can then check out their symbolic meaning.

NIBBLING ON SOMETHING FORBIDDEN Dreaming about secretly nibbling on something forbidden, and enjoying it, may have sexual connotations. Catching somebody else in the act of nibbling implies that the dreamer is envious of that person's success.

NICHE Dreaming about a niche always points to secrets that could cause the dreamer problems in real life. (See also "Grotto" and "Cave.")

NIGHT The night is a symbol for the unconscious, which lies in darkness and induces insecure feelings and denials that need to be addressed during our waking hours. The night hides the secret will of the soul and the dreamer's shadow, which often manifests its self in moodiness during the day. In addition, the night may represent the beginning of a new phase in life of which we are afraid. (See also "Darkness" and the other times of the day.)

NIGHTGOWN (SEE "PAJAMAS")

NIGHTINGALE Dreaming of a nightingale soaring in the sky and singing its song implies that you are in high spirits in real life. Sometimes the nightingale also announces good news. A nightingale locked in cage, however, shows that you are down in the dumps. (See also "Cage.")

NIGHT WATCHMAN A night watchman in a dream indicates that in real life you are groping about in the dark. Being the night watchman yourself in the dream suggests that you are insecure, or can't see that your family or business is in danger. When someone else is the night watchman, this could mean that there is a glimmer of hope for a particular problem; after all, the night watchman is carrying a lantern that illuminates the surroundings. (See also "Lamp," "Streetlight," and "Night.")

NINE The number nine, an uneven, mainly male number, stands for total harmony (3×3) and the quest for absolute truth, as well as for thinking and emotions. Because a mother carries her child for nine months, the number nine also stands for rebirth or the beginning of new, satisfying developments. (See also "Number.")

NOISE Hearing noises in a dream, unless they are the actual noises in your environment, shows that you are restless and agitated about something in your private life. Sometimes the unconscious uses noise in a dream to warn us of impending danger.

NOON In many dreams, noon refers to the middle years of our life.

N Or, like the other times of the day, it may also point to a situation in which we now find ourselves. Because the sun is at the highest point in the sky, a dream about noon could also refer to the station we occupy right now in real life. In addition, dreaming about noon could be an indication that we have reached the height of our vitality.

NORTH (SEE "FOUR POINTS OF THE COMPASS")

NOSE A nose in a dream may represent your ability to "smell out" what could be the proper decision for you right now, especially one that could lead to advancement and success. However, if you "stick your nose in something that is none of your business," this means that in real life you are also too nosy, or even tactless toward other people. A nose in a dream often has sexual connotations: If a woman dreams about a nose, she is satisfied with her partner—unless the nose in the dream is injured or ugly, which, of course, would mean the opposite. When a man dreams about a nose, this is a signal that he will attain an intimate partner.

NOSEBLEED Seen in a sexual context, dreaming about a nosebleed could point to the loss of a man's virility; in the case of a woman, such a dream may have to do with the fear of losing her partner. (See also "Blood.")

NOTE A dream about a note that you wrote on a piece of paper, but can't make out, implies that you aren't very attentive to a person who is close to you in real life. Dreaming about taking notes, or watching others take notes, could be a warning from the unconscious to take note of a certain person. Such a dream may also be a suggestion to pay more attention to everyday matters. If you can remember what the note actually said, look up the symbolic meaning of the words for further interpretation. (See also "Paper.")

NOTEBOOK Dreaming about a notebook related to schoolwork could be a reminder of something important that you need to write down, otherwise you might forget it. Such a dream could also be an encouragement to be more determined or to take charge of a particular situation.

NOVEL The meaning of reading a novel in a dream can be found in the title of the book and its content. However, a more general interpretation is that you are too externally oriented and do not trust your own judgment enough.

NUCLEAR POWER Nuclear power was invented by people, and could easily overpower us if not handled with care and skill. This image often appears in a dream when we find ourselves in a fearful situation in real life.

NUMBER Numbers in a dream do not refer to the winning numbers in the lottery. The symbolic meaning of numbers is as old as humanity itself. If you are wearing a number in a dream, this could be a sign that you are not as great a "number" as you would like to be. (See also specific numbers.)

NUN The meaning of a nun in a dream is similar to that of a "Monk."

NURSE A nurse in a dream (here, we are referring to a female image) doesn't necessarily point to a person who provides care and support. In a woman's dream, a nurse is often a rival; although, in a positive dream, she may be a "soul sister." In a man's dream, she represents his anima (the inner, feminine part of his personality) in a negative as well as positive sense. Sometimes a dream about a nurse is a sign that we are looking for someone who will care for and console us. (See also "Mother" and "Sister.")

NUT A nut needs to be cracked! Because the soft meat of the nut is hidden inside a hard, rough shell, this image has to do with seeking happiness. In erotic dreams, a nut is often a symbol for the female sex organs. The ancient Egyptians believed that dreaming about eating nuts meant that the dreamer could expect to receive a gift.

NUTCRACKER Dreaming about cracking nuts with a nutcracker shows that the dreamer needs outside help with intimate problems or problems at the job.

NYMPH A nymph in a dream stands for the dreamer's vitality and attachment to nature. However,

dreaming about such an ancient nature divinity today may also reveal the dreamer's romantic inclination. Only rarely are nymphs in a woman's dream a sign of nymphomania. (See also "Goblin.")

OAK The oak is a symbol for exaggerated masculinity, but also for an overpowering strength of will. The oak as the "tree of life" reveals the steadfastness of our opinions. Some psychoanalysts believe that when women dream about an oak tree, they are expressing sexual dissatisfaction. (See also "Tree.")

OASIS Dreaming about an oasis usually means that we have found a way out of a difficult situation and can now rest. Dreaming about leaving an oasis could indicate that you are returning from a place of peace to a world filled with adversaries, or that you seek adventure at any price. (See also "Desert.")

OATS Feeling one's oats alludes to being overly exuberant—perhaps like a horse that has been fed too many oats. According to folklore, dreaming about eating a bowl of oatmeal means that the dreamer needs more patience and wisdom in life. (See also "Grain.")

OBELISK The image of the obelisk has sexual/phallic connotations. When an obelisk appears in a dream, this could be a sign that you are putting too much stock in your intimate affairs.

OBOE As with all other wind instruments, the oboe symbolizes male sexuality. Dreaming about hearing the often plaintive sound of an oboe implies that the dreamer is lovesick or suffers from a lack of understanding in interpersonal relationships.

OBSTACLE Encountering an obstacle in a dream can always be translated directly into one in real life. A more detailed interpretation depends on the type of obstacle that is come upon in the dream and the way that the dreamer is confronted with it. (See also "Barriers.")

OCEAN The ocean, with its constantly moving waves, is an archetypal symbol for life lived fully with all its highs and lows. However, the ocean is also a symbol for the collective unconscious, making the ocean's shore the boundary between the collective unconscious and the personal unconscious. Dreaming about a journey on the ocean with its high waves represents the quintessential journey toward new shores, meaning the search for a new phase in life or even a change in the dreamer's personality. The destination of the journey, which is often dangerous, can only be surmised from other symbols in the dream. In any case, something new is about to happen, but how this will manifest itself even our unconscious doesn't know. But the message that we do have is that from now on everything that we are,

meaning our full potential, is needed for our success. (See also "Captain," "Sailor," "Ship," and "Water.")

OEDIPUS COMPLEX (SEE "MOTHER COMPLEX" UNDER OTHER CLUES)

OFFICE If you are visiting an office in a dream, this indicates that in real life you want to accomplish something or confront somebody. If you are assuming a high position or office, this shows that you want to be more than you are in real life, or are being admonished to keep your feet on the ground.

OIL Dreaming about massaging oil into the skin (or a wound) may be a indication that you can pursue your work in real life in peace and quiet, and ignore whatever is bombarding you. The image of oil may also point to the dreamer's thoughts being "well oiled" and focused on the future. If the oil in a lamp burns with a bright flame, much joy can be expected; a smoky flame, however, foretells frustration. (See also "Fire," "Flame," and "Wound.")

OLD AGE The image of an old woman at the roadside spinning the thread of fate is a primeval maternal symbol. The image of an old man indicates that the soul of the dreamer is near the source of a strong cleansing power. If you see yourself as the old person, this means that a process of maturing is near completion. Aging in a dream is often equated with gaining wisdom, and may mean that we hope to get a message to guide us in daily living. Aging is also a reminder to be more reflective. When old people are attacking you maliciously in a dream, this could be a message to check and possibly correct your bad habits. If an old person in a dream is a witch, a torturer, or some kind of snarling person, this could be a confrontation with your own nasty side, and a sign to try to improve it. (See also "Mother" and "Father.")

OLD MAN/WOMAN (SEE "OLD AGE")

OLIVE The fruit of the olive tree is a singular erotic symbol. Dreaming about eating an olive shows that you want to solve a problem that arose from a forbidden or adulterous love affair, no matter what the cost. Collecting olives means that you can count on a passionate relationship. The olive tree is considered the "tree of knowledge" in Asia.

ONE An indivisible unit, the number one stands for the beginning of love, affection, or friendship, or for work or an enterprise. However, the number one could also represent a loner who is struggling hard to get through life. (See also "Number" and specific numbers.)

ONE-WAY STREET Dreaming about a one-way street is a message from the unconscious to proceed straight ahead without looking back at the past. Driving in the wrong direction on a one-way street means that the dreamer is looking back and can't

let go of the past. (See also "Street.")

ONIONS We know that onions are good for our health. Dreaming about eating onions means that we can count on having an abundance of energy that will make any job easier to complete. Crying while cutting onions shows that we are shedding false tears in real life.

OPERA Dreaming about being in an opera house and listening to the singers indicates that you are looking forward to especially harmonious experiences in real life. Dreaming about being onstage and singing, even if you have a good voice, suggests that you are fooling yourself and hoping to impress others. (See also "Music.")

OPERATION Dreaming about an operation indicates some kind of intrusion in your emotional state. Being operated on, or watching somebody else being operated on, shows that you need to drastically change your lifestyle in order to regain your emotional equilibrium. Only rarely does such a dream point to actual psychic disturbances. (See also "Physician," "Amputation," "Hospital," "Anesthesia," and "Injury.")

ORANGES Dreaming about oranges could be a promise of an especially joyful love relationship. (See also "Fruit.")

ORCHESTRA Dreaming about an orchestra playing is a promise of harmony within your family or in your intimate relationship. Playing in an orchestra yourself shows that you are longing for more harmony in your life or for people to whom you can feel connected. Being the conductor is a sign that you want to force an issue. (See also "Conductor," "Music," and individual musical instruments.)

ORGAN MUSIC Dreaming about organ music often points to spiritual problems and their solutions. Although sometimes such a dream may have undertones of sadness, listening to organ music indicates that we are generally happy with ourselves and the world. (See also "Music" and "Musical Instruments.")

OVEN According to Freud, the oven is a female sexual symbol, and equivalent to the uterus. In modern dream interpretation, something in the oven stands for something in life that is reaching maturity. Fire in an oven could be a hint that a passionate love affair is in the making and that the outlook for the future is splendid. Dreaming about a warm oven indicates that you are living in a friendly, warm environment; a cold oven points to heartlessness and frigidity. If the flame in the oven goes out, this could mean that you are unable to complete a task at this time, or that business is taking a downturn. (See also "Stove.")

OWL Dreaming about an owl has nothing to do with the sounds that owls make that supposedly announce impending death or bad luck. The owl is a creature of the night, a time when we can see things only dimly. Thus, this image could point to the deep urges that rob us of our peace. It could also denote the inner peace or the emotional stability that we are searching for in a hostile, gloomy world. (See also "Darkness," "Night," and "Forest.")

OX When an ox appears in the dreams of men, it may indicate their fear of losing their virility. In the dreams of women, it often expresses a sense of inferiority, or a fear having to do with not yet being emancipated. (See also "Yoke" and "Steer.")

OYSTER The oyster is a symbol for fertility, usually in an erotic sense. Depending on the other symbols in the dream, the message could be either positive or negative.

PACKAGE Dreaming about sending a package alludes to someone whom you wish would be with you, or to being a gift to yourself. Receiving a package in a dream points to a friend who has not quite shown his or her true face. Sexual matters might also be "packed" into this symbol. Having to carry heavy packages in a dream suggests having to overcome family problems. (See also "Packing.")

PACKING Dreaming about packing generally indicates that the dreamer is preparing for a new job, a new house, or a journey. But such a dream could also show that the dreamer might have to "pack it in"— in other words, face defeat of some kind. What is being packed is also important to remember, and indicates a change for the better or the worse in the dreamer's life, depending on its symbolism. (See also "Suitcase," "Package," "Traveling," and "Train Station.")

PAGE BOY (SEE "BELLHOP")

PAIN Dreaming about pain in general indicates that you are overly sensitive. If the pain is in the diaphragm area, you may have problems in your love relationship that need to be addressed. When a dream about pain suggests amputation, this may point to changing partners. Dreaming about pain usually doesn't refer to physical problems in real life. (See also "Physician," "Hospital," and "Amputation.")

PAINT BOX (SEE "PALETTE")

PAINTER A painter usually appears in dreams as a fun-loving, but somewhat reckless, man who, brandishing a brush (considered a sexual symbol by most experts), is painting a colorful picture about what he secretly hopes will transpire in real life. Anything painted in black-and-white might refer to the dreamer's bleak situation in real life. (See also "Painting," "Palette," and "Artist's Brush.")

PAINTING A painting in a dream is a reflection of our emotional state. It's important to note which colors are dominant (see also "Color" and specific colors). Paintings often portray a distorted image of ourselves, which could be pointing to charac-

ter weaknesses that we should try to rectify. Seeing a portrait of a friend in a dream means that you want to get a "picture" of a person, perhaps even of yourself. If the picture is a caricature, the unconscious is reflecting your sense of emotional helplessness. Looking at your own picture mounted in a beautiful frame conveys your vanity. (See also "Photography" and "Gallery.")

PAINTING (SOMETHING) A dream about putting a coat of paint on something often indicates that the dreamer would like to cover up something in real life. The colors that the dreamer is using as well as what is being painted will supply additional information about the meaning of the dream. (See also "Colors" and specific colors.)

PAJAMAS People who dream about walking around with nothing on except pajamas or a nightgown may be afraid to lose face in real life. (See also "Dress" and "Nakedness.")

PALACE Dreaming about a palace indicates that you want to be seen in a better light, because a palace is a house with a fancy facade. But this image could also mean that people see you as conceited or vain. In the dream of a young man, a palace represents the big house he hopes to be able to afford someday. In the dream of a woman, a palace signifies that she is looking for "Prince Charming"; but this figure usually stands in for her own partner, whom she wishes would be more like a prince. Sometimes a dream about a palace points

Pto the dreamer's need to create more space in his or her life for spirituality and emotions. (See also "Facade" and "House.")

PALATE The palate in a dream always promises culinary enjoyment; people have reported that they could literally taste the food that they dreamt about.

PALETTE A palette is a board or a tablet that a painter holds and mixes paints on, and has to do with ideas not yet realized in real life. Remembering the dominant colors on the palette is helpful for a reliable interpretation of the dream. A palette without colors means that you are running out of ideas in real life, or that you have no clue as to how to proceed. (See also "Painting," "Artist's Brush," and "Drawing.")

PALM TREE A palm tree frond is a sign of peace, and, according to Artemidorus, promises parents many children. People living in regions where the winters are very cold and harsh often dream about palm trees, because they long for a sunny beach.

PANTHER The black panther, an animal that sneaks up on its prey, ready to pounce, makes its prey restless and wary. Dreaming about a black panther is always a signal of impending danger. Possibly you are being warned about getting involved in a shady transaction. Or, you have a less-than-noble secret that should not see the light of day. (See also "Cat" and "Lion.")

PANTS (SEE "TROUSERS/PANTS")

PAPER Dreaming about writing on paper is a message from the unconscious to finish what has been started. Pay attention to what was written on the paper in order to further interpret the dream. Tearing up paper means that the dreamer wants nothing more to do with a certain subject or issue. (See also "Note.")

PARACHUTE When a parachute opens, it breaks a fall. Dreaming about a parachute that opens shows that you are carried by positive thoughts and enjoy life. If the parachute doesn't open, this means that you shouldn't start anything new in the near future, because success is not a sure thing. (See also "Crashing," "Falling," and "Flying.")

PARADISE Dreaming about being in paradise means that you are longing for peace and happiness in your solitude or at the side of a loved one.

PARALYZED Being paralyzed, or seeing somebody else paralyzed, in a dream shows that you are emotionally or mentally blocked, and are having trouble dealing with certain difficulties, despite your desire to do so. Sometimes such paralysis is a warning from the unconscious to take it easy and take fewer risks. (See also "Arm" and "Leg.")

PARASOL A parasol in a dream points to a need for protection from people who are too insistent or people who show off under bright lights. (See also "Umbrella.")

PARENTS Our mother and father often appear in a dream when we are longing for the security we experienced in our home when we were growing up. The unconscious uses the image of our parents sometimes when conflicts arise in our own immediate family. In dreams during puberty, parents often appear as opponents of the dreamer, which is a sign that the adolescent wants to separate from his or her parents. Dreaming about parents who are deceased means that the dreamer is looking for help or advice in a difficult situation. However, when parents appear in a dream of someone whose parents were not good role models while that person was young, this means that the dreamer is defending him- or herself against people who he or she believes don't give good advice. (See also "Mother," "Father," and "Family.")

PARK Whereas a garden in a dream mirrors our "inside" that we want to protect, a park is about our external appearance. Walking in a park means that the dreamer wants to appear in a favorable way to other people. Dreaming about a park could also be a message to move about more freely or to take a break from everyday worries. (See also "Garden.")

PARKING A CAR Dreaming about parking a car implies that you want to take a well-earned break. Parking a car in a certain spot, although a no-parking sign is posted

for all to see, shows that you want to get your own way, even if logic obviously speaks against it. (See also "Automobile.")

PARROT Dreaming about a talking or screaming parrot is a warning that you are being gossiped about in real life and that this could to be harmful to you.

PARTY (SEE "BALL/PARTY")

PASSPORT Dreaming about a passport that has your picture on it is a signal that a new phase in your life is about to begin. People often dream that they have left their passport at home and are standing at a border being refused entry; should you have this dream, someone is probably interfering in your life and making life difficult for you.

PASSAGE/PASSAGEWAY Dreaming about a dark passage or passageway without seeing the exit indicates that you are faced with a crisis in real life, to which there seems to be no solution. The dream can also describe a feeling of helplessness in real life regarding being asked which door would lead out of a chaotic situation. (See also "Darkness," "Narrow Space," "Hallway," and "Door.")

PASTA Pasta is a symbol for mental nourishment that is lacking but necessary to carry out one's tasks. Dreaming about pasta points to a deficiency that needs to be addressed.

PASTOR (SEE "CLERGY")

PASTRY CHEF A pastry chef is a person who makes sweets. Dreaming about a pastry chef indicates that you will have less to worry about in the future. (See also "Baker," "Baking," and "Cake.")

PASTURE A pasture is where animals graze. The image of a pasture in a dream refers to the dreamer's far-ranging thoughts or to a world of rapt passions. If the dreamer or others in the dream are told to herd animals from a pasture back to a barn, this means that the dreamer is under the control of others or that he or she lives under emotional stress. (See also "Cow," "Ox," "Steer," "Animals," and "Lawn.")

PATENT Discovering something in a dream, and having it patented, indicates that you neglected something in real life whose worth you have suddenly realized.

PATH When people drive down a rocky path in a vehicle, they are frequently "shaken up." But a path can also be where people walk leisurely and have time for reflection. (See also "Trail," "Walking," and different vehicles.)

PAWNSHOP Dreaming about being in a pawnshop, or seeing somebody else in a pawnshop, is a sign that you soon have to give up something very special. A pawnshop can also indicate that you feel insecure and perhaps upset over of what you are afraid others think about you.

PEACH The peach, which is sweet and full of juice, is an erotic symbol.

In a dream, it may have to do with a desire to join with a partner. For some dream interpreters, the round shape of the peach is reminiscent of the female figure. (See also "Fruit.")

PEACOCK Seeing a peacock in a dream shows that you delight in the multicolored world that you live in. Seeing this image also points to being able to balance disharmonies or tune in to the emotional state of the person close to you. In addition, the peacock, like the legendary phoenix that rose from the ashes, is an archetypal symbol for rebirth.

PEARL According to ancient dream interpretation, dreaming about pearls indicates sorrow. Receiving pearls as a gift is a sign that your family will soon experience sadness. Pearls appearing in dreams in regular intervals supposedly show that the dreamer has gall-bladder or kidney problems (pearls represent stones). Breaking a pearl out of a shell means that you have no problem being friendly to people. Giving pearls as a gift is like "throwing pearls before swine," meaning that no matter how generous you are and how much you try, people still don't like you. (See also "Jewelry.")

PEAS The pea plant, a member of the Papilionacea family, grows upward and accomplishes its task of bearing peas regardless of what goes on around it. Therefore, dreaming about this plant shows that you are determined, and promises success. Counting peas in a dream, however, means that you can expect a prolonged and difficult period in your life.

PEDALS (SEE "BICYCLING")

PENIS (SEE "PHALLUS")

PEPPER Seeing, using, or tasting pepper in a dream is not all that uncommon. The dream might be a message from the unconscious not only to be more lively, or have more pep, but to also enjoy the beauty of life more. However, carelessly throwing pepper on the floor shows that you want to send your competition down there too.

PERFUME Dreaming about perfume indicates that you want to be liked by people. However, spraying perfume means that you want to hide your weaknesses from the people around you.

PERJURY When you commit perjury in a dream, most likely you want to prevent someone in real life from "seeing your cards." Dreaming about somebody else committing perjury is a warning that you are going to be deceived in real life.

PERSON (SEE "MAN" AND "WOMAN")

PERSPIRATION Dreaming about perspiration often means that we must work hard before we can enjoy success. Sometimes dreaming about perspiring announces an illness that we must deal with sooner or later.

PESTS Dreaming about pests is similar to dreaming about "Insects" (see also that symbol). In antiquity, people believed that pests in a dream pointed to foolishness in matters of money, which is won as quickly as it is lost. In combination with other symbols, a dream about pests could also point to false friends and their intrigues.

PETS Pets roaming about in our dreams suggest being deprived of tenderness in real life. When the dreamer is the pet him- or herself, this is a reminder from the unconscious not to be so closed or withdrawn emotionally. Stroking a pet in a dream could point to your partner, whom you have neglected in the past or with whom you have fought too much. (See also specific pets.)

PHALLUS For people of so-called primitive tribes, the phallus is a symbol for masculinity. According to Freud, the phallus appears in dreams in many different guises, such as piercing weapons and rigid objects, like tree trunks and walking sticks. In contrast, he said that things like closets, boxes, wagons, and ovens are symbols of the female genitals. In India, the phallus is a symbol for fertility, and in dreams it represents productive work and the intellect. According to Jung, the phallus is the source of all life or the great, magic creator who is worshiped everywhere. People in ancient Babylon believed that dreaming about an oversized penis meant that the dreamer had no rivals; they also believed that if the dreamer was eating his own penis in the dream, one of the dreamer's sons would die. (See also "Vagina.")

PHEASANT This bird was considered a sign of love in China. In the West, the pheasant symbolizes emotional highs, or high-flying thoughts that can easily disappear in thin air. Take note of the color of the bird. (See also "Birds.")

PHOTOGRAPHY Dreaming about taking pictures indicates that you want to record something in order to get a clear picture of certain people or situations, which can be gathered from other parts of the dream. Dreaming of a photograph of yourself that you thoroughly dislike is a message to take a good look at yourself and at what you stand for; something is not right. Dreaming about someone taking your picture indicates that you like to show off and play a role that is different from the one you have to play in real life. Taking pictures, but being unable to handle the camera or to find the tripod, suggests that you lack perspective.

PHYSICIAN The appearance of a physician in a dream has to do with a diagnosis of your emotional state, or is an indication that something needs to be healed. Here, the soul is trying to contribute to the healing of conflicts that cause illness.

PIANO The keys of the piano represent the scale of emotions. The left hand plays the keys that produce the darker tones that stand for the inner, emotional part of us, whereas the right hand plays the keys that stand for the external, conscious part. Stuck keys indicate the dreamer's inhibitions. As with all other instruments, the piano also has erotic connotations. (See also "Music" and "Stringed Instruments.")

PICTURE (SEE "PAINTING" AND "PHOTOGRAPHY")

PICKING A LOCK Dreaming about picking a lock indicates that someone wants to "steal" him- or herself into the dreamer's house or heart. (See also "House.")

PIG A pig in a dream is usually a lucky sign, and means that one's situation is changing for the better. A pig with its nose in dirt or muck points to financial gains. Frequently a male pig, or boar, stands for the same as the steer. (See also "Wild Boar" and "Steer.")

PIGGYBANK Dreaming about putting money in a piggybank refers to the dreamer's good intentions. A broken piggybank, however, could indicate financial gain.

PILGRIMAGE Dreaming about taking part in a pilgrimage shows that in real life you are willing to create emotionally closer ties with people.

PILL (SEE "MEDICINE")

PILLORY Dreaming about being put on the pillory, naked or barely clothed, indicates that you have to endure the derision of others. This could also be a message from the unconscious, making you aware that you have acted improperly in a serious matter. Dreams like this implore us to shift gears, change our ways, and make good on past digressions.

PILLOW One interpretation of a pillow in a dream alludes to the saying "You made your bed—now lie in it!" Fluffing up a pillow implies that you are worried about your home. Putting a fresh pillowcase on a pillow foretells good luck and joy, or means that you like guests. In the Middle Ages, a soft down pillow was considered a promise of an impending wedding or a new job.

PINCUSHION A pincushion is an object in which we bury pins quickly. Is there something in your life that you want to bury in a hurry?

PINE TREE According to dream books from antiquity, dreaming about a pine tree standing tall signifies a healthy, satisfying life in later years, after a life of hard work and many worries. (See also "Tree.")

PIPE The pipe we smoke in a dream with great pleasure suggests a peace pipe that is giving us a restful moment in comfortable surroundings. The smoke from the pipe conjures up memories from the past from which we have something to learn. (See also "Smoke.")

PISTOL For Freud, a pistol is a male sexual symbol and a sign of sexual tension. Pointing a pistol at someone without shooting it in a dream indicates that you are afraid of failing in an intimate relationship or in other areas of life. (See also "Shot" and other weapons.)

PITCHER Dreaming about a pitcher often refers to the dreamer's personal problems: A broken pitcher points to family fights, an overflowing pitcher tears, an empty pitcher a lack of ideas, and a full pitcher a kind and generous heart, as well as giving without getting anything in return. Psychoanalysts believe that, like all other containers, the image of a pitcher has sexual connotations; thus, a broken pitcher could indicate defloration. Dreaming about drinking from a pitcher points to receiving lots of new energy. Trying to drink from an empty pitcher indicates that something is wrong with the dreamer's health. (See also "Container.")

PITCHFORK Dreaming about using a pitchfork indicates that you want to get rid of something that you think is preventing you from becoming wealthy. (See also "Manure" and "Feces.")

PLANING WOOD A plane is a tool for smoothing or shaping wood. Dreaming about planing a piece of wood refers to changing something in real life, or trying to influence the world around you. Seeing somebody else use a plane indicates that you are afraid that someone wants to shortchange you. Often the image of a plane indicates that we must adjust our ideas or thoughts in order to make them more useful. (See also "Wood.")

PLANTS The frequency with which animals and plants appear in our dreams is not difficult to understand, for they are important in our

Plives and our interaction with them is often intense. Some psychoanalysts claim that animals in our dreams represent our physical urges, whereas dreams about plants are an expression of our spirituality. However, they believe that plant images can have sexual meanings too; this is something that can't be denied if we consider certain shapes and colors—take, for example, the opening of a calyx.

PLATE A plate in a dream refers to a circle of congenial people who come together for good companionship as well as a good meal. Empty plates show that a get-together will be spoiled due to some action on the part of the dreamer. A broken plate is supposed to be a sign that the dreamer will be lucky in love. (See also "Circle" and "Dishes, Broken.")

PLAYING HOOKY Dreaming about playing hooky implies that you are in emotional conflict. You could be resisting necessary changes in real life, or be subconsciously denying a precarious situation, which you have gotten into due to something that you did or failed to do. Even elderly people still dream about playing hooky, which, for them, could stand for a fear of the future.

PLAZA Many streets lead to a plaza, which is usually the central point in a city. Dreaming about a plaza translates into the center of the psyche. (See also "Marketplace.")

PLEDGE Dreaming about pledging something is a message from the

unconscious that you need to compensate for something in real life; what you have pledged is also important. Giving away what you have redeemed indicates that you are not very sure about a friendship. Dreaming about playing a game of forfeit, by the way, expresses the desire to get closer to someone for a very specific purpose. Pledging something may also indicate your intention to break with an old habit. (See also "Pawnshop.")

PLIERS Dreaming about handling a pair of pliers means that you want to put a double lock on someone. (See also "Plumber.")

PLOW The plow is an archetypal symbol for the power that produces good. Dreaming about walking behind a plow means that you are industrious in real life, and, therefore, nobody can make a fool of you. Watching someone plowing shows that you want to harvest the fruits of the labor performed by someone else. A broken plow is a sign that you can't expect progress in certain ventures right now. (See also "Field," "Farmer," and "Harvest.")

PLUM The plum is often compared to the female sexual organs, so this image frequently has a sexual meaning. Men dreaming about seeing or eating plums are promised good luck in matters of love; women, on the other hand, are said to become envious of the opposite sex. Since ancient times, the plum has been seen as a symbol for good luck and virginity, that is, if the fruit is unblemished. In

Asia, the plum tree is considered the "tree of knowledge." (See also "Fruit.")

PLUMBER The plumber is the person who uses pliers and repairs what doesn't function. Translated, this means that a somewhat unsuccessful phase in your life has concluded and that you want to start something new; here, pliers represent forceps used during birth. (See also "Pliers.")

POCKET The meaning of a pocket in a dream depends on its contents. According to ancient Egyptian dream interpretation, dreaming about pulling something out of a pocket meant that the dreamer ought to stop being wasteful in real life. (See also "Purse/Pocketbook.")

POCKETBOOK (SEE "PURSE/POCKETBOOK")

POCKET WATCH Dreaming about putting a pocket watch back into a pocket indicates that you may be groping in the dark in real life. (See also "Clock/Watch.")

POISON Dreaming about poisoning someone means that in real life you want to eliminate bothersome competition. When somebody is poisoning you, this is a warning to watch out for people who want to do you harm. Some dream researchers believe that being poisoned indicates that the dreamer is being cured of a serious illness, because some medications are actually poisons.

POLAR BEAR The symbolism of the polar bear is similar to that of

"Bear." But more is implied, because the polar bear also connotes cold weather and unpredictability.

POLICE Dreaming about the police could be a sign of conflict, which suggests a change in lifestyle. Or this image could mean that something about your thoughts or actions is outrageous. But the police in a dream can also have a positive meaning: They could be showing you the right way, or telling you what is against the law and what is not; it is up to you to heed the message in real life.

POND A pond in a dream represents your depth of thought, which is even more profound if the water is clear. If the water is muddy, you are said to be "fishing in troubled waters" or doing something outside the law.

PORCELAIN, BROKEN Broken pieces of porcelain indicate good luck. However, dreaming about breaking porcelain has to do with avoiding a family fight. (See also "Dishes, Broken.")

POSTAGE STAMP Dreaming about collecting postage stamps indicates that you want to create your own social circle. Attaching a postage stamp to a letter or a card shows that you are fantasizing about taking a trip.

POSTER When dreaming about a poster, it's important to remember the message that the poster conveys. (See also "Note" and "Paper.")

POSTERIOR According to Freud, the posterior is a symbol for infan-

Ptile sexuality. But in a dream this image could also mean that we are looking back to our youth, where we hope to find the roots of all our problems. Exposing your posterior in a dream may indicate that you are showing your ignorance in real life or that you have an inferiority complex.

POSTMAN (SEE "MAILMAN")

POT   A pot with a lid can always be considered a sexual symbol. The saying "There is a lid for every pot" could be interpreted to mean that every person finds his or her partner. If the contents of a pot boil over, this could be a message not to be too enthusiastic in real life. Mixing all kinds of things together in a pot indicates that you do not distinguish between good and bad enough in real life. (See also "Container" and other types of containers.)

POTATOES   The potato is a plant with edible roots. When potatoes appear in a dream, something could be growing and flourishing inside us that is strengthening our character. Seeing the potato as a sexual symbol, in our opinion, is a bit far-fetched. (See also "Earth.")

POTTER   A potter in a dream may be a message to give a different shape to your life or to "shape up." If you are the one making the pottery, you need to find a different "form" of lifestyle on your own.

POULTRY (SEE "FEATHERED ANIMALS")

POWDER   Dreaming about powdering your face or body indicates that in real life you are trying to hide or cover up something that is unattractive, naked, or you don't like about yourself. (See also "Gun Powder.")

POWER   Dreaming about lusting for power implies that in real life you are pretty impressed with yourself but nobody else is. So-called wimpy people often dream about lusting for power.

PRAIRIE/PLATEAU   If you are gazing at a prairie or a plateau in a dream, your journey through life will be uncomplicated—in other words, you will get on in life without much trouble. On a plateau or a prairie, we can see far and recognize possible obstacles early, enabling us to get around them before they become problems. Dreaming about a prairie indicates success at work and at home, but this image is also a warning not to become too comfortable in life.

PRAYING   Dreaming about praying is usually the unconscious trying to help us get out of an unhappy or problematic situation.

PRECIOUS STONES   Dreaming about precious stones shows that the dreamer is suffering from either an inferiority or a superiority complex, and suggests that a lot of polishing of the self still needs to be done. (See also "Diamond.")

PREDATOR   A predator in a dream stands for physical urges that need to be kept in check, otherwise they will take over and all codes of decency and morality will be cast aside. It's important to look at other symbols in the dream for a complete interpretation. (See also specific predators.)

PREGNANCY According to Artemidorus, a woman's dream about pregnancy means that a certain wish of hers will be fulfilled; of course, it could be the wish to conceive. When a man dreams about "giving birth" to something, he can expect money and wealth, or perhaps even a woman to love. Dreams about pregnancy often refer to an emotional rebirth that also promises good fortune in life. Dreams about pregnancy and birth frequently point to the beginning of a new chapter in life, as do dreams about death. Such dreams imply that the dreamer is becoming a new person and that the past seems forgotten. They can also indicate the end of a crisis in which the dreamer is afraid of what is to come. In such dreams, the unconscious is suggesting that life, as the dreamer knows it, is irrevocably over, that limiting thoughts and emotions need to be discarded, and that new insights need to be gained in order to give the new life meaning. (See also "Birth.")

PRIEST Ancient Egyptian dream scholars believed that seeing a priest in a dream meant that the dreamer would soon be appointed to a high position in real life. (See also "Clergy.")

PRINCE Unless the dream is about a legitimate prince, in women's dreams he is usually the fairy-tale prince, who turns out to be the woman's partner or the man of her dreams.

PRINCESS Dreaming about a princess means the same as dreaming about a prince, except the princess is primarily the object of a man's dream. (See also "Prince.")

PRISON Dreaming about being in prison indicates that you are starting a simpler way of life, which you have long sought. Other symbols in the dream will indicate whether you will be happier in your new life or not.

PRISONER Dreaming about being a prisoner shows that you feel tied to certain circumstances or people. The message of such a dream is to free yourself from them.

PROSTITUTE Dreaming about a prostitute is often an indication that the dreamer is ignoring customary morals and seeking amusement and carefree play in "bad" company. But sometimes such a dream might just be the desire for more freedom in one's own relationship; people often dream about permanent bachelorhood for this reason. (See also "Brothel.")

PUB (SEE "GUEST HOUSE" AND "RESTAURANT")

PUDDING Dreaming about this dessert, with its somewhat wobbly texture or consistency, could stand for the dreamer's psychological weak side, which makes him or her appear to be somewhat fragile.

PPUDDLE A puddle is the dirty water that describes the little blots on our soul. Dreaming about stepping in a puddle means that bad luck will "stick to the soles of our shoes." (See also "Water.")

PULLING OUT (SEE "TEARING/PULLING OUT")

PUMP Dreaming about a pump often alludes to the heart pump, and could be a message from the unconscious to take better care of the health of your heart. Dreaming of a water pump that doesn't deliver water indicates that you should get yourself out of a truly hopeless affair. A pump dispensing a lot of water implies that you are probably also overreaching. Only if the pump handle is moving quietly and steadily, and the water is clear and flowing evenly, can you hope to conclude a difficult matter successfully. (See also "Water.")

PURPLE Dreaming about wearing purple, the color of royalty, says that you are in control of your emotions in real life. The color purple bolsters the meaning of the color red. (See also "Red.")

PURSE/POCKETBOOK A purse, or pocketbook, often contains something having to do with erotic love. Pay attention to the amount of money in the purse, if the money was used to pay for something, or if the purse was closed. (See also "Pocket.")

PUTTING OUT A FIRE Putting out a fire in a dream indicates that

you will have just enough time to free yourself from an unhappy situation in real life. People in antiquity believed that turning off a lamp or a lantern for somebody else meant that the dreamer was about to hurt another person. (See also "Fire," "Fire Department," "Lamp," "Streetlight," and "Light.")

PUZZLE A puzzle in a dream is a symbol for problems in real life. If you solve a puzzle in a dream, not only will you solve some problems but you might also make a fortune. However, a puzzle remaining unsolved suggests that certain problems will be around for some time.

PYRAMID The configuration of a pyramid is made up of a square and four equilateral triangles. Dreaming about a pyramid therefore shows that the dreamer acts very methodically. According to ancient Egyptian belief, seeing a pyramid in a dream meant that the dreamer was about to discover a secret.

PYRE A pyre in a dream points to guilt and an inferiority complex. If the pyre is on fire in the dream, this means that you should lay low in real life. Seeing yourself standing on the pyre means that you should reflect on your actions in order to redirect your efforts. The image of a pyre also suggests approaching strangers with caution rather than trust.

QUACK Here, we are referring to a bungling physician. When this quack appears in a dream, it is likely that the dreamer has treated others unfairly. The dreamer is the quack him- or herself.

QUACKING (SEE "GOOSE")

QUAGMIRE (SEE "SWAMP")

RABBIT (SEE "HARE")

RACING Racing in a dream is usually about racing after something. So, in this sense, the dream implies that in real life you are running hard to catch up, or wanting to take advantage of a missed opportunity (but running hard often leaves us breathless and unable to succeed). (See also "Running a Race" and "Running.")

RAFT A raft is a water craft that is dependent on the current but steered by us. Dreaming about a raft is a message from the unconscious that you will reach your goal if you trust in your own power or in the power of your benefactor or good friends. (See also "Boat" and "Ship.")

RAGGED CLOTHES Shabby clothing in a dream is the equivalent of a badly wrapped package: Both make a poor impression. Tattered garments are a sign that something in your emotional state is out of kilter. If you are buying or selling tattered clothes in the dream, this means that you want to hide something from people that would make you look bad. (See also "Dress.")

RAILROAD TRACKS Railroad tracks serve as a symbol for the predetermined journey of the dreamer's life, and show that his or her fate cannot be changed. (See also "Train.")

RAIN If you dream of rain falling down from the sky and fertilizing the soil, this means that you can expect to receive the fruits of your labor or that your hopes and desires will be fulfilled. A driving rain hitting the face is a sign to prepare yourself for conflicts and futile efforts. Feeling a warm rain on the skin means that you can expect improvements in your financial situation—because a rain shower is always followed by sunshine. (See also "Heaven" and "Clouds.")

RAINBOW Dreaming about a rainbow, where all the colors of the spectrum are united, indicates a resolution of the contradictions in your life.

RAIN GUTTER Dreaming about cleaning a rain gutter indicates that you are looking for a specific idea to help you get ahead. A clogged rain gutter shows that you are very despondent right now. Holding on to a rain gutter to avoid falling off the roof implies that you are clinging to certain ideas even though you shouldn't be. (See also "Roof" and "Roof Tile/Shingle.")

RAM (SEE "ARIES")

RAPIER As a phallic symbol, the rapier stands for exaggerated masculinity. When a woman dreams about a rapier, this means she could have extravagant sexual expectations. Dreaming about pulling a rapier out of its sheath indicates that the dreamer may experience drastic changes in real life; this could also be a message from the unconscious to control one's thoughts. From a psychoanalytical point of view, a broken or rusty rapier indicates a lack of vigor, or possibly some illness in the abdominal area.

RASCAL (SEE "ROGUE/RASCAL")

RASPBERRY The sweet, red raspberry is the fruit that promises love. Dreaming about picking raspberries shows that the dreamer is secretly in love. Dreaming about eating raspberries is a sign that the dreamer can expect hours of happy intimacy. (See also "Fruit" and "Red.")

RATS What is described under "Rodent" could be intensified when fear is part of a dream about rats. The fear usually has to do with illness. Dreaming about rats often is a warning that should be taken seriously.

RAVEN A black bird flying in a dream is a messenger of bad luck or of dark thoughts that threaten our ego. Dreaming about this mythological bird of death is also a message to lighten up, or to turn around and choose a different road in life, because the one you have been traveling on will lead nowhere. (See also "Crow" and "Birds.")

RAVINE A ravine is a narrow valley between two mountains, as well as a threatening sight. Dreaming about being in a ravine could be translated into emotional distress from which there is only one way out: your own honorable behavior. Seeing someone else in the ravine implies that you are prepared to free a person close to you from some predicament. (See also "Hill," "Narrow Space," and "Mountains.")

REBEL The rebel creating the furor in a dream is the dreamer him- or herself. When you have such a dream, you probably feel treated unfairly in life and want to do something about it. But this could also be your own voice raised against yourself, because you acted despicably toward others. (See also "Revolution.")

RECEIPT Dreaming about a receipt is a message from the unconscious to take care of a certain obligation. When you are handed the receipt, this could stand for something that you are responsible for in real life. Handing the receipt to someone else occasionally means that the dreamer is faced with financial burdens.

RECEIVING GIFTS (SEE "GIFTS")

RECIPE Dreaming about a recipe for cooking a dish is a reminder to have a good recipe for living and to follow it. Often the ingredients in the recipe are symbols for what the dream is recommending. (See also "Cooking.")

RECLUSE (SEE "HERMIT/RECLUSE")

RED Red is the color of blood and fire. Red conveys aggressiveness and passion, but it is also a warning sign and the color of signals. When less intense, red is the color of love and mercy. As a symbol for emotions, it can point to devotion or distress, or virtue or vice, depending on the other symbols present in the dream. (See also "Blood" and "Fire.")

RED CURRANTS Dreaming about zesty red currants, which are more tart than sweet, points to a secret love affair without a happy ending.

RED PENCIL/PEN Dreaming about using a red pencil or pen means that you want to eliminate something that you were enthusiastic about at one time. (See also "Red.")

REDUCING Dreaming about making things or people smaller is a message from the unconscious to stop discounting yourself. Appearing like a midget in a dream if in reality you are fairly tall indicates that you are angry, because someone has "put you down."

REEDS Caution is the watchword when you are dreaming of standing amid reeds. Although solid ground may be near, you are still standing in a swamp that threatens to swallow you up. Does this image bring to mind a predicament you are facing in real life? Of course, the situation is much less onerous if you are cutting reeds and carrying them on dry land; this means that you are pulling yourself out of a quagmire, to continue your journey successfully on solid ground. (See also "Swamp" and "Mud.")

REFLECTION Dreaming about seeing our own or somebody's else's reflection indicates, according to Artemidorus, that we will find friendship that could eventually lead to an intimate relationship.

REFUSE (SEE "GARBAGE" AND "RUBBISH")

REINS A dream about taking up the reins of a saddled horse, for instance, indicates that somebody is "taking you by the hand" in real life, or that you will have to accept the inevitable. (See also "Leash" and "Horse.")

REPAIRING (SEE "SEWING")

RESCUE Dreaming about being rescued from a dangerous situation could be a warning of impending dangers in real life. But rescuing someone else in a dream should make you feel good, because you can expect to receive praise or to be honored for something.

RESIGNING If you dream of resigning from an important position,

R this could be a message from the unconscious to let go of some illusion, no matter how wonderful. This image can also be a sign that you are trying to be on better terms with the realities of life.

RESTAURANT Not only are we fed at restaurants, but our overall sense of well-being is catered to there as well. Dreaming about a restaurant also indicates that we are faced with an emotional emergency. Only rarely does such a dream refer to this pleasurable pastime that in real life can take up so much time and cost so much money. For more symbols to decipher, you need to pay attention to the type of restaurant it was and the people with whom you were eating (if there were any). (See also "Guest House.")

RESTING Dreaming about resting means that you are either physically or emotionally exhausted, perhaps to the point of being disabled. Or, this image could indicate that you are simply in need of a break to collect yourself.

REVOLUTION Dreaming about a revolution is a sign that the unconscious is rebelling against something. However, this image could also be pointing to something in your life that needs urgent attention. To determine the cause of the rebellion, examine additional symbols in the dream. (See also "Rebel.")

REVOLVER (SEE "GUN" AND "PISTOL")

RIB Counting every rib in a dream is a sign to take better care of your

health. A broken rib implies that you can't make something out of nothing or that you don't know how to handle a certain situation. Adam's rib, from which Eve was created, appears rarely in dreams today. If it does appear, the dream is considered to be about sexual matters; seldom does it describe a man's superiority over a woman.

RIBBON A colorful ribbon is often the tie connecting a man and a woman. A ribbon fluttering in the wind is a sign of inner unrest, which will occur even with people who are in very contented relationships.

RIFLE A rifle is a symbol not only for "hitting the mark" but also for missing it. Translated, this means to keep a cool head and wait for the right moment to do the right thing. Shooting fairly accurately at somebody in a dream means that in real life you are trying to eliminate a rival or a competitor. Some psychoanalysts consider a rifle to be a sexual symbol. If a man is carrying or aiming a rifle in a dream, they believe that in real life he is very sure about his intentions but too bashful or cannot satisfy his desires for a number of other reasons. (See also "Shotgun" and "Pistol.")

RIGHT When you go right (as opposed to left) in a dream, this is a reference to intellectual interests, masculinity, activity, and the ability to act. (See also "Left.")

RING Dreaming about wearing a ring describes the bond as well as the faith that exists between two people or within a community. Commitments that are made are kept. Removing a ring in anger in a dream indicates that you are losing something that you love, or that you yourself are having an illicit affair. A broken ring indicates a broken relationship. (See also "Circle" and "Wreath.")

RINSING (SEE "DISHES, DOING")

RIVAL Dreaming about a rival usually points to unfounded jealousy that can turn life with one's partner into sheer hell.

RIVER Dreaming of a river that is carrying debris to its shore, or a river that is gray and muddy, shows that you have troubles and worries that the unconscious would like to wash away. A river that is going over its banks is an indication that your everyday worries may be justified. A quietly flowing river with clean, clear water, on the other hand, stands for a trouble-free life. A dream about a river in a valley may describe a decisive point in your life; depending on how fast the waters are moving, you are either being swept away or watching what is going on around you from the riverbank. (See also "Boat," "Ship," "Stream," and "Water.")

ROAST Preparing a roast in a dream shows that you want to contribute to a worthwhile project in real life; however, this could also merely indicate that you want to impress your guests. Burning a roast

in a dream shows that in real life you may have lost all credibility.

ROBBERY Being robbed in a dream points to your character weaknesses or to an inferiority complex in the sexual area. Dreaming about a robber being caught in the act may refer to mistakes that you made. Such a dream may actually be very helpful, because once you have recognized your mistakes you can do something about them.

ROCK Dreaming about climbing a rock indicates that many obstacles in real life have to be overcome. The ancient Greeks also believed this. Modern psychology has added another level to this interpretation: Climbing a rock in a dream implies striving for something higher and better, and being able to reach this goal only with much effort. Dreaming of building on a rock shows that you have a solid foundation for your plans.

ROCKET The image of a rocket in a dream stands for fleeting and confusing memories or thoughts. Dreaming about firing a rocket could be a reference to your inconsistencies or your unelaborated, incomplete ideas. (See also "Fireworks.") A space rocket in a dream, on the other hand, symbolizes lofty thoughts concerned with God and the world. In a nightmare, a space rocket indicates that you are wandering around aimlessly without a goal.

RODENT Rodents darting through our dreams rob us of vital nutrition,

Rparticularly if they appear in a storage room, which in dreams represents the soul. Dreaming about rodents almost invariably indicates that something uncomfortable is secretly nagging at us; it might be a hidden grief, a worry concerning not having enough to eat, or a fear of losing our vitality. (See also "Hare," "Mouse," and "Rats.")

RODS (SEE "BARS/RODS")

ROGUE/RASCAL Rogues and rascals appearing in a dream stand for dishonest people in real life who want to put something over on you. Be on the lookout for them!

ROOF Dreaming about a roof usually refers to the head of the dreamer. If something seems wrong or out of kilter with the roof, this is a message to examine your thoughts to see whether or not there is something that you need to straighten out. Dreaming about places under the roof is often a reminder of early sexual experiences. A burning roof in a dream could be a sign to seek advice from a psychotherapist. People waking up from such a dream often have a headache. (See also "Fire" and "House.")

ROOF TILE/SHINGLE Dreaming about a roof tile falling off the roof is a clue that in real life you are dealing with an opponent who is trying to defeat you intellectually.

ROOM Considering that dream interpreters equate the image of a house with the body, then a dream about a room, being on the inside of a house, refers to the dreamer's psyche. A dream about a room may point to your reluctance to share yourself and your space with others. Pacing restlessly from room to room could mean that in real life you are constantly changing your point of view, which itself could be an indication of a change in your emotional makeup. Walking from a dark room into a brightly lit room implies that something you had been unconscious of is now conscious and might embody a lesson for you. Seeing a room in a dream as it actually is in reality might indicate that you are getting bored and want a change of scenery, or that you want to go someplace where life is more exciting. (See also "House," "Hall," and "Apartment.")

ROOSTER This animal is thought to be a male sexual symbol, particularly in the dreams of women. In the case of men, it points to their amorous intentions. Dreaming about a crowing rooster is a hint that one's partner might be unfaithful. A rooster with bright-red feathers refers to the dreamer's fiery passion. (See also "Feathered Animals.")

ROOT Roots always push upward toward the light. Translated, this means that the dreamer is reaching to the "light of knowledge." Roots describe the hope that we will push through, or be assertive in life. Dreaming about digging up a root implies that you want to get to the "root" of a matter or alludes to "the root of all evil." A root that is not yielding to your efforts means that you won't be able to satisfy your curiosity.

ROPE A rope tied around something, or connecting things, in a dream could describe the all-encompassing thoughts you have about a certain person or subject, or express your longing for a permanent bond with another person. If you see someone tying a rope in a dream, this could mean that you have become too dependent on a certain person. Dreaming about a tug-of-war game— either watching it or participating in it—means that you want your partner to be on your side. Dreaming about dancing on a rope indicates that you have taken on a task that will be difficult to finish. Falling to the ground while walking on a rope is a warning to let go of a plan that could only end in an unresolvable conflict. (See also "Wire.")

ROSE The rose is known to be the flower of love, and describes happy emotions. If the blossom is large, this points to a big heart and a generous spirit. The image of the cross, symbolized by the thorns, is a reminder of how close happiness and love are to deep sorrow and fading beauty. It's also important to pay attention to the color of the rose, because it will give you further information about the meaning of the dream. (See also "Cross," "Flowers," and specific colors.)

ROULETTE The meaning of a dream about playing roulette is often confusing in terms of winning or los-

ing. Losing a game of roulette in a dream indicates that in real life you are involved in some kind of adverse situation, but you may learn something from the dream that will improve the situation. However, winning a game of roulette could also point to a loss; perhaps you will lose the arrogance with which you tend to approach the people around you (so, in a sense, you are winning here too). Other parts of the dream can give you additional information about the meaning of the dream. For instance, pay attention to the movement of the roulette ball rolling around the edges in circles, as well as to the number at which the ball comes to rest. (See also "Ball," "Circle," and the relevant number.)

ROWING Rowing is the action that moves us forward in a boat on water—a boat where there is little to rely upon in case of trouble. How do these images resonate with the condition of your life or a particular situation you are facing? Rowing in a dream may also refer to heavy work that demands sweat and tears but also promises rewards, despite the many ups and downs that are part of the journey. Dreaming about rowing, but making slow progress or none at all, shows that you are muddling along in life and not feeling very much like working. (See also "Boat.")

RUBBISH When you or someone else is sweeping up rubbish in a dream, this means that you must deal with an emotional issue that has already "collected too much dust." Looking for something in a heap of rubbish is like "looking for a needle in a haystack." Rubbish in a dream could also be a reminder from the unconscious to "sweep in front of your own door." (See also "Garbage.")

RUBBLE Dreaming about looking for something among the rubble that once was your own house means that hard times are behind you, or that you can take advantage of whatever remains useful to build something new.

RUIN The image of a house or another building in ruin may refer to your body, and could be a message that you need nutritional "building blocks" in order to avoid being weakened too much during an illness. The image of a castle or a palace in ruins is a reminder that nothing is permanent, including the human body. (See also "House.")

RUMBLING GUNS Dreaming about hearing rumbling guns usually implies that the dreamer is worried. (See also "Thunder" and "Noise.")

RUNG (OF A LADDER) Dreaming about a rung of a ladder breaking means that the "bottom is dropping out" from under you or that you are losing the support of a loved one. (See also "Ladder.")

RUNNING Being a determined runner in a dream shows that in real life you are using every effort to "get to the finish line." But running could also indicate that you are frantic. Ancient Egyptian dream books stated that running in place

meant that the dreamer had to wait a long time for success, and that sometimes the wait was in vain. (See also "Running a Race.")

RUNNING A RACE Dreaming about running in a race expresses your worry that time is going by too fast. Such a dream also has to do with the constant chase after success and recognition, and the big prize that only a few will win.

RUNNING THE GAUNTLET Running the gauntlet, a punishment for deserters practiced until the beginning of the 19th century, describes your fear of making mistakes and being ridiculed for them by the people around you.

RUN OVER People who dream about being run over will at most suffer emotional injuries in real life. Such a dream could also indicate that you feel literally "taken over" by people who want to put you "under their thumbs."

SABER The meaning of a saber in a dream is similar to that of a "Sword." However, the meaning here is more intense.

SACK Dreaming about carrying a loaded sack over your shoulder shows that you are suffering under the weight of a great responsibility in real life. An empty sack stands for poverty and deprivation, and occasionally for diminished vitality.

SADDLE A saddle makes horse-back riding more comfortable, so its meaning has to do with comfort, but it also has a sexual meaning. Dreaming about saddling a horse implies that you are looking forward to a sensuous experience, which also promises great excitement and speed. A saddle also indicates that long-sought-after ideas might finally become clear. Seeing someone else saddle a horse, or seeing only a saddle, means that you can look forward to someone sharing the burdens of your life. (See also "Horseback Riding" and "Horse.")

SAFE (SEE "WALLET")

SAILBOAT A sailboat is kept in motion by the wind, or by the spirits. Dreaming about a sailboat thus is a reminder to examine the spiritual contents of events. (See also "Boat" and "Ship.")

SAILOR A sailor in a dream plays the role of a helper in our life's journey. The sailor sees to it that nothing goes wrong. Dreaming about having a fight with a sailor points to losing a good friend or a colleague. (See also "Captain" and "Ship.")

SALAD GREENS/LETTUCE

Salad is seen as having female attributes. When a man dreams about salad, this supposedly means that he thinks he can have any woman he wants. To him, they are all like a side dish. Dreaming about planting lettuce neatly in straight rows means that you want to bring more order into your intimate life. Wilted lettuce

indicates that a friendship might come to an end. Every now and then, dreaming about salad greens means that the dreamer is happy leading a simple live. (See also "Vegetables.")

SALESPERSON (SEE "MERCHANT")

SALT Salt is an important substance in dreams. Dreaming about spilling salt is a clue that you have some kind of stomach problem. Such a dream should be taken seriously if you want to avoid health problems. Dreaming about having soup containing too much salt indicates that you have to take the blame for something in real life that is not your fault. (See also "Soup.")

SALVE Salve also heals in dreams. Dreaming about using a salve indicates that you will soon forget the pain that a present situation is causing you. Applying a thick layer of salve, on the other hand, refers to your fruitless efforts having to do with another person who is undeserving; this image is a hint for you to let go. (See also "Balm" and "Medicine.")

SANATORIUM A sanatorium is a place where one regains strength after an illness or a stressful event. This dream image suggests that you are in need of help in real life. (See also "Hospital.")

SAND Dreaming about seeing, or getting caught in, a sandstorm indicates that you might suffer severe losses due to your lack of judgment of others. Digging a hole in the sand, or lying down in a sandy hollow, shows that you are undermining yourself. (See also "Storm.")

SAW Dreaming about a saw points to a radical event in real life. Sawing in a dream indicates that you want to free yourself from a bad situation or separate yourself from someone. Seeing someone else handling a saw means that you may be faced with a separation for which you are responsible. A dull saw implies that the sorrow and the grief in your life won't go away soon. (See also other tools.)

SCAFFOLD Dreaming about a scaffold, meaning the platform on which a criminal is executed, indicates that a fateful period, during which you did not always act properly, is behind you. Looking at a scaffold in a dream is a warning to be prepared for so-called friends preventing you from making potentially profitable changes. Climbing up on a scaffold suggests that you have left things from the past behind, or have gained new insights that promise a profitable future. (See also "Hangman" and "Execution.")

SCAFFOLDING Dreaming about scaffolding, a system of platforms temporarily erected for workers such as bricklayers and painters to stand on, usually refers to a new beginning, in which the dreamer can rebuild something that has decayed. However, seeing a house with scaffolding put up around it could also be a message from the

unconscious to pay more attention to your health. Scaffolding that is difficult to climb upon is an indication that you will have a difficult time in getting ahead and being successful. Working on scaffolding without getting dizzy, on the other hand, points to a positive conclusion of a project. (See also "House.")

SCALE If the two sides of the scale in the dream are balanced, this shows that you are a fair and thoughtful person. If one side is lower than the other, other symbols in the dream will indicate whether a particular situation in your life is to your advantage or not.

SCAR Dreaming about looking at a physical scar usually has something to do with an event from the past, from which we should learn in order to be more successful in the future.

SCARECROW A scarecrow in a dream could stand for someone in your life who wants to harm you, or someone who wants to push him- or herself into your life and create havoc.

SCARF Dreaming about wearing a scarf could be a message not to talk so much. After all, the voice originates in the throat.

SCHOOL Dreaming about school is a message from the unconscious telling us that we are never finished learning. Such a dream points to the "school of life" and to the work that we have to do on ourselves. Cheating or playing hooky in this school is not possible. Here, the dreamer is asked to be responsible. (See also "Teacher," "High School Graduation," and "Test.")

SCISSORS Dreaming about scissors describes your fear of having made a mistake; a cut is permanent. Cutting something with a pair of scissors in a dream is a hint that you should think twice before acting. A pair of scissors may also refer to a disagreement or to anger. Receiving a pair of scissors as a gift from someone implies that you are thinking of cutting the tie to that person, which would be a permanent loss. Cutting with scissors stands for the intention of making a clean break. Watching someone else using scissors suggests that that person refuses to have anything to do with you. (See also "Cutting.")

SCORPION This insect will poison us with its bite even in our dreams. It could be that the unconscious is warning us of a secret enemy who wants to do us harm. Scorpions are rarely seen, but we are afraid of their sting nevertheless.

SCOUT, BOY OR GIRL Both boy scouts and girl scouts are positive images in dreams. They show us the way to the right path in life.

SCREW Dreaming about putting a screw into something implies that you want to secure and strengthen a relationship that means a great deal to you. Failing to find the hole for the screw is a sign that a love affair or a professional connection is less

secure than you had thought. Seeing a rusty screw is an indication that a relationship has suffered over the course of time.

SCULPTOR A sculptor can be seen as a person who, with a hammer and a chisel, can bring out the best in something. Dreaming about a sculptor could mean that the unconscious is concerned that you are not showing yourself well in real life, or that you are trying, at any price, to get more out of life.

SCYTHE A dream about using a scythe points to cleaning up something that is long overdue. Seeing others using a scythe indicates that someone would like to "chop off your head," because you are "holding your head too high," meaning that you are too arrogant. (See also "Cutting.")

SEAL Seeing a seal on a letter or a document in a dream indicates that you might be confronted with facts that you can't do anything about. When you are attaching the seal yourself, this suggests that you have completed a phase in your life successfully. (See also "Document.")

SECURITY The desire for security is expressed often in dreams. A dreamer who feels insecure or is not all that reliable him- or herself may be searching desperately for security, like the drowning man reaching for a life preserver.

SEEDS Dreaming about seeds about to sprout refers to your desire for a new beginning. At the same time, it is a warning to be very careful not to damage the tender seedling, which represents the new life or world that you are seeking. However, seeds may also refer to your emotional energies, which, falling on fertile ground, are laying the groundwork for a successful venture in real life. Dreaming about buying seeds, but not sowing them, indicates that your inhibitions will lead to difficulties in your personal life. (See also "Sowing," "Farmer," "Grain," and "Field.")

SEEING YOUR OWN IMAGE

Seeing your own image in a dream indicates that you want to get a better picture of yourself, or perhaps you want another identity. (See also "Painting," "Photography," and "Mirror.").

SENTRY The image of a sentry in a dream is a reminder from the unconscious to go through life with great care and with your eyes wide open, because many dangers could be lurking.

SERMON When dreaming about listening to a sermon, it is important to remember the words of the sermon, because they will give you information about the meaning of the dream. If the sermon is in the form of a reprimand, then the meaning would be obvious. (See also "Speech.")

SERPENT According to C.G. Jung, the image of the serpent is an archetypal symbol for something significant in our unconscious, pointing to either danger or healing. Deeply buried emotions and equally deep-seated emotional energies, which are often in conflict, burst forth from the unconscious in either a positive or a negative direction. Since the expulsion from Paradise, the serpent is often encountered with fear. A serpent appearing suddenly in a dream stands for our fear of being forced to reveal a carefully guarded secret. When a woman dreams about a yellow serpent, this indicates that she is afraid of male sexuality. A red serpent often takes on the shape of a phallus, a white serpent suggests deep emotions, and a green serpent refers to our physical energy. Dark-colored serpents often forecast a change in our lifestyle. Dreaming of making friendly contact with a serpent means that we might be betrayed or cheated. Together with other symbols in the dream, a serpent could also be positive, in the sense of predicting healing. It is not by accident that a serpent has wound itself around the staff of Aesculapius, the Greek god of medicine. A serpent shedding its skin in a dream is considered a sign that we will be healed from an illness or freed from suffering.

SERVANT Dreaming about being a servant who must work hard could mean that in real life you are the boss, or are an example for others who are not as industrious. Only rarely does the servant in a dream translate into the dreamer's being subservient or always giving in.

SEVEN According to a secret teaching, the number seven has magical power like no other. The number seven is a symbol for completion (the seventh day of Creation). It also stands for the magical transformation of the self. Every now and then, seven in a dream is a reminder from the unconscious to use time wisely and allow for a day of rest.

SEWING Sewing is an activity that requires patience and exactitude if the aim is to produce something wearable and useful. Dreaming about sewing on a patch means that in real life your work will be a patchwork, and not last long. (See also "Thread," "Yarn," "Needle," and "Darning/Mending.")

SEXUAL RELATIONS Dreaming about having sexual relations doesn't always refer to sex in real life. Artemidorus, who wrote a book about dreams in the second century, was of the opinion that a dream about sleeping with one's wife when she is willing could only be a good omen for both partners; an unwilling wife, however, had the opposite meaning. According to many modern psychoanalysts, sleeping with the boss in a dream indicates that the dreamer can expect advancement on the job, because both the dreamer and the boss in the dream seem to pursue the same goal. However, generally speaking, dreaming about intercourse says something about the dreamer's virility. A dream about "unsuccessful" intercourse might have something to do with the dreamer's lack of sexual drive. When we dream about sleeping with a stranger, often the stranger is standing in for our partner, because we are hoping for more intimacy. (See also "Sexual Dreams" under Other Clues, and "Intercourse.")

SHACKLES Dreaming about being shackled could be a message from the unconscious that we are shackled to something negative in real life that does not bode us well. The image could also indicate that we are shackled to somebody, perhaps in an unhappy marriage or friendship. (See also "Chain.")

SHADOW The shadow represents those things that we can't see quite clearly or the unknown that frightens us. Seeing a shadow in a dream, even if it is your own, is a sign that in real life you feel lost, lack courage, or are afraid of everything and everybody (this fear could even border on a persecution complex). However, dreaming about sitting in the shade when the sun is shining is an indication that a certain issue has been cleared up satisfactorily. (See also "Sun.")

SHARDS (SEE ALSO "DISHES")

SHARPENING If you are sharpening something in a dream, this indicates that you need to take care of a few shortcomings. Seeing someone else do the sharpening suggests that someone is after you to do you harm. However, much depends on what is being sharpened in the dream. Seeing a person who is sharpening a pair of scissors could refer to someone in your life who wants to create a conflict between two people who are close to each other. Such a dream could also point to a rival of yours. If someone is sharpening scissors or knives to make them more efficient, this could indicate a change in old habits or a loss of something very dear to you. (See also "Knife" and "Scissors.")

SHAVING When sporting a beard was more in fashion, dreaming about shaving one's beard meant great trouble lay ahead. Today, shaving or trimming one's beard tends to mean that the dreamer would like others to consider him a gentleman. If someone else is shaving the dreamer's beard, this indicates that he will have to pay for some action or situation. If the dreamer cuts himself or is being cut while shaving, this is a sign that he has acted badly. (See also "Beard," "Hair," and "Cutting.")

SHEAVES Sheaves represent something that you have acquired, and want to tie up and hold on to. Dreaming about binding sheaves of wheat can mean that you are looking for a new partner, whom you can "bind" to yourself.

SHED A shed in a dream stands for a poorly built house and describes the poverty of your interior or exterior state. Translated, this image could also mean that you feel sorry for yourself. (See also "House.")

SHEEP Sheep represent patience and tolerance in dreams, which you would do well to imitate if you want to be successful. According to

Artemidorus, even black sheep are a good omen, foretelling that a task will be completed or an important job will progress well. Incidentally, even though sheep are not thought of as very smart, this image doesn't carry over into dreams. (See also "Dog" and "Shepherd.")

SHELTER Dreaming about a shelter could be a message for you to take a break. (See also "Roof.")

SHEPHERD The shepherd is a figure that the unconscious is using to remind you to be more accommodating or to obey the law—as sheep are reminded by the shepherd not to stray. (See also "Herdsman.")

SHIELD The shield was a means of protection that our ancestors used when fighting an enemy. Translated, it means that in real life you can't be careful enough in protecting yourself from harm. A traffic sign, when considered like a shield, tells you the direction to take in life. For example, a stop sign would translate into a warning not to continue in your old ways, but to stop and think about a new approach. (See also "One-Way Street" and "Street.")

SHINGLE (SEE "ROOF TILE/SHINGLE")

SHIP The image of a ship in a dream stands for the "ship that carries us through life," and could be thought of as a "lifeboat." Carrying the dreamer's personality on the waves of the ocean, the ship is continuously finding new shores or new opportunities for learning. The ancient Chinese book *I Ching* emphasizes the psychic value of a ship in a dream, stating that it is "good to cross the waters." Additional symbols in the dream will make it easy to determine whether the dreamer's journey is going well or not. Often the smoke from the ship's chimney is a meaningful symbol, as is the ship's engine. Is the ship in your dream moving at full speed ahead? This too will tell you something about your life journey. (See also "Smoke," "Engine," "Embarking," "Harbor," "Traveling," "Shore," "Water," and "Boat," as well as other vessels.)

SHIPWRECK Dreaming about a shipwreck suggests that your life journey is suddenly being interrupted or that certain emotions are being endangered. Escaping the threat of sinking in a dream indicates a temporary setback in a certain area of your life. If you are drowning or see others drowning, this is a sign of a nervous breakdown, which has negative effects not only on you but also on others. However, being able to reach the shore safely after a shipwreck indicates that a dangerous or otherwise troublesome situation in real life will take a turn for the better.

SHIRT Dreaming about wearing nothing but a shirt means that in real life you are afraid of being exposed or found out, perhaps regarding a sexual matter. Washing your shirt shows that you want to make a good impression, possibly in sexual matters. Wearing a dirty or torn shirt

implies that you care about nothing. Changing your shirt means that you are about to change your opinion about something. (See also "Dress" and "Ragged Clothes.")

SHOEMAKER The shoemaker repairs the holes in the soles of shoes, and appears in the dreams of people who are ill or recovering from an illness as a warning that they must do something themselves if they want to get better. Sometimes a shoemaker also points to the dreamer's character weaknesses that can be "repaired." If you are the shoemaker in the dream, this could be a message to try to be friendlier toward others in real life and help them get ahead, even if you might never be paid back for your generosity. (See also "Shoes.")

SHOES According to Freud and his followers, slipping on a pair of shoes stands for the sexual act or the desire for intimacy. Indeed, many dreams about shoes point to an impending love relationship. Most of the time, however, shoes describe the dreamer's emotional and mental states. Dreaming about a shoe that pinches and doesn't fit indicates that something is bothering you, or that you would like to change, to be somebody else. A shoe that is too big or too small could be a message to try to adapt more in life. Wearing well-fitting shoes suggests that you can be satisfied with your actions and that everything will go smoothly. Shoes in need of repair point to weaknesses in your character that you have known about for a long time but done very little to correct. (See also "Slippers," "Shoemaker," and "Boots.")

SHOOTING (SEE "SHOT," "PISTOL," AND OTHER GUNS)

SHOOTING STAR (SEE "METEOR")

SHOP When we enter a shop, we have the expectation of being served if we know what we want. If you don't know what you want when you go into a shop in a dream, this shows that you lack decisiveness in real life; if you do know, this means that you are making decisions that will advance your cause. A shop without customers indicates that you have misjudged a situation in real life. Dreaming about being the salesperson shows that you are offering yourself, even to the point of being ridiculed. Only rarely can you, as the owner of the shop, expect that the dream foretells financial rewards. Passing by a shop indicates that you are missing a good opportunity in life. (See also "Business," "Shopping," and "Merchant.")

SHOPPING Dreaming about going shopping is an expression of your secret desires. You may desire some kind of social contact that has been withheld thus far. Or, you may want to buy the love of a person. Dreaming about shopping can also simply indicate a need to get recognition from a partner or be assured that all is well. But such a dream raises questions, such as, Is it possible to buy love and recogni-

tion? Buying new clothes could be a hint that in real life you want to slip into a "another skin" or are not satisfied with a present situation. (See also "Money," "Dress," and "Shop.")

SHORE A shore in a dream usually represents a place where we can rest and get together with good friends. If the shore is flooded, you can expect to fall into dire circumstances. (See also different bodies of water that have a shoreline.)

SHOT A dream about hearing a shot stands for an impending decision that you need to make fast. This also points to bringing order to a certain matter. Sometimes a shot can backfire, which is said to be a sign of a lack of energy. Hearing individual shots implies that radical changes are imminent. Dreaming about a real gunfight in progress is an indication that you will find yourself in a tricky situation. (See also "Pistol," "Rifle," and other guns.)

SHOTGUN The shotgun is the gun of the common man, and is supposed to foretell good luck in matters of love when fired. It is also thought to be a phallic symbol, and, in this sense, it can sometimes get jammed. (See also "Rifle.")

SHOVEL Dreaming about using a shovel to bury something not only means that you are avoiding work in real life, but also hiding from higher authorities in order to keep their goodwill. Carrying a shovel, but not using it for work, indicates that you want to convince the world of how industrious you are.

SHOWER A dream about a cold shower indicates that most likely some of your hopes will be dashed.

SHREW Xanthippe, the supposedly quarrelsome wife of the wise Socrates, appears in our dreams every now and then when the unconscious wants to remind us not to get involved in petty fights.

SHRUBS Shrubs are the ideal place to hide things; dreaming about them means that you want to hide yourself and your actions from others. (See also "Bush.")

SIBLINGS Dreaming about siblings often refers to people in real life who have different opinions but still get along. In the case of a man, a brother in a dream is his own shadow, which represents his weak side as well as that part of himself that has remained worthy. In the case of a woman, a sister in a dream is the shadow of herself, whereas a brother represents the masculine side of her emotional world. Fighting with one's siblings indicates frustrations in real life or a worsening of a present situation. Speaking about or with siblings should be taken as a warning not to get caught up in misunderstandings. Dreaming about losing a sibling may indicate that a crisis is looming. (See also "Brother" and "Sister.")

SICKLE The meaning of a dream about a sickle is similar to that about a "Scythe," except that the sickle rep-

resents less dramatic issues that the dreamer should address.

SIEVE A dream about a sieve indicates that you let something in real life slip through your fingers because you felt so sure about it. Putting something through a sieve is a signal that you are trying to sort or filter out something at your job. But this image also carries the implication that something could "fall through." This interpretation is more likely if you are using the sieve in the dream to remove water or any other liquid from a container; at the very least, you are being made aware how futile your real-life attempts are to deal with a certain issue or situation. If somebody else in the dream is putting something through a sieve, this could point to how much you gloat over someone's shortcomings.

SIGNPOST A signpost is used by the unconscious to show us which direction to take. However, sometimes signposts lead us astray, so it is important to examine them closely. If you can't see anything written on the signpost at all, this could itself be a message that you are going in the wrong direction in life.

SILHOUETTE A silhouette in a dream may have the same meaning as that of a "Shadow." However, looked at as a positive image, it could mean that you can count on a rather ominous matter becoming clear and eventually being resolved to your satisfaction.

SILK Dreaming about silk refers to the tender emotions that you have for someone in your life. Wearing silk in a dream means that you can be assured of a time of happiness with a reliable partner and friends. But the image of silk also has a negative connotation—namely, that a beautiful exterior may cover up a lot of heartache. (See also "Velvet.")

SILVER The silvery disc of the moon is a symbol for femininity, whereas the sun symbolizes masculinity. A dream about silver, regardless of its form, always points to positive female values. Other symbols in the dream will provide additional information about the meaning of the dream. (See also "Moon.")

SINGING Dreaming about singing is usually a positive sign. Singing as part of a choir means that you are surrounded by a circle of happy people who are in accord with each other. Additional interpretation is possible when the words of the song are also considered. (See also "Choir" and "Song.")

SINKING Sinking in a dream may stand for losing courage in real life. The unconscious is using this image to make the dreamer aware of this lack of lack of courage, and to encourage him or her to do something about it. Sometimes people want to sink through the floor, because they feel embarrassed or ashamed.

SISTER A sister in a dream is usually not the dreamer's actual sister, but rather a sympathetic person, such as a nurse. The sister in the dream often represents a good friend or a social worker, who can help the dreamer or provide advice. Dreaming about fighting with a sister indicates that you are dissatisfied and are complaining; you want someone to listen to you and lessen your burden, which you believe has become too heavy. (See also "Nurse" and "Sibling.")

SISTER-IN-LAW (SEE "BROTHER/SISTER-IN-LAW")

SIX The number six expresses a balance of power. Take, for example, the six squares making up a die. Another example is two equilateral triangles that together form a six-pointed star. Many psychoanalysts believe that the triangle pointing upward symbolizes the male sex organ, whereas the triangle turned downward symbolizes the female genitals. The number six, which in the multiplication table is the result of two (which is said to represent the female) times three (the male), also describes the constant conflict between emotional tendencies and reasoning. The latter always wants to shut out any feelings.

SKELETON The skeleton is a symbol for everything that is impermanent. The skeleton is usually part of a nightmare, and very frightening to the dreamer. Often the dreamer's fears have to do with him- or herself, and may relate to having made certain mistakes. The skeleton in a way is the self laid bare. (See also "Bone" and "X Rays.")

SKIING A dream about skiing down a slope successfully indicates that you are free of worry and problems in real life, or that you can sit back comfortably, because you can get by without much work or effort. Sometimes the skier becomes aware of how easy it is to go downhill but how difficult to go up, meaning to reach the more affluent side of life. Taking note of other symbols in the dream will, of course, shed more light. (See also "Snow" and "Winter Sports.")

SKIN The skin is the first place where we feel the pain that is inflicted on us from the outside, but it can also protect us from serious harm. Dreaming about burning your skin is a sign that someone wants to hurt you in real life or place you in a bad light to the outside world. Dreaming about skinning an animal or even another person indicates that in real life you have to face nasty people without protection. Stroking your skin tenderly with your hands in a dream shows that you want to achieve something (possibly an intimate relationship) that can't be accomplished with force.

SKY The sky is the mythological home of the gods. Dreaming about the sky indicates that you have lofty thoughts or creative ideas, or feel very good about life. A blue sky promises good luck; a cloudy sky is a sign that you are depressed, perhaps by the lack of success in your life. In antiquity, people believed that dreaming about a clear, star-studded night sky promised success and money.

SLAP IN THE FACE Dreaming about being slapped in the face could be a message from the unconscious pointing out your carelessness or negligence. Perhaps you are egotistically pursuing certain plans that could cause all kinds of problems.

SLAVE The archetypal image of the slave appears in dreams not only when we have been betrayed by others, but also when we have "sold out" ourselves in life. In the case of the latter, the lot of the slave is of our own doing, because we are saying yes and amen to everything and never expressing what we truly believe.

SLED/SLEIGH Dreaming about moving blissfully ahead in a sleigh means that you can count on a "smooth ride" in life and on a successful journey. A sled standing still in a dream indicates that you are embarrassed in real life, or it points to the chilling of emotions. (See also "Ice" and "Sliding.")

SLEEPING Dreaming about sleeping is usually a hint to wake up and take care of our problems. But this image could also be a reminder not to forget something important, and that, if we did, it would have dire consequences. Dreaming about sleeping may also mean that we can sleep well, because our conscience is clear. Seeing others asleep means that we can count on the fact that they are also not very alert in real life and that we can thus overtake them (perhaps co-workers). Sleeping with a partner shows that we are good friends. (See also "Bed.")

SLEEPING CAR When you are in the sleeping car of a moving train in a dream, this could be an indication that you don't want to miss out on the comforts in life. However, this image could also mean that you will, in fact, miss out on many other things in life (because you will be sleeping through the many stops that the train makes). Upon awakening from such a dream, you might shake yourself and make a commitment to pursue your work more vigorously. (See also "Train.")

SLEIGH (SEE "SLED/ SLEIGH")

SLIDE A children's slide in a dream represents the ups and downs of life, with which most of us are confronted. Of course, the dream might also refer to a present bumpy or troublesome situation in the dreamer's life.

SLIDING The image of sliding implies downward movement, so dreaming about sliding may indicate that you won't be able to hang on to a certain position. This image may also point to a lack of courage.

SLINGSHOT David killed the Goliath with a slingshot. Dreaming about a slingshot then means that you want to fight someone who is stronger than you are with your mind.

SLIP A slip has the same meaning as "Underpants," only in a woman's dream.

SLIPPERS People dreaming about wearing slippers tend to be idle in real life, and this can easily be the cause of a family or marital conflict. Walking around in worn-out slippers in a dream is a sign that you have trouble embarking on a new venture. Slippers in a dream may also stand for a weakness or a sense of inferiority, and thus also allude to feelings of shame. (See also "Shoes.")

SMOKE Dreaming about seeing smoke is often a sign that we are confronted with a confusing situation in real life that is causing us considerable headaches. Whether the smoke is dark gray or whitish gray is also important. Dreaming about smelling smoke usually points to a passion that could cause us to get burned. In this case, it is wise to search your conscience for troubles you have had in which your emotions have played a role. (See also "Blaze" and "Fire.")

SNAIL The snail's proverbial slowness is significant in dreams. Dreaming about a snail could mean that you would like to take it slow in a particular situation, although other circumstances could possibly overtake you. Crushing a snail underfoot is a sign that you are at the end of your patience; you want to act, but might do so carelessly. Removing a snail from its shell points to wanting to separate from an overly sensitive person. If the snail disappears into its shell, patience is asked for in a certain situation. In addition, a snail shell, like a mussel shell, can stand for aloof virginity. (See also "Mussel.")

SNAKEBITE Being bitten by a snake in a dream means that you need to "move your heels" in real life in order to get away from danger. This image could also indicate that a change is necessary at work or in other areas of your life. In an erotic interpretation, someone is poisoning or destroying your love life.

SNARE Setting a snare (a contrivance by which birds or mammals are entangled) in a dream denotes setting a trap for your real-life competition to stumble over. Of course, this also works in reverse: You could get caught in the snare—but this could always mean a "love trap."

SNEEZING Dreaming about sneezing, and not waking up from it, is a good sign, showing that you want to free yourself from something offensive.

SNOW When interpreting a dream about a blanket of snow covering the earth in winter, this image is often compared to a shroud covering the body of a deceased person, which expresses emotional coldness or a fear of impotence and loneliness. Positive messages from such a dream are rare (see "Snowball Fight"). Dreaming about sinking into the snow indicates that your feelings for someone you thought you loved have grown cold. In ancient Egypt, people believed that dreaming about snow foretold a change in the dreamer's personal life, and that trudging arduously through snow meant that the dreamer could expect great difficul-

ties in the near future. (See also "Ice," "Glacier," and "Avalanche.")

SNOWBALL FIGHT Dreaming about having fun in a snowball fight is a message from the unconscious that it is time to relax, stop isolating yourself, and enjoy the company of good friends. However, such a dream could also point to a rivalry between certain people close to you.

SNOWMAN You are the snowman you are building in the dream, which means that you should display more tenderness and warmth toward your partner. On the other hand, a snowman already built and decorated means that your partner is showing little interest in you or could be giving you the "cold shoulder."

SOAP A dream about soap isn't a reminder to clean yourself physically in real life. From experience, we know that a piece of soap can easily slip out of our hands. Therefore, when soap appears in a dream, it may be a message that it is impossible to clean up a particular situation, because you don't yet know all the facts.

SOAP BUBBLES Dreaming about soap bubbles implies that your hopes or illusions might burst like soap bubbles. If you or someone else are blowing the bubbles, this could add more meaning to the dream.

SOAPY WATER Soapy water is used to clean our dirty laundry, so this image may point to a less-than-pleasant phase in your life coming to an end. You can take a deep breath and get a fresh start. (See also "Dress" and "Laundry Room.")

SOCKS Socks cover our feet; so, for some psychoanalysts, socks in a dream describe a sexual act that a neurotic person is repressing. However, we believe that dreaming about socks means that you can expect life to progress comfortably (walking with socks is easier). In line with this, a dream about new socks means that you can look forward to an unburdened future. Dreaming about a hole in a sock or a stocking points to a character weakness or to a bad decision that the unconscious wants you to recognize and correct.

SOFA A dream about a sofa usually has something to do with the past. Seeing the sofa that belonged to your grandmother, for instance, may bring up a memory of a former boyfriend or girlfriend, or remind you of an object that you had been looking for a long time ago and thought was lost.

SOLDIER A soldier is an archetypal symbol for discipline and obedience, and appears even in the dreams of conscientious objectors, reminding us that these virtues concern everyone, unless the soldier in the dream is a hothead obsessed with shooting. In that case, the soldier stands for the person who creates chaos out of everything that was in good order before. Unrest and anxiety are indicated in real life when a whole company of soldiers appears in a dream; some psychoanalysts believe this image occurs primarily with single women. (See also "Fight" and "War.")

SON When parents dream about their son, the dream can be a way of making them more aware of their son's problems, and of their own incorrect behavior that contributed to them. A man's dream about a son, whom he might not even have in actuality, could be a message that something is not quite right in his emotional life. (See also "Daughter" and "Child.")

SONG When dreaming about listening to a song, pay attention to the words, because they will indicate the meaning of the dream. People who dream about music usually wake up happy. However, generally, only people with musical talent dream about music. (See also "Choir," "Music," and "Singing.")

SOOT Dreaming about a sooty oven or chimney usually refers to problems in the dreamer's intimate life. Soot that is settling down on things describes our emotional troubles that we can deal with without outside help. (See also "Oven" and "Chimney.")

SOUP Dreaming about thoroughly enjoying a bowl of soup is a sign that you will get a boost of energy in real life. Forcing the soup down shows that you have to "eat what you have cooked"; if you are exhausted when you are done, this is a message to take a break or go on vacation when everything is taken care of. Cooking soup for one's partner translates into wanting to show him or her how to do something in lovemaking. (See also "Cooking.")

SOUTH (SEE "FOUR CORNERS OF THE COMPASS")

SOWING Sowing a field in a dream stands for growth and success. Sowing may also refer to sexual matters, especially when the seeds are deposited in a furrow. In ancient Babylon, people believed that a dream about sowing meant that the dreamer would be blessed with many children. (See also "Harvest" and "Seeds.")

SPA (SEE "SANATORIUM")

SPARK When sparks are flying in a dream, the dreamer is bursting for joy. These are the sparks that kindle enthusiasm or that light the flame of love. In the case of the latter, they foretell a wedding and a glorious marriage. But sparks can also have negative connotations and can allude to something that is about to burn down. (See also "Fire" and "Blaze.")

SPARROW Sparrows in a dream are the birds that sing from every rooftop, which means that in real life the most fervently kept secret has ceased to be one. The person who dreams about hiding a sparrow in his or her hand or in a net is considered to be very impolite in real life.

SPEAR Although this weapon belongs to a bygone area, psychoanalysts still hold on to the notion that a spear is a sexual symbol. They see it

as a reference to intimate relationships between men and women, and specifically as the dreamer's attempt to overcome some difficult sexual situation. In the dreams of some people, the spear is the one that killed Christ. In this sense, it stands for the dreamer's present suffering, either physical or emotional, which can, however, be overcome. A broken spear might mean that the dreamer is "going to bat" for someone.

SPEECH Dreaming about giving a speech shows that you want to be ahead of the crowd in real life, or at least that you want to influence the people around you. If someone else is giving a speech, be warned: Someone wants to talk you into something. The content of the speech is also important, and contains symbols worth looking up. (See also "Sermon.")

SPICES If a dream about spices is not the result of having consumed a spicy meal before going to bed, the pungent taste could be an indication of your irritability or aggressiveness. However, it could also be a suggestion to pay more attention to a particular person or situation.

SPIDER The spider symbolizes seduction, destruction, or dangers lurking everywhere. If other symbols in the dream are positive, the spider may stand for the one who spins the lucky thread of your life, or may show focused thinking and action, and what is possible—all of which are described by the artful web the spider is spinning. However, if the dream is about a spider hanging by a single thread of its web, the luck of the dreamer is also hanging on a thread. (See also "Spiderweb" and "Insects.")

SPIDERWEB Sometimes a dream about a spiderweb is a reference to a present situation that shouldn't be put to a test. Brushing against a spiderweb in a dream could be a clue that you tend to be inconsiderate or preoccupied with inconsequential things. (See also "Spider.")

SPINE Dreaming about the spine may indicate that something treacherous is in the making, particularly if you see vertebrae sticking out or if there are other abnormalities. If the spine is absolutely straight, the unconscious is telling you to face a difficult situation straight on (have a "backbone") and to be persistent. (See also "Back" and "Bone.")

SPINNING WHEEL Dreaming about a spinning wheel turning industriously means that you would like to have a matter of importance to you or your family underway expeditiously. Seeing yourself at the spinning wheel indicates that you are preoccupied with a matter in real life that requires your undivided attention.

SPITTING A person spitting on somebody in a dream means that that person not only lacks refinement, but also insults or slanders people, or puts them in a bad light. If you are the one who is spitting, you need to do some serious soul searching and quickly clean up your

act, as well as stop insulting the people around you.

SPONGE A sponge in a dream suggests that you want to squeeze something out of something in real life; this often refers to financial matters, such as "squeezing the last penny." Dreaming about using a sponge to wash yourself could mean that you want to wash away an uneasy feeling or could be a warning about a certain person or a critical situation.

SPOTLIGHT Seeing a spotlight turned to a specific object in a dream is an indication that you should pay attention to this object, for it could be alerting you to something important. Headlights or spotlights turned on could mean that someone has found out what you are up to, and believes you are free game. (See also "Light" and the relevant object.)

SPRING A spring in a dream is usually understood to represent the "fountain of youth," and indicates vitality and a joyful life. If the water is clear, good luck is almost guaranteed. Cloudy water, on the other hand, points to less-than-favorable prospects or conflicts in personal matters; this image could also be a hint that you are dealing with people of dubious intentions. (See also "Water.")

SPRINGTIME Dreaming about springtime, when nature is budding and blooming, alludes to creative power, growth, and youth. For older people, springtime indicates a care-

free, youthful, sexual spirit.
Springtime, however, can also be a
warning that things won't always
remain as they are or that we should
prepare for winter or old age. (See
also "Summer," "Fall," and "Winter.")

SQUARE The square is a symbol for
the space where competitive games are
held, like the boxing ring. Dreaming
about a square is a signal that you
need to come to terms with threatening forces within yourself, for which
simple solutions may exist. However,
drawing a square in a dream probably
means that you have a well-developed
sense of order, which manifests itself
in your private life.

SQUIRREL This comical animal
also entertains us in our dreams. But
dreaming about a squirrel is a warning to be aware of people who flatter
you, for they might not be trustworthy. Getting bitten by a squirrel in a
dream means that somebody is planning to deceive you. Dreaming about
killing a squirrel doesn't imply that
you torture animals, but rather is a
signal that you should recognize and
avoid false friends.

STAG The stag is a symbol for
redemption, its antlers representing
the stairs leading to heaven. Fights
during the rutting season are a sign
of the stag's virility, which is why this
dream image also has sexual connotations. In the dreams of women, a
stag is sometimes a promise of an
amorous adventure; in the case of
men, it points to brilliant ideas or
success, not just in erotic or sexual
matters.

STAIN A stain, particularly on a
dress, represents the dark part of
your soul, which makes you insecure. (See also "Dress.")

STAIRS Stairs are a symbol for the
connection between the different lay-
ers of our personality. A missing step
or a damaged banister points to a feeling of insecurity, with which the
dreamer needs to deal. A spiral staircase tells us how difficult it is to reach
the top. Freud compared a staircase to
sexual relationships (in which the
penis goes up and down). We, how
ever, agree with the notion that stairs
represent the dreamer's efforts to reach
ever higher states of consciousness, or
desires to climb to higher intellectual,
social, or financial levels. Going
upstairs in a dream then would mean
an improvement in the position that
we hold in real life. Going downstairs
in turn would indicate a loss in a present position. (See also "House," "Back
Stairs," "Ladder," and "Floors.")

STAKE (SEE "PYRE")

STALL A stall in a stable or a barn
houses animals. Therefore, this
dream image points to the place
where insatiable urges are tamed,
which means that the dreamer is getting the upper hand over his or her
sexual appetite. (See also " Fire,"
"House," and "Animals.")

**STAMP (SEE "POSTAGE
STAMP")**

STARS Stars lighten up the darkness
of the unconscious, and thereby give
us a glimpse of our next goal in life.

Although seeing a clear, star-studded night sky is a positive sign pointing to illumination, stars falling from the sky, according to the Indian dream book *Jagaddeva,* indicate that an illness will soon break out. (See also "Meteor.")

STEAM Dreaming about steam is a sign that your hopes are disappearing or your plans are vanishing into nothing. When steam is preventing you from seeing into the distance in a dream, you have trouble seeing into the future. (See also "Landscape," "Smoke," "Fog," and "Water.")

STEAMBOAT A steamboat stands for restlessness or anxiety, or indicates that you are afraid that your life's journey might take off into unknown waters. If the steam being emitted prevents you from seeing clearly, you may see the future poorly; but don't be discouraged, for your journey may still end happily. (See also "Traveling" and "Ship.")

STEER Usually when a steer appears in a dream, untamed urges are being addressed. The steer is a symbol for lust. Being thrown by the horns of a steer can be taken as a warning: Your vitality is in danger, or you are allowing your physical urges to go beyond what is allowed. Fleeing from a steer indicates that you are afraid that you will lose your energies. If you are able to tame the steer, you are able to stand up for yourself in real life, because you can use your energies wisely on the job and in your personal life. Psychoanalysts believe that a steer in a woman's dream expresses her sexual desires. Because the steer also symbolizes creative, godly power, in a dream it may also stand for the power of the genius.

STOCKINGS (SEE "SOCKS")

STOCKS Buying stocks in a dream means that you are seeking security in an unstable situation. Destroying or selling stocks means that you don't want to depend on false friends.

STOMACH (SEE "BELLY")

STOMACH PAIN Dreaming about having a pain in the stomach that isn't present when you wake up is a signal that something is upsetting you. It could be a worry that shouldn't be ignored, a love affair gone bad that needs to be ended, or anger over having been treated unfairly, and of which you are unable to let go. (See also "Abdominal Pain.")

STORK Seeing a stork in flight in a dream shows that you have "high-flying," or "lofty," ideas about how to achieve financial success for yourself and your family. Seeing a stork's nest, with or without chicks, has less to do with the number of children you will have than with the children you are dealing with now or will have to deal with in the future.

STORM Like the wind, a storm in a dream is a reference to the intellect. The dream means that, like a storm, your powerful mind is hurling you toward success. Of course, many exciting and anxious moments are part of the journey. (See also "Wind.")

STOVE Since antiquity, a stove has been a symbol for the warmth and the security of the family. Dreams about a stove say a great deal about the condition of the dreamer. For instance, if the flame in the stove is going out, the dreamer is emotionally out of sorts. Some psychoanalysts believe that the image of a stove, in a man's dream, represents his wife, because the stove provides fire and fire in turn renders warm sustenance. They also see a stove as a sexual symbol, because the fire in the stove must be tended constantly and fed in order to be maintained.

STOVEPIPE If the stovepipe in the dream is particularly long, you might have to wait a long time for your dreams to come true.

STRAW Sleeping on straw in a dream shows that in real life you cannot expect to win, or that you must economize. (See also "Hay.")

STRAWBERRY The strawberry, often compared to a nipple, is a positive sexual symbol that alludes to marriage and motherhood. Strawberries also refer to "sweet" expectations and indicate that erotic wishes may be fulfilled. (See also "Breast.")

STREAM Dreaming about a stream indicates that your life is moving into a new channel, or course, and that your vitality is being renewed. (See also "River.")

STREET A street is a symbol for the path of your life. A street where you are building a house points to a good future. A street winding through the mountains refers to the difficulties that you can expect along the way to the top, or to success. A road through a forest may refer to your inner conflicts. The appearance of robbers, vagrants, or wild animals on the street means that you need to recognize those people who stand in the way of your progress and success. For a more complete interpretation of the dream, also pay attention to the street signs. Roads in poor condition and narrow paths indicate that progress will be difficult. (See also "House," "Mountains," "Forest," "Path," "One-Way Street," and "Signpost.")

STREETCAR (SEE "TRAIN")

STREETLIGHT A streetlight that is just coming on indicates a sudden insight, such as the need to change the course of your life if you want to avoid a bleak future. This image may also be a sign that you are becoming aware of a particular situation or of the intentions of certain people. (See also "Darkness," "Lamp," and "Lighthouse.")

STRETCHER A stretcher being used in the context of a hospital or an ambulance is not necessarily a bad omen, and may point to something being brought to you or even to a joyful event. However, an empty stretcher connotes an emotional crisis, or perhaps the emptiness of a relationship. Sometimes a stretcher in a dream describes the dreamer's feelings of helplessness on the job or in interpersonal relationships; but, wherever the problem lies, it easy to solve with the help of other people. Seeing another person on a stretcher could be a message to help someone through a burdensome situation.

STRINGED INSTRUMENTS

Whereas wind instruments are considered to be male, stringed instruments stand for so-called female emotions. But the bow could represent the penis, which could be influencing the rhythm. Dreaming about tuning the strings of an instrument indicates that a minor inconvenience in real life will most likely be forgotten quickly. (See also "Music" and specific stringed instruments.)

STUDENT Dreaming about being a student, if you are long past that stage in real life, indicates that a new learning phase or period in life is beginning. You need to pay close attention to other symbols as well, so that you will understand those things that will be important in your future. (See also "School.")

STUMBLING Stumbling in a dream could be an indication that some minor thing in your character is out of kilter, because when we stumble we fall over our own feet. Stumbling may also point to a mistake that you don't want to admit. If you dream about stumbling without falling down, this means that you can count on having luck on your side.

STUTTERING A dream about stuttering, if you aren't a stutterer in real life, indicates that you are dealing with some type of physical discomfort. Usually, the dreamer wakes up from such a dream with some kind of pain (perhaps a headache). Meeting a person who stutters in a dream indicates that someone is worried about your health. Incidentally, a person who actually stutters often dreams about speaking fluently.

SUBMACHINE GUN Like a pistol, a submachine gun represents sexual tension; this image, however, has the added meaning of aggression, with dangerous consequences. People who dream about a submachine gun generally have difficulty controlling their sexual urges. (See also "Rifle" and "Pistol.")

SUFFOCATING Dreaming about not being able to breathe activates a natural defense, and the dreamer wakes up. The relief that the dreamer feels might last through the entire day. We know of very ill people who dreamt that they were about to suffocate, and this generated so much drive in them that they were able to overcome their illness.

SUGAR The sugar we dream about is not sweet, but points to possible deficits in our condition. This image may reflect a wish for life to be "sweeter" and more beautiful, although the grind of everyday living won't allow it. (See also "Sweets.")

SUICIDE Don't be scared over a dream about suicide! Such a dream is simply a message from the unconscious to be mindful of how your energies are spent, or to possibly change your lifestyle. (See also "Death.")

SUITCASE A suitcase in a dream stands for the burdens that you are carrying through life. However, not only are there worries and problems inside the suitcase, but also original thoughts and ideas that you can "unpack" and profit from someday. (See also "Luggage.")

SUMMER Summer symbolizes the best years in a person's life. The image of summer indicates that something has matured, or describes the wise sense of reserve that you use around the people in your life. It could also indicate that the time is "ripe" to deal with a certain situation.

SUN The sun is a positive symbol for the power of the soul and for vitality, creativity, and fertilization. Most cultures consider the sun to be male. When the sun rises in a dream, success is almost guaranteed. The splendor of the sun gives us strength to face new challenges. Only the blinding sun of the desert scorches the earth, reminding us of pain and the end of all things. Seeing a sunset in glorious colors is said to be a promise of a wonderful old age. (See also "Gold," "Moon," and "Desert.")

SUNDIAL The sundial follows the sun, and promises all the good things described under "Sun."

SUNFLOWER The sunflower is a plant whose flower turns toward the sun. A sunflower in a dream indicates that you are a very trusting person. Or, it can mean that you are hopelessly in love. A sunflower may also connote great success, and your tendency to look down on people who have less than you do.

SUNSET In certain countries, the glow of a sunset is a good omen. Seeing a sunset in a dream signifies that a wish of yours will be fulfilled, that you will be lucky in love, or that your financial situation will improve. This image is almost always connected to a happy event, which also influences emotions.

SWALLOWS Dreaming about watching a swallow build its nest means that you want to make changes in your life that will make you happier. If you are unmarried, such a dream could show that you have found a partner and that the two of you plan to start your own household. (See also "Nest" and "Birds.")

SWAMP Dreaming about being in a swamp shows that you would do well to discontinue or rethink something that you have just started, otherwise little will be accomplished. Getting stuck in a swamp is a sure sign that you feel helpless in a confusing situation. (See also "Moor.")

SWAN The swan in Richard Wagner's opera *Lohengrin* also appears in dreams, and stands for the secrecy with which a couple in love is approached, and the caution never to ask them for the date of their marriage. A swan attacking you in a dream means that a certain matter does not bode well for you in real life. Dreaming about a swan song (ancient legend has it that the swan sings just before it dies) suggests that something in your life has passed and is being replaced by something better.

SWARM OF BEES Dreaming about a swarm of bees is a positive sign, and implies that the dreamer is playing an important role in society. However, such a dream is also supposed to indicate little sexual pleasure. (See also "Bee.")

SWEEPING Sweeping the floor in a dream is a message from the unconscious that something in your emotional state is out of kilter.

SWEETS People who dream about sweets are longing for love or a relationship. When the sweets don't taste good in the dream, this points to problems in an intimate relationship. A dream about sweets can also indicate that the dreamer is keeping a "delicious" secret. More can be learned about the secret from other symbols in the dream. (See also "Sugar.")

SWIMMING The meaning of a dream about swimming largely depends on the condition of the water in which you are swimming. Clear water denotes success through your own initiative; murky water refers to the lack of purpose with which you go through life. The images of swimming aimlessly and being afraid of drowning allude to your fear that your work is losing its purpose.

SWING Sitting on a swing in a dream generally means that we are unsure of our feelings. You may be vacillating in making a choice between two people. But such a dream could also point to being between jobs. Seeing others on a swing indicates that you are surrounded by people who constantly change their minds. In a woman's dream, swinging is also thought to be an expression of erotic desires. We find that interpretation rather unlikely, but believe that a swing in a dream may also signal danger or point to careless actions, particularly if the swing is attached to a flimsy tree branch or is too high off the ground.

SWITCH/CANE Dreaming about making a switch or a cane, but not succeeding, indicates that you are in a state of confusion at the present time or that work is not going well. Being punished with a switch shows that you are being subservient, even if you are finding it difficult to be so. Hitting others with a switch suggests that you have difficulties adapting. Or, this image may refer to how trivially you view certain things.

SWORD The sword can be seen as the defensive weapon of the soul, or as pointing to the need to defend oneself against emotional problems. It is also a symbol for the will to assume power or to govern. It is the "sword of justice" that is dispensed with precision (a sharp blade). Sometimes the meaning is the same as that of the rapier. (See also "Rapier.")

TABLE Dreaming about a table set for company has always meant that in real life guests are coming who need to be well fed and entertained. According to modern dream interpretation, the food on the table represents the vitality that we need in order to deal with emotional and spiritual matters. Dreaming about clearing the table means that you don't think very much about emotional and spiritual issues. You are a realist in life, and you want to have a "clean table." As far back as the Middle Ages, it was believed that the person who placed a clean tablecloth on the table in a dream was keeping a spotless house in real life, and that a dirty tablecloth meant the opposite.

TAILCOAT (SEE "EVENING ATTIRE")

TAILOR/DRESSMAKER It can be said that a tailor is the person who does something for us that we are afraid to do ourselves. A tailor in a dream therefore shows you your lack of courage and your timidity regarding doing something creative in real life. Sometimes a tailor also indicates that we are at "the end of our rope." If you are the tailor in the dream, this means that you need to take a risk in a certain matter if you are to reach your goal. (See also "Dress.")

TAKING OFF Taking off your clothes in a dream means that you have nothing to hide in real life, but should still be careful of not becoming too vulnerable. Taking off your shoes may mean that you would like to live a more natural lifestyle. Taking off, in the sense of leaving a house or an apartment, is a message from the unconscious that you are unhappy with your present lifestyle. This image also shows that you want to make changes so that you can live more freely.

TANK Dreaming about driving a tank means that in real life you want to use all of your powers to achieve something, regardless of the cost. Tanks approaching you in a dream are a message to be strong and face impending hardships with courage.

TAPE MEASURE (SEE "MEASURING")

TAPS Dreaming about this military signal means that you have concluded something in real life that could give you cause to celebrate. Perhaps you have completed an exam successfully or concluded a good business deal. Taps, however, are also a reminder that something has to come to an end.

TAR Dreaming about this gooey, oily, brownish-black substance is an indication that progress in real life will be slow. Dreaming of walking, and getting your shoes stuck, on a freshly tarred road points to terminating a relationship that has gotten "stuck." Dreaming about being spattered with tar is a message to be wary of people who would like to prevent you from getting ahead or could even be throwing obstacles in your way.

TASK Dreaming about a task is usually a "test dream," possibly testing the task that needs to be tackled. If the task is not identified in the dream, this means that you have a difficult problem to deal with in real life. A task in a dream is often a message from the unconscious to attack our life's task with more gusto. (See also "Test.")

TEACHER A teacher in a dream could represent the "wise man," whose advice and direction we usually don't follow because we simply don't have the energy; however, a teacher could also stand for the father, boss, or old man whose advice we should take to heart. But often the image of a teacher is the unconscious trying to teach us something. The teacher could be warning us about a muddled situation and showing us a way out. If the teacher is particularly tough, the dreamer is facing a serious situation. People in ancient Egypt believed that seeing a teacher in a dream was a message to the dreamer to be more serious. Sometimes people dream that a teacher is looking over their shoulder, which means that in real life something that they wanted to keep secret is out in the open. In dreams about taking a test or an exam, the teacher is usually only there to give the dream a reference point. (See also "Boss," "Father," "School," and "Test.")

TEARING/PULLING OUT Dreaming about tearing or pulling

something out indicates that you want to free yourself of something and to do so on your own. Tearing out your hair shows that you could be trying to rid yourself of guilt, a particular situation in your life, or a partner.

TEETH Teeth grind the food that we eat to get energy, so the image of teeth conveys a certain aggressiveness. A dream about tooth loss points to a loss of energy and, in some cases, even to impotence, which gives teeth a sexual meaning as well. Dreaming about wanting to bite into something could mean that you love someone so much that you want to "eat him or her up." When young girls dream about having lost their teeth, this might mean that they have lost their virginity, or might point to problems in their interpersonal relationships. Dreaming about teeth falling out also refers to having committed misdeeds in a relationship and the resulting guilt feelings. Some people believe that tooth loss also points to menopause (male menopause too), particularly if a person going through menopause has a dream about tooth loss repeatedly. Ancient Egyptian dream researchers believed that dreaming about teeth falling out indicated bad luck for the dreamer, or that a member of the dreamer's family could die.

TELEGRAM Dreaming about receiving a telegram, but not being able to read the text, suggests that you might become involved in a rather obscure adventure. If the text is easy to read, the contents will give further clues about the meaning of the dream. Sending a telegram implies that you are acting in haste.

TELEPHONE A telephone call in a dream might be a call from the unconscious, alerting you to the threat of something dangerous. If there are no danger signs in your life, the dream may simply point to a "connection" (positive or negative) to something or somebody. Getting a call may also mean that you are being accepted or rejected for something on the job or in your personal life. If you made the call, try to remember the individual numbers, and determine their meaning, in order to understand the significance of the dream.

TEMPLE According to an ancient Egyptian interpretation, seeing a temple or a similar structure in a dream indicated that the dreamer was enjoying life. (See also "Church.")

TEN The number ten, especially when seen as a combination of one and zero, reflects loneliness. But ten also has to do with possessions and advancement that can only be achieved by one's own efforts. (See also "Number.")

TENT A tent in a dream is the equivalent of a house, and conveys a message from the unconscious to think about living closer to nature. A tent can also be seen as fulfilling the same purpose as a roof, and because the roof of a house stands for the head, a dream about a tent could also be a sign to make things less compli-

cated for yourself. (See also "Roof" and "House.")

TEST Dreaming about tests, according to Adler and Freud, refers to indelible memories of punishments that the dreamer received for childhood misdeeds. But modern psychoanalysts believe that tests and exams appear in nightmares, and have to do with tests for survival in the present. But such dreams just as well could be about a fear of the future. By the way, the test in the dream is usually one that the dreamer passed successfully a long time ago. (See also "Task," "High School Graduation," and "Teacher.")

THEATER A dream about the theater is usually about life depicted in abstract or bizarre forms, and may describe certain hopes and desires of the dreamer. Missing a cue in a dream means that you will also fail to act in real life. If you have a part in the play, this alludes to the role that you have chosen in life. The type of play, either comic or tragic, reveals your basic attitude toward life. Some people dramatize things that they should smile about or, conversely, laugh about something that is serious. Pay attention to the title and the text of the play, because they contain a wealth of information about the meaning of the dream. (See also "Opera" and "Actor.")

THEATER SCENERY Dreaming about theater scenery as a backdrop means that in real life you are imagining things that are unlikely to come to pass. Scenery may also point to wanting to see a person whom you consider to be a friend in a way that is different from how he or she actually is. The colors of the scenery and what it describes will give you additional information about the meaning of the dream. Constantly changing the scenery is a sign that you are restless. (See also "Theater.")

THERMOMETER This device has nothing to do with illness in real life. The temperature readings are a reflection of the ups and downs in a relationship or a community. They may also show how intense our longings are or how coolly we react to certain people and things. (See also "Fever.")

THIEF Dreaming about a thief is a warning that losses can be expected if you don't take proper precautions. Such losses may not only be material but also moral or emotional. A thief in a woman's dream often means that she wants to "steal" away, or hide secrets from her lover. Catching a thief means that you may be able to rescue your possessions or reduce your emotional stress. It's also important to pay attention to where the thief came from in the dream. (See also "Burglar" and "Burglar's Tools.")

THIN Dreaming about being thin is not a reference to the size of your body but rather to your depleted emotional or mental state. Through this image, the unconscious is encouraging you to consider the advice that people give you as food for the mind and the soul, and to use this advice to your advantage. Seeing yourself looking like a broomstick, even if in real life you aren't underweight, means that you can't count on success in the near future. (See also "Rib.")

THIRST Thirst in a dream can be interpreted as an inner restlessness, and may have to do with thirsting for more balance in your life. Being thirsty also points to being afraid of being left alone, or without hope that your situation will improve. In addition, thirst is a sign that you need to make contact with faithful friends and avoid false friends. Dreaming about quenching your thirst means that you can count on an improvement to take place soon in a mishandled situation. A dream about thirst is often not concluded, because the feeling of thirst awakens the dreamer. (See also "Hunger.")

THIRTEEN Thirteen symbolizes death and thereby rebirth, so in a dream this number has nothing to do with having bad luck.

THISTLE Dreaming about being pricked by a thistle is the unconscious making you aware of people who are secretly envious of you. This image may also indicate that you have been hurtful to someone and want to make up for it. According to Artemidorus, dreaming about a thistle meant that the dreamer will worry about, or have difficulty with, some male in his life.

THRASHING Dreaming about getting a thrashing indicates that in real life the successes that you have achieved are due to self-discipline with a bit of recklessness thrown in. Even giving somebody a thrashing is not a negative sign, because it describes your ability to carry through.

THREAD Having difficulty threading a needle in a dream means that you have difficulty in real life keeping your nerves under control, and that this could possibly turn successes into failures. Human relations often "hang on a thread" in times of crisis. The color of the thread is also important. (See also "Colors," "Needle," and "Sewing.")

THREAT A threat in a dream in itself means very little. It doesn't point to any danger that we have to be afraid of, but at most is a warning not to do anything irrational.

THREE Three has always been considered to be a sacred number (the Trinity), and is an expression of creativity. Three describes our will, our ideas, the result of a union between a man and a woman, and giving birth to the future. The number three can have positive or negative connotations. When the dreamer sees the hand of the clock almost at three, this is considered a negative sign.

THREE-LEGGED STOOL A stool with three legs has always been considered a positive sign, and points to professional advancement as well as a happy family life.

THORNS Reflecting a Christian idea, thorns in a dream may convey the message that suffering is necessary when you want to help others. When a woman dreams about thorns, this often points to a fear of sex with a man with whom she is secretly in love. Being pricked by a thorn, or getting caught in one, points to being in a crisis or the loss of love. According to Artemidorus, thorns represent obstacles in the dreamer's life, or have to do with a difficulty with a woman.

THRUSH Dreaming about this bird implies looking out for something better. This is why, in the Middle Ages, when a woman dreamt about a thrush, it meant that she would meet a new acquaintance; in the case of a man, it meant that he would meet an admirer whom he had not expected. (See also "Blackbird" and "Birds.")

THUMB Although Sigmund Freud associated the thumb with sexual passion, he saw dreaming about the thumb having more to do with the dreamer's creativity or artistic talents, because it is the thumb that gives humans manual dexterity and nimbleness. Dreaming about a short thumb would therefore mean that one's artistic talents are not well developed, or that the person has too little energy to use his or her talents fully. (See also "Hand" and "Finger.")

THUMB SUCKING Dreaming about thumb sucking indicates that you are afraid and ashamed of something that you have done. Some psychotherapists believe that thumb sucking stands for masturbation.

THUNDER Thunder comes after lightning, and may have good or bad connotations. Additional dream symbols need to be analyzed in order to determine the reason for the thunder. Thunder without lightning, according to an ancient Egyptian dream interpretation, indicated that bad news was in store for the dreamer. (See also "Lightning.")

THUNDERSTORM The destructive power expressed in a dream about a thunderstorm always stands for the cleansing power of the soul. (See also "Lightning" and "Thunder.")

TICKET Receiving a ticket for a train, bus, or even a concert in a dream is a hint from the unconscious to be more outgoing in real life. (See also "Train Ticket.")

TICKLING Dreaming about tickling someone means that you want to insult that person. (See also "Laughter.")

TIGER As with the other predators, when a tiger appears in a dream, it stands for the enormous physical urges in human beings. The meaning of the tiger is similar to that of the steer, except that the tiger points to greater levelheadedness or being consciously more focused. People who dream about tigers tend to be vigorous, and their appetites often cause them to "overshoot" their targets. A caged tiger, or a tiger with which the dreamer is fighting successfully, indicates that the dreamer has his or her appetites under control.

TIME OF DAY (SEE "MORNING," "NOON," "NIGHT," AND "MIDNIGHT")

TIN Dreaming about tin indicates that in real life you might be wasting precious time on the wrong subject.

TINKER Dreaming about a tinker repairing something is an indication to be ready to make compromises in life.

TOILET Dreaming about a toilet is not unseemly, and means that we want to rid ourselves of burdens. A dream of being in a toilet stall has to do with getting our emotional household in order. Sadly, people repress such dreams, and thereby fail to benefit from this useful picture of their overall emotional state. (See also "Bowel Movement" and "Constipation.")

TOMATO This juicy, red fruit from the garden is equated with the apple of Paradise and with love. Eating a tomato in a dream is a sign that the dreamer has an excellent relationship with another person. (See also "Red.")

TONGUE A dream about the tongue, an instrument of language, refers to speech. Dreaming about looking at your own tongue in a mirror is a message from the unconscious advising you to keep your lips buttoned in a certain situation rather than simply chattering along. Seeing somebody else's tongue is a message to watch out for people with a sharp tongue in your immediate surroundings or for chatterboxes who want to make you look bad. French kisses, by the way, do not refer to sexual matters, but rather are a suggestion to find common ground with a partner or another person in order to solve a problem. (See also "Kiss.")

TOOLS Dreaming about carrying tools around carefully indicates that you want more order in your life. This is also a message from the unconscious to fix something that is faulty. (See also individual tools.)

TOOTHACHE Dreaming about a toothache is rare, even if we have one in real life. Such a dream might have to do with trying to find out something about a particular person by "drilling" him or her. Or, this image could be revealing that something that we can't reconcile with our conscience is bothering us. Sometimes a toothache in a dream refers to nothing more then being lovesick. (See also "Pain.")

TORCH A torch is a symbol for marriage, because, in earlier times in certain countries, a torch was used to light the hearth in the house of newlyweds after their marriage ceremony. A torch in a dream either ignites or extinguishes the fire of love. Or, it has to do with bringing light, or letting us sink into darkness. A torch also stands for psychic energy, in a positive as well as a negative sense. (See also "Fire.")

TORTE (SEE "CAKE")

TORTOISE The tortoise represents the shield we use to protect a threatened ego, and also stands for reflec-

tion and self-examination. Sometimes the tortoise is considered a warning to be more restrained in order to avoid being harmed.

TOWEL Dreaming about using a towel to dry the skin, or to rid it of something uncomfortable, means that you want to forget something sad or distressing in real life.

TOWER In a dream, a tower with enough space for people to live can be compared to a tall, sturdy house, which translates into the strength to defy all temptations, particularly those relating to spiritual and intellectual matters. A tower in ruins indicates that, against our better judgment, we are about to give in. Looking down from the spire of a tower means that our boundless dreams will come to pass. However, here, the unconscious is also sending a warning signal—namely, that those who reach for the stars might fall twice as hard, should an envious person stand behind them and push. A fall from a tower might be an indication that we are afraid of failing an exam or of performing a responsible task at work. Psychoanalysts consider a tower to be an oversized phallic symbol, but we don't agree with this interpretation.

TOWN HALL/CITY HALL Dreaming about a town or a city hall has nothing to do with a position of honor, but is a message to burden yourself less, both emotionally and physically. This image is also a sign to listen to the advice of the people close to you. A town or a city hall, like a house, represents the body. For additional information about the meaning of the dream, try to remember the number of floors and rooms in the building.

TOYS Particularly for older people, dreaming about lots of toys lying around suggests that they are remembering the past and wishing they could be young again. Playing with toys means that we long for a life free of burdens, like the life of a child; additional symbols in the dream will indicate whether or not this longing will be fulfilled.

TRACKS A dream about following in someone's tracks means that you want to get even with somebody in real life. Or, it could mean that you are extremely jealous and suspicious, and are checking up on your partner. Following the tracks of your anima (in this case, your true inner self) indicates that you want to steal away from your present life or a current situation and try to calm internal tensions by being out in nature.

TRAFFIC LIGHTS When the traffic light is green in a dream, this means that you hope that you will see the "green light" in your life, which would make it possible for you to deal successfully with a certain problem or a difficult job. When the traffic light is red, this shows that you are struggling with some thoughts. A red light can also be an indication that not all is well physically. (See also "Green," "Red," "Burning," and "Fire.")

TRAFFIC SIGN (SEE "SIGNPOST")

TRAIL Dreaming about a trail through difficult terrain is some kind of warning. If the trail disappears suddenly, be prepared for fate to deal you a blow. A trail turning into a path that is easy to navigate means that the chances of finding a solution to a dilemma are good. Walking up a trail on a mountain describes a life burdened with many difficulties. (See also "Mountains," "Street," and "Path.")

TRAIN Because the train is a means of transportation, in a dream it refers to the journey through life. It could mean that we want to get away from a present situation, leave everything behind, start anew. But sometimes we miss the connection; then we must make due with the present situation. If the train doesn't reach its destination, this means that you are adrift in life, have given up, and live every day without purpose. Reaching the destination in the dream means that you will also reach your goal in real life. Being late and missing the train means that you should quickly deal with the anger in yourself that has accumulated over time; this image could also point to having some difficulty in your contact with the people around you. (See also "Departure," "Arriving," "Train Station," "Train Ticket," "Ticket," "Railroad Tracks," and "Sleeping Car.")

TRAIN (ON A GOWN) (SEE "BRIDE")

TRAIN-CROSSING BARRIER A closed barrier at a train crossing in a dream shows that you are stuck right now on the road of life, or that your emotions are at zero. When the barrier opens, this indicates that you look to others ahead of you, believing that they have accomplished more than you have. (See also "Barriers," "Train," "Border," and "Border Gate.")

TRAIN ENGINE Dreaming about a train engine is usually a positive sign, and means that you have plenty of energy to forge ahead or that you can look forward to good times (unless the train is moving backward). A steam-driven engine emitting white smoke indicates a positive outcome and continued success; dark smoke, on the other hand, shows that your future is also dark. The pistons that operate the engine represent virility and a passion for life. (See also "Steam," "Darkness," "Train," and "Traveling.")

TRAIN STATION A train station could stand for the unconscious itself, which is trying to keep you from "missing the train." A train station can also be regarded as the point from which you are embarking on a new phase in your life. Whether the subsequent journey will be positive or negative can only be gathered from other symbols in the dream. (See also "Bus/Train Stop," "Train," "Departure," "Arriving," and "Train Ticket.")

TRAIN TICKET Dreaming that you can't pay for the train ticket indicates that right now you simply don't have the means to realize your personal goals; therefore, this could be a message to consider postponing any changes in your present situation. If you have the money for the ticket, you will go forward and accomplish your goals with great success. If you are traveling without paying, you are trying to get something for nothing. (See also "Ticket," "Traveling," "Train," and other means of transportation.)

TRAP A dream about trapping somebody points to reaching your goal by resorting to some kind of ruse. If you dream of being trapped yourself, you might find yourself in real life in a seemingly hopeless situation.

TRAVELERS Dreaming about people traveling with us refers to those hidden parts of our personality that, when exposed, shed light on our emotional makeup and our lifestyle. Such a dream is also a message to pay attention to the type of people we are attracted to, and what aspects of their personality appeal to us.

TRAVELING Dreaming about traveling usually refers to changes in our emotions and goals. On the journey, you are presented with places where you would like to linger as well as places from which you want escape. Traveling may also indicate a desire to assume some responsibility. Or, it may point to the will to keep going forward on your life's journey. Traveling could indicate your quest for true values as well. (See also "Automobile," "Train," "Airplane," "Boat," and "Ship.")

TREASURE Dreaming about searching for a treasure opens up untold possibilities. Coming up empty-handed in spite of an intensive search shows that you are chasing an illusion in real life, but without suffering significant consequences. Digging up a treasure indicates a dashed hope, or perhaps a serious financial situation in which you are "reaching for a straw." Burying a treasure is a message from the unconscious that you want to taunt someone who has always been friendly to you. If someone else is burying the treasure, this means that somebody wants to play a trick on you.

TREE The tree is the archetypal symbol for life. Adam and Eve picked an apple from the tree of knowledge, and this lesson influenced the rest of their lives. Therefore, dreaming about a tree means that you can expect to gain insights that will be helpful in your life. A tall tree points to a high honor, a tree in bloom to luck in your personal life, and a fruit-bearing tree to success in the near future; a scrawny tree, on the other hand, indicates little success in business. Falling off a tree is a sign that you have difficulties recognizing your true situation. Climbing a tall tree shows that you are taking on more than you can handle in life; this also implies a good chance of falling off. (See also "Branch," "Leaves," and Forest.")

TRENCH (SEE "DITCH/TRENCH")

TRIAL Dreaming about a trial could be a way that the unconscious is making you aware that a particular issue in your life can only be resolved by your being aggressive and courageous. If you are losing in a trial, the message here is to confront a real-life opponent and agree on a compromise. Winning indicates that you have gained new insights that could prove to be invaluable in a certain situation. (See also "Court.")

TRIANGLE The triangle is considered a female sexual symbol and must be seen within the context of other symbols in the dream. An equilateral triangle in a dream shows that you are thinking clearly and creatively.

TRIPOD (SEE "THREE-LEGGED STOOL")

TROLLEY (SEE "TRAIN")

TROMBONE Unlike the other wind instruments, the trombone is not always seen as a sexual symbol. Dreaming about a trombone could also mean that you are announcing something with fanfare, or that you are broadcasting something that would be better left unsaid.

TROOPS (SEE "SOLDIER")

TROUSERS/PANTS Dreaming about putting on a pair of trousers indicates that in real life you are easily insulted. This could also point to an exaggerated need for power (after all, you are wearing the pants). Dreaming about taking off your pants means that you are revealing your ignorance, and that your reputation therefore will suffer. Dreaming about using suspenders means that you are making sure that in real life you get help.

TROUT This seemingly happy fish, swimming in crystal-clear waters, describes your love of life and the flair and spontaneity with which you delight in the world around you.

TRUCK The truck represents the self, and in a dream shows that you are being asked to carry an especially heavy burden. (See also "Automobile.")

TRUMPET The trumpet symbolizes formidable male sexual power. Interestingly enough, the sound of the trumpet is seldom heard in a dream; but when it is, it may announce a secret love affair. (See also "Wind Instruments.")

TULIP This flower, whose petals open up in great beauty, stands for the affection that you have for someone. The tulip is also a sign of an ever-deepening relationship between two people, either marriage partners or two friends. Wilting or wilted tulips indicate that such positive feelings are fading. (See also "Flowers.")

TUNNEL Entering a tunnel in a dream indicates that you are afraid of sudden darkness, or are going through a period of some type of affliction, which will, however, soon be over.

TWO The number two is a symbol for opposites, such as good or evil and being or non-being. Two in a dream may also stand for obstacles in real life that are in the way. Or, it may represent infinite femininity, as seen when a woman gives herself to a man so that he can fulfill his intrinsic purpose. (See also "Number.")

UDDER Dreaming about an udder only occasionally points to our urges. It most likely refers to receiving intellectual nourishment. It could also have a negative connotation—namely, that you are naive and will receive less than what you had hoped for. Artemidorus saw a full udder as the promise of a full purse.

ULCER Dreaming about an ulcer shows that something in your personality needs attention and should be rectified quickly, in order for you to have a clear conscious again.

UMBRELLA An umbrella in a dream describes protection from natural forces. An old man who is desperately looking for the umbrella he has lost is trying in real life to regain his sexual powers. A woman who is unfolding an umbrella might be trying to fend off a pushy admirer.

UNDERPANTS When men dream about underpants, this expresses their fear of not behaving appropriately when in the company of others. (See also "Dress" and "Nakedness.")

UNEARTHING (SEE "DIGGING UP")

UNIFORM A dream involving a uniform points to your feeling of monotony in real life or to the constant conformity from which you want to escape. If the uniform fits badly, you are afraid that you aren't meticulous enough in real life. If the uniform fits well, you might be too self-assured. (See also "Dress" and "Soldier.")

URINE As is the case with dreams about feces, dreams about urine are far from negative. Dreaming about urinating tends to be a sign of sexual tension in real life, unless the dreamer suffers from incontinence. It is also possible that such a dream means that the dreamer is "fertilizing" emotional or intellectual ideas, or stimulating fruitful activities. (See also "Feces.")

URN When the container that holds the ashes of a deceased person appears in a dream, it has nothing to do with death in real life. Instead, it refers to your emotional state at the present time, or perhaps to your moody behavior. (See also "Deceased Person.")

VACCINATION The unconscious also equates a vaccination with protection. Dreaming about a fear of being vaccinated indicates that in real life you are against something that could be to your benefit. Vaccinating somebody in a dream suggests that you want to force your own will on someone. A child being vaccinated could refer to your desire to protect a defenseless person from the dangers of his or her environment.

VAGABOND The vagabond who strolls through your dreams represents your longing for freedom and independence. It is the vagabond of the soul who is described here, and what is alluded to is a rebellion against hypocritical morals in real life.

VAGINA Many indigenous tribes consider the vagina to be a symbol for both femininity and motherhood. According to Freud, all kinds of round, hollow objects represent the vagina. Modern psychology views the vagina as a symbol for feminine power, which is also part of the male; in other words, the vagina is not seen exclusively in sexual terms. (See also "Phallus.")

VALET Even a beggar might dream about a valet, a person who keeps things in order, except that in dreams the unconscious uses this image as a means of describing emotional matters. Dreaming about being a valet yourself could be a hint to look at your behavior and your actions, to see if you are offering help to others too generously.

VALLEY Dreaming about walking through a valley indicates that life right now is rather easy; however, a valley also implies that soon the road will rise again. The only time that a dream about a valley is negative is when the valley is surrounded by mountains that are so high that no sunshine is able to reach the ground. Such a dream may even point to a serious illness or bitter losses. (See also "Mountains" and "Narrow Space.")

VAMPIRE This bloodsucking monster of Slavic tales also visits our dreams. The vampire stands for a person in your life who wants to get "the last drop of blood" from you. Or, this image could be a hint that you are allowing others to take advantage of you and are not even aware of it. (See also "Monster.")

VAN The image of a van in a dream suggests that your opinion of yourself is changing. However, the shifts that have taken place in your personality are not for the better.

VANITY FAIR (SEE "FAIR")

VARICOSE VEINS (SEE "BLOOD VESSELS")

VASE Because this container is used to hold flowers, in a dream the image of a vase holds our most splendid feelings, which is why a vase is often connected to sexual desires. If the vase is empty, love is not mutual. Filling the vase with flowers promises that an existing relationship will be strengthened. A vase filled with beautiful flowers refers to your healthy emotional state. But should the vase break, there is a possibility that you will be leaving a person with whom you thought you were in love.

VEGETABLES Some vegetables, like some fruit, point to female or male sexual organs. Dreaming of growing vegetables that are reminiscent of certain parts of the body indicates that sexual pleasures may be awaiting you. Dreaming of vegetables that cause flatulence might indicate physical or emotional discomfort. Even growing these vegetables has negative connotations. (See also different kinds of vegetables.)

VEHICLE A dream of using a vehicle or other means of transportation expresses our hope of getting ahead a little faster in life. In ancient Egypt, it was believed that those who dreamt about riding in a vehicle wanted to get ahead of their competition. (See also "Traveling" and individual means of transportation.)

VEIL A veil in a dream points to virginity as well as to a secret. Covering yourself with a veil means that there is something in your life that you want to hide, so that others won't see it as it truly is. If someone else is wearing the veil, this means that you are being fooled or deceived. A torn bridal veil may indicate that the loving feelings you thought you had for someone are now gone. Similarly, a black mourning veil is only a window dressing or a showpiece, because in real life you have ceased loving a certain person. (See also "Bride" and "Virgin.")

VELVET Dreaming about caressing a piece of velvet cloth means that you are longing for softness and love, or simply for a few gentle, understanding words that indicate affection and caring. On the other hand, dreaming of being dressed in velvet and silk is a message not to act so smug and superior. (See also "Silk.")

VICTIM A victim in a dream is an image harking back to the mythological cult of sacrifice. Therefore, if you dream of a victim, you are probably making sacrifices in real life. This image can also point to abstaining from, or forfeiting, something in order to appear faultless to others. Or, it could be a message to leave some bad habit on the altar of sacrifice, so that you can again be at peace with yourself.

VIEW The best view is from a high mountain, a tower, or any other high structure. Dreaming about any of these places indicates that you look down on people who are less successful than you are, and therefore implies a certain degree of arrogance that should quickly be abandoned. When there is an obstructed view in a dream, you need to ask yourself if you are exercising proper control in a certain matter.

VILLAGE If you are a city person dreaming about a village, this not only indicates a desire to return to a more natural lifestyle but also a feeling of being boxed in emotionally. According to an Egyptian interpretation, dreaming about living in a village meant that the dreamer intended to live a quiet life in the company of good friends and family members.

VINEGAR Dreaming about vinegar usually means that something does not sit well with us. But vinegar may also point to something (intellectual or emotional) that has yet to be "digested."

VIOLENCE Dreaming about being attacked, and not doing anything about it, is an indication that in real life you feel unworthy and suffer from an inferiority complex. Acting violently yourself is a message from the unconscious that your attempts to reach your goals or desires are futile.

VIOLET Violet is the color of reflection and contemplation. When interpreting the meaning of the color violet, you might also consider the symbolic meaning of red and blue. (See also "Red" and "Blue.")

VIOLETS These delicate flowers, with their compact root stocks, speak of restraint and humility, seclusion, and a secret love. (See also "Flowers.")

VIOLIN Like the cello, the violin in dream interpretation is compared to the soft curves of a woman's body, and expresses erotic charisma and yearning, including that for a joyful union. The tone of the violin indicates how harmonious the interaction is between two people in love. (See also "Stringed Instruments.")

VIRGIN The virgin stands for purity and for being untouched. In a man's dream, a virgin is the embodiment of the anima, or the inner feminine part of his personality. In a woman's dream, this image is her own shadow, which is pointing to the past or to a strong attachment to her father. It might also indicate her emotional strength. Men who dream about virgins usually suffer from a mother complex (see "Mother Complex" under Other Clues), because they see their own mother as the model for femininity. For young men in particular, a virgin represents a flawless woman, whom they want to marry. (See also "Defloration," "Woman," "Girl," and "Mother.")

VISE Dreaming about working with a vise, the tool with two jaws used in woodworking, is a message to hold on to what we have right now. Seeing others working with a vise is a clue that somebody is "bearing down" in a particular situation, and that a quick change of mind can get us out of this situation.

VISITOR If we consider a visitor as someone who creates discomfort, when one shows up in a dream he or she might point to allergies or a dislike of something or somebody.

VOLCANO A dream about a volcano stands for character flaws in ourselves that we should get rid of. The lava that burns everything on its path stands for uncontrolled jealousy, outbursts of temper, or thoughtless actions. (See also "Mountains," "Blaze," and "Fire.")

VOMITING Dreaming about vomiting means that you are getting rid of something that was uncomfortable or "indigestible." Sometimes this can be a warning from the unconscious

not to say things that might injure others. (See also "Disgust.")

VULTURE The vulture is an archetypal symbol for danger. Dreaming about a vulture often refers to the dreamer's extreme self-centeredness. The vulture may represent "having it in for" somebody, which results in feeling a sense of aloneness. Killing a vulture in a dream is a signal from the unconscious to break with bad habits and find strength from within. (See also "Cadaver.")

W

WAGON A fully loaded wagon in a dream points to successful and profitable activities; an empty wagon, on the other hand, implies losses and futile efforts. Something falling off the wagon shows that you are looking at financial circumstances, or can expect diminished worth in the future.

WAITER/WAITRESS Dreaming about being served well is a positive sign, and means that you can count on good health and advancement in life. When you are the waiter yourself, this indicates that you will have to work very hard and often for the benefit of others.

WAITING ROOM A waiting room in a dream stands for a break that you are taking in your life's journey. The break may be due to a certain matter or an illness. It's important to determine whose waiting room you were in; was it a physician's, a lawyer's, or the waiting room in a train or bus station? (See also "Physician," "Lawyer," and "Train Station.")

WALKING People who dream about taking a walk generally enjoy a leisurely lifestyle and take care of themselves (we all know that walking is good for our health). However, such a dream could also be a message from the unconscious, reminding us that any excess in work or love could do us more harm than good. If you watch yourself or others walking slowly in a dream, this is a message to be cautious in real life. Walking fast implies that a problem you are facing is being resolved quickly. Taking a stroll points to good luck and contentment, and expresses an optimistic attitude. (See also "Path.")

WALL Looking for protection behind a wall in a dream indicates that in real life you are hiding your emotional pain from the people around you. Standing in front of a wall without a gate or a door means that something in your life is being blocked, especially if the wall is high. According to Freud, a gate in a wall describes the dreamer's sexual desires; the dreamer would like to go through but hasn't yet found the courage. Standing on top of a wall and jumping off is an indication that you are about to go on an adventure in real life. Falling off a wall, however, is a message to think twice before taking a risk in real life.

Dreaming about a wall that is about to fall down on you (or dreaming about narrow streets, or hills or mountains that suddenly seem too close) is said to indicate breathing or thyroid problems.

WALLET A dream about a wallet describes the emotional state of the dreamer. An empty wallet or safe may indicate a loss of affection or a lack of willpower. (See also "Money.")

WALLPAPER Dreaming about hanging wallpaper means that you want to live someplace else or make a radical change in your life.

WALTZ Dreaming about a waltz implies that you are moving joyfully through life, even if you might step on other people's toes every now and then. Watching others dance the waltz indicates that you feel left out and think others are better than you are. (See also "Dancing.")

WANDERING ABOUT
Dreaming of wandering aimlessly about (which is usually part of a nightmare) indicates that you are in severe emotional trouble, especially if you awaken soaked in perspiration and don't know where you are. (See also "Lost.")

WAR If a dream about war doesn't refer to a childhood memory or an actual war experience, it could point to a fear of being dragged into something against our will. Or, it could denote a difficult emotional state or a conflict that appears to be hopeless, but can be overcome if we are willing to put up a good fight. (See also "Fight.")

WARTS Dreaming about having warts, or seeing someone else with them, points to negative characteristics. When the shortcomings are our own, they are not all that difficult to deal with. But when they belong to someone else, we need to give them careful consideration so that we can deal with them properly.

WASHING A dream in which you are washing yourself indicates that you need to be absolved of some kind of accusation in real life.

WASP A wasp causes fear in dreams as well. Its buzzing, and its black-and-yellow coloring that is reminiscent of the stripes of a tiger, throw us into anxiety. A dream about wasps describes the state of our nerves, which have been weakened by the fears and the stresses of daily living. Sometimes a wasp in a dream stands for a parasitic person who has crossed our path in real life. (See also "Insects" and "Bee.")

WATCH (SEE "CLOCK/WATCH")

WATER A symbol for the unconscious, water also cleanses and bestows and sustains life. Dreaming about water that is calm or moves gently is always a positive sign. But water that breaks in waves over the shore, flooding the surrounding area, points to danger. The kind of danger can be deduced from other symbols in the dream. Clear water means good luck, murky water bad luck.

(See also "Moor," "River," "Ocean," and "Flood," as well as other symbols having to do with water.)

WATER CLOSET (SEE "TOILET")

WATERFALL A tumbling waterfall in a dream promises success or quick results from good investments; this image also stands for encouragement coming from above.

WATER SPIRITS (SEE "GHOSTS," "GOBLIN," AND "NYMPH")

WEAPON Dreaming about weapons is a sign that you are defending yourself against something that could drain your emotional energy. Sometimes weapons are seen as sexual symbols, which, of course, is the case in psychoanalysis. (See also specific weapons.)

WEATHER VANE In general, a weather vane in a dream stands for the dreamer's moodiness, something that doesn't win anybody many friends. Determining the direction from which the wind was coming will add to the interpretation of the dream. (See also "Flag.")

WEAVING LOOM Dreaming about a loom shows that a job in real life will progress slowly, which means that its rewards will also not come quickly.

WEDDING A wedding implies an end and a beginning, at the same time. Therefore, a dream about a wedding is about a change in your life. A wedding is also a symbol for union. If you are celebrating your own wedding—even if in reality you have been married a long time—this indicates that your lifestyle is changing. Dreaming about being a guest at a wedding indicates changes in personal relationships. The Indian dream book *Jagaddeva* says that dreaming about a wedding points to an impending death or at least to great pain. (See also "Bride.")

WEDDING RING The general meaning of a wedding ring has already been discussed under "Ring." But something else comes into play here—namely, that a person can never be a hundred percent sure of his or her partner, and there is always some fear of losing him or her. The image of a wedding ring thus could be seen as a message from the unconscious not to ever take one's partner for granted. (See also "Marriage.")

WEEDS If the field in your dream is overgrown by weeds, this indicates that you may become disheartened in real life. This image could also be a hint that in real life you overestimate your status. Another message could be that you should take care of the weeds in your own garden before criticizing the gardens of others. (See also "Moor.")

WEIGHT LOSS Dreaming about weight loss could mean that an argument regarding a certain issue is rather "thin." Weight loss also points to the "lean years" being almost over, and to an increase in status. If

you dream of a number of complete strangers who are very emaciated, this could be a message from the unconscious that there are many people who are much worse off than you are.

WEST (SEE "FOUR CORNERS OF THE COMPASS")

WET NURSE A wet nurse suckling a baby, when the dreamer is a woman, is often a sign of a repressed desire to be a mother. This image could also be a message from the unconscious that you need outside help in dealing with something. When you are the wet nurse in the dream, this is a warning that in real life others are taking advantage of you.

WHEAT Wheat, like other types of grain, is considered a fertility symbol, and in dreams also stands for growing and maturing. (See also "Farmer," "Harvest," "Grain," and "Seeds.")

WHEEL The greatest invention in human history alludes to the power to move everything, the focal point around which everything rotates, and that which helps us to get ahead. In some dreams, the wheel also stands for the intellect, or the words that were there at the beginning of everything. (See also "Circle" and "Words.")

WHEEL OF FORTUNE Dreaming about a wheel of fortune that is turning is the unconscious telling us that luck is capricious and it is better to rely on our skills.

WHIP Dreaming about cracking a whip indiscriminately indicates that you pretend to be nastier than you actually are. At the same time, such a dream is a sign of inferiority and inhibition, probably due to the way that you were raised. Dreaming about being whipped (usually without feeling any pain) shows that you shrink back often in real life, letting others take the initiative.

WHIRLING A whirling spring or fountain in a dream is a reference to volatility. Such a dream may be a message to first have a conversation with a possible opponent before deciding to act. The dream might also address your unrestrained personality, which you need to get under control if you don't want to ruin your chances for something. (See also "Fountain" and "Spring.")

WHISPERING GOSSIP
Whispering gossip or information to the student next to you in school could get you into trouble. Dreaming about whispering into someone's ear is the unconscious alerting you that trying to court favors is useless, particularly when what is being whispered is unwelcome gossip. This image may also imply that you like to listen to gossip yourself, even though you know that it can be hurtful. (See also "School" and "Teacher.")

WHITE White represents purity, which is why in many countries a bride stands before the altar in a white gown. But white also represents abstinence, calmness, and infertility, and in certain cultures signifies grief.

WIDOW/WIDOWER Dreaming about being a widow or a widower has nothing to with losing your partner, but rather alludes to the new and happy experiences that life has in store for you. Meeting a widower or widow in a dream shows that you are part of a happy family that sticks together no matter what. Only in dreams that have many negative symbols is the image of a widow or a widower a sign of your loneliness in real life or your having been deserted at a time when you needed someone desperately.

WIG Sometimes dreaming about a wig is a message to the dreamer not to pretend to be something that he or she is not. Dreaming about wearing a wig may indicate a fear of having lost a sense of yourself and an attempt to regain it. Seeing others wearing a wig may be a warning to be on guard when making new friends. (See also "Hair.")

WILD BOAR The wild boar in a dream stands for untamed physical urges that you need to manage better; it also points to the luck that you may find with the opposite sex. Being attacked by a wild boar in a dream could be a warning to be on guard against ruthless people who live close to you. Of course, this animal also stands for your own untamed driving forces and energies that can get you into trouble in interpersonal relationships. Although the steer represents untamed urges as well, the wild boar is a more positive symbol. (See also "Steer.")

WILL Dreaming about a last will and testament might mean that you have successfully concluded some assignment in real life. When the dreamer is the one making out the will, this could point to getting everything in order for a more relaxed future, or for a long and restful old age in the case of older people.

WIND Wind in a dream brings a breath of fresh air into our personal issues and relationships. Wind drives the ship of life, and is the intellectual engine that moves us to act. It provides us with energy to reach our goals, particularly when the wind is at our back. Gently moving air directs us into calmer waters. (See also "Storm.")

WIND INSTRUMENTS Wind instruments have to do with male sexuality. When a woman dreams about wind instruments, she is promised a cheerful sex partner; in the case of a man, wind instruments allude to his own eroticism. (See also "Music" and specific instruments.)

WINDMILL (SEE "MILL")

WINDOW A window in a dream is connected to the image of a house, and, by being either open or closed, describes the personality of the dreamer. A window can also point to an opening in the body, and then has a sexual meaning. (See also "Door" and "House.")

WINE Drinking wine in a dream refers to having insights regarding emotional and spiritual issues. Drinking wine also indicates that everything will be positive, that the magic of love is at hand, or that you can look forward to an increase in wealth. Spilling wine, on the other hand, points to the end of luck. Pouring clear wine is a message to tell the truth, even if doing so is difficult. (See also "Alcohol," "Grape," and "Grape Harvest.")

WINNING Even if the dream specifically refers to winning money (perhaps winning the lottery), it has little to do with financial success in real life. What is alluded to is almost always something that is nonmaterial, like a new friendship, a passionate, all-consuming love affair, or good luck for the family or in one's personal life.

WINTER Winter is the time of year that corresponds to the last stage of a person's life. But even if you are still young, dreaming about a winter season that is particularly cold may indicate that you feel lonely, because the love you felt for someone has grown cold. If this indeed is the case with you, another message that is implied is to try to change your overall outlook and pursue new contacts, thereby gaining a new perspective. A dream about winter can also be a message to be patient while waiting for better times. (See also the other three seasons.)

WINTER SPORTS Dreaming about skiing or sledding down a

snow-covered mountain silently and smoothly indicates that your life is going well, and that when there is a mishap you are able to retain your balance. Obstacles and crashes indicate that there are emotional problems in your life that need to be taken care of, possibly with professional help. (See also "Skiing," "Sled/Sleigh," "Ice," "Snow," and other winter-related symbols.)

WIRE Dreaming about a wire has to do with encircling something in order to possess it. You could be tying down the person you love, or even keeping out a person who is no longer a friend. Barbed wire can injure us, but in dreams it is the soul that gets hurt, or the ego. Possibly your ego feels mocked by people who are resentful of you. (See also "Rope.")

WITCH Dreaming about a witch, who is usually an ugly, old woman, is a warning to beware of unscrupulous people. She is the quintessential evil fairy who wreaks havoc with our emotions, as well as a symbol for the negative mother who interferes in our personal life. A man dreaming about sleeping with a witch suffers in real life from a destructive passion or possibly is sexually dominated by a woman. (See also "Fairy" and "Broom.")

WOLF A wolf in a dream refers to those forces within us that can't be tamed, or to that part of the self with which we are in constant conflict and tension. Dreams about wolves are a sign that you need to come to terms with your inner self. A wolf can also

stand for a person in your life who supports you as long as you don't make him or her your enemy. According to Artemidorus, somebody was after the dreamer when a wolf appeared in a dream. But this ancient Greek dream interpreter also said that the danger is easy to recognize, giving the dreamer a chance to get to safety. (See also "Animals.")

WOMAN According to Carl Jung, strange women appearing in the dreams of men symbolize the anima (the unconscious female side of the psyche), and provide information about their emotions as well as their capacity to love. The behavior of these women also says something about the characteristics of the men. A woman appearing in a woman's dream can be any number of personalities, and can only be interpreted within the context of the entire dream. According to Freud, women in a man's dream usually point to sexual desires that cannot be satisfied because of moral reservations. Throughout time, a woman appearing in a dream has been considered a messenger of good luck, her kisses indicating increased wealth. It is particularly important to pay attention to the woman's actions, and to how she moves and where she is; even the color of her hair should be noted. In ancient Egypt, the image of a beautiful woman was considered a warning about spending too much money.

WOOD Dreaming about wood points to the difficulty you have in real life producing something. Stacking wood shows that you are willing to bring your life to order. Chopping wood indicates that you can expect to be rewarded, because you are willing to share. Watching somebody else chopping wood suggests an impending separation. Throwing wood in a fire implies that you are fanning the flames of passion. (See also "Wooden Board" and "Planing Wood.")

WOODEN BOARD Dreaming about working with a saw to reshape a wooden board indicates that you want to change your life. Using wooden boards to build a cabin shows that you want to clean up your act and make more of yourself. (See also "Wood," "Cabin," "House," and "Saw.")

WOOD SHAVINGS Wood shavings in a dream represent the small things that we seem to forget, leave behind carelessly, or simply ignore. The dream is a reminder that even the small things in life have value.

WOOL Wool in dreams represents that which keeps us warm and helps to support the circulatory system. A dream about wool reflects the genuine, heartfelt warmth that you will receive from others. Wearing a woolen garment in a dream means that you can look forward to financial gain as a result of your own hard work. (See also "Dress.")

WORDS Words in dreams are very important, because in themselves they are often significant symbols. If you are unable to "get a word in edgewise" in a dream, this points to not having found the proper words

to express your opinion in a certain situation in real life. If someone is interrupting you in a dream, in real life you may not have enough to say or may fail to express yourself clearly.

WORK When you dream about work, it is likely that you have taken the burdens of the day to bed with you, where they have been dealt with by the unconscious. Dreaming about work also has to do with testing your emotional stamina or testing how competitive you are in everyday life. In addition, this image could be an encouragement to be more productive during the day and to stop wasting time, or to deal with your emotions more effectively so that you will be less vulnerable when things get tough.

WORM Dreaming about this invertebrate animal points to your helplessness in a certain situation or to your being generally spineless. It might also mean that someone is trying to "worm" him- or herself into your life. If something in the dream is being eaten by a worm, this indicates that you feel weak and worn-out.

WORSHIP (SEE "CHURCH SERVICE/WORSHIP")

WOUND A wound in a dream is not about pain, but rather is a signal that your emotions are out of sync. The wound could also be a message that you need to change your lifestyle, in order to better deal with the misery you have created. (See also "Blood," "Scar," "Oil," and "Bandage.")

WREATH A wreath stands for the bond between you and other people, a connection that may entail grief or joy. Making a flower wreath in a dream means that you can count on a happy future. A wreath with wilted flowers, on the other hand, indicates that hard-to-handle disappointments may be looming ahead. A wreath can also be a symbol for a ring, indicating that you are longing for a relationship and marriage. (See also "Flowers" and "Ring.")

WRECK Seeing a wrecked vehicle or a shipwreck in a dream is an indication that a project in real life is doomed to fail. (See also "Automobile," "Ship," and "Shipwreck.")

WRESTLING MATCH Often the outcome of a fight in a dream is unclear, which shows that we need to come to terms with a situation in real life where the upshot is also not clear. Sometimes a wrestling match indicates that we are wrestling with ideas that could help us get ahead, or with our image or the one we want to present.

WRINKLES Dreaming about wrinkles is a reminder of past experiences in real life. Seeing wrinkles or having wrinkles yourself could also mean that you are carrying around gloomy thoughts that you should shake off quickly to avoid falling into self-doubt.

WRISTWATCH (SEE "CLOCK/WATCH")

WRITING Dreaming about writing may be an indication not to count on verbal agreements, because they can be easily changed, by us or by others.

X Seeing this letter in a dream often refers to the Roman numeral for ten; therefore, look up "Ten."

X RAYS Because most people have had X rays taken, this image also turns up in our dreams. It indicates that we would like to get to know someone better in real life. Sometimes X rays indicate that our own shadow is being examined. Looking at our own X rays in a dream means that we are being made aware of our shortcomings and encouraged to eliminate them.

Y The second-to-the-last letter in the alphabet is a symbol for male and female joining (the Yang and the Yin of Chinese mythology), which eases the burdens we carry. Dreaming about a Y-shaped piece of wood, such as a forked branch, placed under a heavy load indicates that a certain burden that life has placed on your shoulders will be easier to carry or be taken away entirely. The "Y" in a dream could also refer to the Y-shaped divining rod, indicating a search for new possibilities.

YARD/COURTYARD If the courtyard is surrounded by attractive buildings, the dreamer is looking for good company. A dark, foreboding yard implies that the dreamer lacks contact.

YARN If you are spinning yarn in a dream, you probably want to convince someone in real life of your trustworthiness. (See also "Thread" and "Sewing.")

YELLOW Yellow is the golden, glowing color of the sun, which brightens life and enlightens us. Golden yellow stands for wisdom and generosity, medium yellow for self-centeredness, and pale yellow for the disappointments that life has in store for us.

YOGI (SEE "FAKIR")

YOKE Dreaming about an ox that is carrying a yoke is a reminder that in real life we too have to endure hardships.

YOUTH People over forty often dream about their youth. Such dreams could be a way for them to examine their lives, and could entail going to school, doing homework, and taking a test (which they have passed long ago). But often such dreams are a sign that they are worrying about their children or grandchildren, or point to their own (unfounded) anxieties. (See also "School" and "Child.")

ZEPPELIN A zeppelin is an airship, and when one is floating about your head in a dream, it might easily resemble a dark cloud, which could refer to something oppressing in your life. Flying in a zeppelin, however, means that you are well on your way to reaching a lofty goal with the help of a mentor or a good friend. (See also "Airplane.")

ZERO A zero in a dream is seen as a sexual symbol. Many zeros stand for erotic experiences that overtax the dreamer's energies.

ZOO A dream about a zoo, where the trees are green and the flowers are in bloom, is proof that you come alive when in good company. But the animals in the cages are a warning to keep your physical urges under control.

OTHER CLUES

DREAM STIMULANTS We know that specific muscles protect the eyes from external stimuli during sleep. The pupils contract and the eyeballs move upward. But if a light is turned on in the room where we are sleeping, the light can still penetrate the eyelids, and this light stimulus can influence our dreams. The same thing happens when car headlights send flashes of light into a room. It's important to know that external stimuli, including eating a heavy meal just before retiring, often make for frightening dreams. (See also "Nightmares" below.)

DREAMS ABOUT CRIMINALS Wilhelm Steckel used dream analysis to explore the reasons for a patient's neurosis. He suggested that one needs to consider the "secret criminal in the human being" if the treatment of a neurosis is to be successful. A neurosis is an emotional disorder that can cause physical symptoms and ailments, such as a migraine headaches, nausea, and vomiting, as well as stomach, intestinal, heart, and circulatory problems. Most neuroses can be traced back to neglect, mistreatment, or overindulgence in childhood, or to a divorce or the loss of one or both parents. A troubled

marriage or continual problems on the job can also produce neuroses. According to Steckel, neurotic people are the criminals in dreams, and in real life they simply lack the courage to display their criminal behavior.

MOTHER COMPLEX Sigmund Freud developed the theory of the Oedipus complex from the special relationship that exists between the infant and its mother. He thought that boys had a sexual desire for their mothers from infancy on. This desire is expressed later on in many dreams where incest is taking place between a mother figure and the dreamer. Freud also believed that troubled relationships between the mother and the child, or exceptionally close relationships during childhood and youth, had psychological consequences, like neuroses. But a dream about incest with one's own mother has little to do with the Oedipus complex, in our opinion. We tend to agree with Artemidorus, an ancient Greek dream interpreter, who thought that if the dreamer was far away from home, it was only natural for him to dream about his mother. If the dream included incest, he thought that this was a sign that the dreamer would soon be returning home. Modern thought on the subject maintains that incest dreams have a positive meaning when the mother—who, after all, is the one the son loves most in life—stands in for the woman in his life whom he loves and longs for. Carl Gustav Jung likened the "mother complex" to unprompted thoughts and memories, or to psychic energies that can last into old age and cause disorders, like neuroses. This comparison makes sense when we consider that we were physically connected to our mothers during our earliest development.

NIGHTMARES We are shaking with fear, somebody is running after us, and we are trying to protect ourselves but cannot find a place to hide. Or, calamities are coming at us from all sides. We are still gripped by fear when we wake up. Nightmares usually appear when we are about to lose something that is precious to us or that has become a comfortable habit. People feeling a sense of crisis at the onset of puberty or menopause often complain of nightmares, because they are beset by physical changes that must be integrated, and the situation they are facing frightens them. Freud believed that nightmares can be eliminated by making sexual repression, which he saw as the source of nightmares, conscious. Many people still hold the view that nightmares are connected to sexual

urges. Jung saw nightmares as symbolic messengers of our primitive, dark sides, which must be recognized in order for the nightmares to be conquered.

PROPHETIC DREAMS Most natural scientists consider prophetic dreams the stuff that fables are made of, and dismiss them outright as occult, mediumistic, or supernatural, or as the delusional musings of parapsychology. However, history reveals numerous prophetic dreams whose contents concurred almost verbatim with significant details of actual events that happened later. Although prophetic dreams are rare, they cannot be ignored, even if they are outside what is considered normal experience.

SEXUAL DREAMS Dreams use sex without embarrassment, often in exaggerated form, such as wild orgies. Many physical urges that are tamed by cultural taboos and the dreamer's upbringing are expressed with abandon in dreams. But sexual dreams are not always an expression of lust and sexual hunger; in fact, often they are a disguise for intellectual and spiritual yearning. The images of crude sexual urges many times are detours used by the unconscious to point out problems in a relationship or inhibitions that block or at least impede human contact.